Joanna Hodgkin is the author fiction and historical fiction (as Jo... translated into ten languages and ... the *Guardian*, has taught creative writing and worked as a Royal Literary Fund Fellow. After living in Cornwall for many years, she has now returned to London, her first home.

'Hodgkin has done both Nancy and herself proud with this fresh portrait of a marriage we thought we knew, and of a woman we have never known well enough'

Miranda Seymour, *Sunday Times*

' . . . a particularly rich and honest account'

Amy Mathieson, *Scotland on Sunday*

'This is not just a memoir of her mother. This is the history of a literary wife. On both counts, Hodgkin succeeds beautifully'

Lesley McDowell, *Independent*

' . . . an enjoyable, revisionist account of a bohemian marriage'

Blake Morrison, *Guardian*

' . . . a cracking story'

Olivia Laing, *Observer*

'Full of arresting details . . . *Amateurs in Eden* is full of good things'

D. J. Taylor, *Literary Review*

Amateurs in Eden

The Story of a Bohemian Marriage:
Nancy and Lawrence Durrell

Joanna Hodgkin

virago

VIRAGO

First published in Great Britain in 2012 by Virago Press
This paperback edition published in 2013 by Virago Press

Copyright © 2012 Joanna Hodgkin

A CIP catalogue record for this book
is available from the British Library.

ISBN 978-1-84408-794-5

Typeset in Goudy by M Rules
Printed and bound in Great Britain by
Clays Ltd, St Ives plc

Papers used by Virago are from well-managed forests
and other responsible sources.

MIX
Paper from
responsible sources
FSC® C104740

Virago
An imprint of
Little, Brown Book Group
100 Victoria Embankment
London EC4Y 0DY

An Hachette UK Company
www.hachette.co.uk

www.virago.co.uk

For my sister Penelope
1940–2010

Think: two amateurs in Eden,
Spaces in the voiceless garden,
Ancestors whose haunted faces
Met upon the apple's bruises,
Broke the lovely spell of pardon.

Lawrence Durrell, 'The Prayer-Wheel'

ACKNOWLEDGEMENTS

Non-fiction, as I have discovered over the past two years, involves much relying on the kindness of strangers, as well as one's long-suffering friends. First of all, my thanks go to Corinne Turner, Zoe Watkins and Matthew Fleming, who suggested the book in the first place: three people I'd never met before who started me on a journey that has been a revelation. My thanks to them for their trouble and perception.

The geographic journeys involved in the research would not have been possible without the financial assistance generously given by the Authors' Foundation and the Arts Council. The money provided a vote of confidence at a time when that was needed, and especial thanks to Gemma Seltzer at the Arts Council, who was enthusiastic and encouraging throughout the process, and to Michelle Spring, who not only guided me through the labyrinthine application process but selflessly gave up her time to join me in my researches in Corfu.

The big guns in the Durrell world have also been unstinting in their help: thanks to Ian MacNiven, Richard Pine and Michael Haag, as well as to Charles Sligh and Gordon Bowker. Also to Lee Durrell, Françoise Kestsman and Anthea Morton-Saner.

Along the way I have been grateful for the help of Liz Hodgkin, Judith Heath, Tim Nicholson, Roger Nashe, Simon and Penny Dawson, Stephanie de Montalk, Peter Potocki, Jean

Radford, Mercedes Pavlicevic, Patricia Earl, Hilary Whitton Paipeti, Perikles Katsaros, Tassos and Daria Athinaios, Eugenia Hanrott, Rebecca Fox, Diana Hogarth, Deirdre A. David, Peter Ellis Jones, Anna Davin, Anthea Holme, Harriet Harvey-Wood, Alexander and Spiros Mercouris, Ray Mills, Katerina Krikos-Davis, Anna Davis, Shelley Cox, Endymion Wilkinson, Mary Williams and Charles Pettiward.

Three women have offered me their pre-war memories, and have also been an inspiration on the grace and joyousness of growing older: to Veronica Tester Dane in Devon, Lotte Geiger in Jerusalem and Alexia Mercouri in Athens, my special thanks.

Sometimes staff go out of their way to be helpful. Thanks to Julie Buck at the Lincoln Archive, Sally Brooke at the Museum of London, Russell Kirk at the *Lincolnshire Echo*, Beverley Kaliati at the British Council in Jerusalem, Alexandra Thornton at Lincolnshire County Council, Leda Costaki at the Gennadius Archive, the staff at the archive at UCLA, at the Morris Library of the Southern Illinois University at Carbondale, the Local Studies centres in Chichester, Holborn and Eastbourne, to Rachel Foss and all who have helped at the British Library, and especially the ever helpful staff at the London Library.

My agent Jane Turnbull has been wonderful throughout, and working with all the staff at Virago is a joy. Which only leaves my family – gently supportive, humorous and loving at all times. Thanks.

CONTENTS

INTRODUCTION

My sister and I had different fathers. Hers was Lawrence Durrell, famous author of *The Alexandria Quartet*. Mine was Edward Hodgkin, also a writer but a journalist and, though well respected within his profession, unknown beyond. In theory Penelope and I had our mother in common: Nancy Myers, Nancy Durrell, Nancy Hodgkin. But it often seemed as though we had different mothers as well – two sisters divided by a common mother, as it were.

Penelope's mother was the young, beautiful and rootless wife of a bohemian poet, with whom she lived in Greece and Paris. In Egypt she left him, and for the next few years struggled to survive in the Near East. The mother with whom I grew up was older by nearly ten years; she had settled in London and the Home Counties, and was secure, respectable and, above all, safe. It made a huge difference, and nowhere more than in the matter of talking. Penelope complained, with reason, that our mother never talked to her, never discussed anything with her, never shared stories of their years alone together. I didn't know how to respond to these complaints because from when I was about eight or nine, and Penelope had left home, my mother and I talked incessantly. Sometimes, when I was in my teens and back from school for the holidays, we would begin a conversation at breakfast, continue through elevenses, segue still chatting into lunch, and carry on for the rest of the day with just a brief interlude to shop for supper. One consequence of these marathon talk-ins was that when she died in 1983 I was spared that most frequent of regrets – 'I wish I'd asked her about So-and-so', or 'I wish I'd got to know her better'. (Though since starting this biography, there have been plenty of occasions when I wished I could check facts with her, fill in gaps.)

What did we talk about? Well, just about everything: my friends, her friends, clothes, religion, furnishings, current events, the books we were reading, sex, films, the meaning of life. And often, very often, she talked about her life before she met and married my father: her childhood and her years with Lawrence Durrell.

At the time I was pleased and flattered by these confidences. She had been a remote figure when I was a small child – seriously depressed, in fact, though I didn't piece that together until later – and it was a wonderful way to grow close to her. Later I realised there'd been a price to pay, but at the time having such an exotic, wise and forthright mother seemed unbelievable good luck.

In 1976 she developed breast cancer and had a mastectomy. Six years later the cancer returned, this time in her bones. She kept the X-rays ('like a Swiss cheese', she said) under her bed. At about the same time a reference to the end of her marriage to Durrell appeared in print, quoting his verdict on the break: 'Nancy is in Jerusalem with the child. We have split up; just the war I guess.' This triggered one of her characteristic snorts of derision. She wanted to put the record straight, or to give her side of the story – delete as appropriate. She began writing a memoir, intending it to be about the decade they spent together, but with her usual thoroughness she started with her own childhood and the early London years, so as to give an idea of the person she already was when they met, which was crucial to the way their marriage developed. It was slow progress, partly because of her huge inhibitions about writing. Her determination to pin down the precise truth about an event or a relationship meant the literary fluency of both her husbands was completely alien to her. As it became obvious that she was running out of time, she decided to talk about her life before the war. She and my father set up a tape recorder, he asked questions and she talked. She died long before the task was complete. It is poignant that her last months were spent grinding up organic carrots for the whole-food Bristol diet and discussing her first husband with her second.

Lawrence Durrell died in 1990, Edward Hodgkin in 2006. In the quarter-century since her death, Nancy has been written about in fiction, academic studies and biographies – always those of other people. She has developed a reputation as someone who didn't have much to say for herself, probably from shyness. In Paris with Henry Miller and Anaïs Nin, she sat on the outside of the circle, sometimes performing the duties of handmaiden, but seldom joining in. Her silence was commented on. In a letter to Lawrence after their first visit to Paris, Anaïs wrote: 'I think often of Nancy's most eloquent silences, Nancy talking with her eyes, her fingers, her hair, her cheeks, a wonderful gift.' But far from being a wonderful gift, her silence was a burden that had its roots in her relationship with Lawrence, and which she wanted, finally, to break. It may seem that, at times, personal details are made public, things which would have been better left private. But having once embarked on this task, the only course seemed to do it properly, as Nancy would have wanted; right to the end she was adding supplements to the tapes, handwritten pages which provide crucial insights into the infinitely variable puzzle of their marriage.

The main narrative ends in 1947, the halfway point in her life, the year she married for the second time and stepped into a different and more private world. To some extent, as I discovered while writing this, after 1947 she became a different person. In this memoir I am writing about both someone I knew intimately and also a young woman who is a stranger.

What follows is my own personal account of a highly unusual woman who lived through fascinating times. A great deal of it is based on her own words, either from private conversations and letters, or the unfinished memoir.

I could not have attempted it before – and indeed it never occurred to me to do so – partly because of the 'two mothers' quandary. But, five years ago, my sister fell victim to the tragic vanishing act that is Alzheimer's, and the contrast in our maternal experience could no longer cause her the grief it once did. More than anything, I wish my sister was still in health, and that I was not free to write these words, but there was no return from the grey land that claimed her. In fact, the idea for the memoir came from a conversation about how to boost interest in her father's work, so the royalties could cover her care – which in the end was not needed for as long as we had expected. She died, by a heartbreaking coincidence, just as I was finishing the first draft, but her researches, the time she spent making friends with the people who had been significant in her parents' lives, her efforts to unravel the conundrum of their time together, are an unspoken presence on nearly every page.

So it is to the memory of my sister Penelope, much-loved offspring of a troubled union, that this book is dedicated.

Nancy, Larry and Penelope in Cairo, 1941

PROLOGUE

Early August, 1937: Lawrence and Nancy Durrell stepped down from the train that had brought them to Paris from the south and made their way to the 14th arrondissement and a quiet cul de sac called the Villa Seurat. They had come to meet Henry Miller, who was already a legendary figure in bohemian circles, and the centre of a fascinating group of renegades and eccentrics. At last, they were going to discover friends who shared their values and goals. All their hopes were staked on this meeting.

The young writer and his artist wife who were about to burst on the Parisian scene that summer morning were in every sense a golden couple. Hair bleached, skin bronzed by the sun, and with the vitality of long afternoons sailing their little sloop and swimming off deserted beaches, they brought, as Nancy said, 'a whiff of open air and Ionian breeze, full of vim and ideas and enthusiasm' to their new circle of older and more sophisticated friends.

At first sight, they appeared an incongruous duo. Larry was short and stocky – 'tiny really', as he described himself – and in some ways he seemed younger than twenty-five, hardly more than a boy, with a boy's beauty and vulnerability. Yet he seemed old, too, old beyond his years. His blue eyes were those of an ancient sage, or even, some thought, of someone who had never been young. This duality, angelic youth and aged seer, was all part of his charm.

Tall and willowy, Nancy was a total contrast to her husband. She had high cheekbones and clear blue eyes, and an androgynous beauty that evoked comparison with Greta Garbo, or else had people reaching for images from the natural world. She was variously described as resembling a leopard, a flamingo and a wild deer, all creatures of grace and elegance, but also with an elusive, feral quality. A child who had known her in Corfu described her as 'innocent', a strange word for a seven-year-old to use about an adult. Years later, another friend remembered her simply as 'the most beautiful young woman I've ever seen'.

Though physically mismatched, they seemed to complement each other admirably. Larry was a fizzing firecracker of energy, witty and challenging, brimming with ideas and passion for literature, a man who dominated any gathering and whose company acted like champagne. Words were the medium in which he moved, his weapons of seduction and exploration and attack. He was fluent without ever being glib. Yet those who were present on that first day in Paris remembered his laughter even more than the talk – wonderful laughter, infectious and stimulating, laughter that resonated round the little studio apartment and signalled to all present that their life had shifted into a higher gear.

Nancy appeared to be the perfect foil. She was calm and serene, apparently content to hold back and let her brilliant partner take centre stage. People regarded her as steadier and more mature, dealing with the practical details of their existence and leaving him free to develop his talents. Yet she was much more than just a manager: an artist who had studied at the Slade, she subscribed wholeheartedly to the bohemian credo that they were set apart, different from other people and bound to live by different rules. In their world, bourgeois restrictions must be sacrificed to the creation of genuine art and literature.

They had come to Paris from Corfu, the island where they had lived for over two years, and where they had made a home for themselves on the remote north-east coast. For them, the White House in Kalami was more than just a good place to work and live: it was a shared joy, a source of strength, the place where they rinsed off the disappointments and frustrations of that bleak homeland Larry always referred to as Pudding Island. The house they shared with a fisherman and his family was primitive, Spartan even. They happily endured infestations of biting insects, the lack of plumbing, restricted food and social isolation because for Nancy and Larry that lonely corner of the Ionian was their own private Eden.

A short walk from their white-washed home was a small, secret bay. No road led to it. Above the rippling, striated rock face and almost smothered in greenery perched a little shrine dedicated to a local saint, Arsenius, and this private retreat was for them a hallowed place. Here they stripped off their clothes, dived naked into the crystal water, swam and sunned themselves and were able to imagine that Arcadias are possible.

It was literature that had lured them north from their island idyll at the height of summer. Two years earlier, Larry had been bowled over by Henry Miller's groundbreaking book *Tropic of Cancer*, a work that was considered so shocking it was banned in Britain and the United States. Only a legal loophole had allowed it to be published in France. Larry had written Henry an ardent fan letter; Henry responded with enthusiasm and a literary friendship was born. Soon Nancy was drawn into the exchange: Larry fished her discarded paintings from the waste-basket – she was always her own fiercest critic – and surreptitiously sent them to Paris. They read manuscripts by Anaïs Nin, whose tempestuous affair with Henry had gone on for years as she pioneered a new kind of writing and poured her sensations and experience into her monumental diaries. And now they had the chance to create their very own literary magazine, *The Booster*. Larry would be literary editor and Nancy was to design the cover and be art editor. Along the way, they intended to have as much fun as they could. And so they did.

That first encounter was everything they could have hoped for, and more. The party went on all day. The sunny room in Henry's studio apartment was soon littered with bottles and glasses, books, the remains of meals and loose manuscript pages. Smoke from their cigarettes curled up towards the ceiling, and from the kitchen came the delicious aroma of the steaks Nancy was cooking. The whole place reverberated with laughter and talk, and Henry was so overwhelmed by the brilliance of his protégé that he was speechless for a while, his eyes shining with tears of pleasure.

No doubt about it, the youthful pair from Corfu were a huge success. At last they were launched in the world where they belonged.

But that was only half the story. In the creative mayhem of the Villa Seurat, nothing was ever quite how it looked. For a start, no one could ever be sure who was sleeping with whom. Was Henry's turbulent affair with Anaïs still ongoing? Was she supporting him out of the generous dress allowance she received from her wealthy banker husband? Who were the mysterious Spanish refugees to whom she devoted so much attention? Soon Nancy and Larry became caught up in the lies and intrigues, but the young couple, apparently so unspoiled and radiant and open, harboured secrets of their own, secrets that remained hidden much longer than those of Henry and Anaïs.

Even then observant friends were struck by a marked dissonance in Larry's personality, a discord that went deeper than the normal contrast between the self we show in public and our inner, more complex reality – that shadow self so beloved of Jungians. Under his brilliance and dazzling charm lay a core of deep loneliness and uncertainty that he never shook off, even after the publication of *Justine* had brought him fame, success and financial security. And he had a vengeful, cruel streak as well. He could charm and seduce with words, but he could also use them to lacerate and destroy. The angelic boy-man could be transformed into a demon in a moment.

It was a dissonance that Nancy might have sympathised with, because it was something she shared. Superficially confident and assured, serene in her beauty and her accomplishments, underneath she was every bit as complex and uncertain as her husband. For much of her childhood she had seen herself as a pariah, and her mother's spite had corroded her self-confidence and crippled her spirit. Even more than Larry, she needed to forge a new identity and leave her family behind. In fact the Durrell clan – his mother, the mildly eccentric Louisa, and her unlikely brood (including Gerald, who in 1937 was still a pond-dipping child running wild in Corfu) – provided a haven for Nancy, a place where she felt accepted as she had never been by her embittered parents. In 1937, as she put it, the leopard had most definitely changed her spots – outwardly – but inside she was as tortured and conflicted as she had always been.

The Paris adventure that began with such laughter and high spirits came at precisely the mid-point of the decade Nancy and Larry spent together. It was the moment of their greatest triumph, but also the moment when the fabric of their marriage started to unravel. Five years earlier they had met in a smoky Fitzrovia pub; Nancy was in love with someone else and drifted into her relationship with Larry almost without noticing. Five years later, angry, heartbroken and uncomprehending in the turmoil of Cairo as Rommel's seemingly unstoppable army approached, they went their separate ways. And that was that. End of story.

Except it never is.

In 1975, when they had been apart for more than three decades, Larry talked to an audience in California about those halcyon, pre-war days in Kalami. He remembered 'that house with its remoteness and the islands going down like soft gongs all the time into the amazing blue, and I shall really never, never ever forget a youth spent there, discovered by accident. It was pure gold. But then of course ... youth does mean happiness, it does mean love, and that's something you can't get over.'

And Nancy, living a new life with new people, far removed from the places and times they had shared, would surely have agreed. Amazing blue, pure gold, youth and happiness and love ... all the ingredients to create the idyll they both craved, but the seeds of its destruction had also been there from the beginning, from their beginnings. To understand, one must turn back to those very different worlds out of which their stories grew, Larry's in Northern India and the remnants of the unique experiment that was the Raj, Nancy's in the social minefield of Edwardian England and her convoluted and mysterious family.

1

OF INTROSPECTION GOT

Taken in the pattern of all solitaries,
An only child, of introspection got,
Her only playmates, lovers, in herself.

Description of Nancy in Lawrence Durrell,
'Cities, Plains and People'

The Reverend Thomas Myers had been rector of Twinstead, a parish near the Essex–Suffolk border, for thirty-two years and was about to retire. One of his last duties in the little church where he had officiated for a generation was a long-awaited pleasure: in July 1910 he presided at the marriage of his only child, also Thomas, to Louise Shaw. Thomas was thirty-seven, his bride a little older, so no one could say the couple were too young to know their minds. After the wedding the rector retired to Bath and the newly-weds set up home in a solidly respectable house in Eastbourne, where Thomas had recently established his dental practice. When their daughter Nancy was born two years later, she was welcomed into a world of apparent affluence and security. Or so it seemed.

Eastbourne in 1912 was, for those of adequate means, a benign place in which to be born. The resort had been developed under the inspired guidance of the seventh Duke of Devonshire and was considered a good example of a town developed 'according to plan', with a long gracious seafront, spacious boulevards, winter gardens and a pier with a fairy-tale palace known as the Kursaal. Behind the town lay the beautiful South Downs, while the white cliffs of Beachy Head were just a short walk away. Edwardian Eastbourne had for some time been known as the Empress of Watering Places and it guarded its reputation jealously, as a contemporary guide made clear: 'Whilst extending a cordial welcome to the bona fide visitor and holiday maker [Eastbourne] … has never regarded the day tripper or the excursionist in any too kindly a light.'

Quite so. The newly married Thomas and Louise would have taken an equally dim view of 'excursionists'. Their home at 28 Gildredge Road was quintessentially genteel. Semi-detached and four storeys high, it had steps leading up to the front door and large bay windows. A butler was installed and his wife did the cooking. After Nancy was born, a Nurse Peacock was employed to take care of her.

Those Eastbourne years were remembered as a time of sunny content for all the family. The child was happy and confident. Tended by Nurse Peacock, she played in the large gardens, made friends with children nearby and chased blue butterflies with her little net on the wide freedoms of the downs. She played on the beach and visited the winter gardens. Even when Britain went to war with Germany in August 1914 the band continued to play on the seafront.

Meanwhile, her mother revelled in her smart home and passed her days arranging curtains and cushions and small tables smothered with little silver objects. She enjoyed presiding over elegant tea parties.

Thomas Myers was in his element; his free time was spent in

the bracing air of the Willingdon Golf Club, where he won competition spoons, and was honoured to be elected its president. He doted on his young daughter and, with the help of his dental technician, made her an enormous doll's house. He learned photography and took endless pictures of the little girl, which he developed and printed himself.

Two photographs taken of Nancy in her christening robes when she must have been about three months old give a first hint of the shadows that were to fall across her life. In the first she is sitting on her young nurse's knee. Calm and pretty in her starched cap and uniform, the nurse glows with calm contentment. In the second photograph Louise herself, dressed for the occasion in the heavily encrusted bodice of the grand Edwardian matron, holds her daughter. Her face, partly in shadow, already has a stricken, almost haunted expression. She is not looking at the baby, which she holds awkwardly and slightly away from her, with her right hand curled into a fist. The baby's former look of myopic self-absorption has been replaced by one of mild alarm.

Nancy in her christening robes with her nurse
Nancy with her mother, rather more anxious

That alarm was eventually to develop into an indelible and guilt-ridden dislike, but for the Eastbourne years at least Nancy was secure in the care of Nurse Peacock, and she grew into a happy and confident child. 'Eastbourne confidence', she called it later.

And then, catastrophe. Overnight, or so it seemed to Nancy, their comfortable world collapsed. The butler and the cook were dismissed, Nurse Peacock vanished, the furniture was packed up and the spacious Gildredge Road house was sold for a fraction of what it would have fetched a year later. In 1917 the family moved north to Gainsborough, a small manufacturing town in Lincolnshire, and to a new life in a little terraced house in a street dominated by a long, high factory wall.

Why? The explanation given by her parents was 'invasion panic', an overwhelming terror that the beastly Hun were about to make landfall on the South Coast and slaughter the good citizens of Eastbourne in their homes. But this doesn't wash: for one thing, the real time of invasion panic had long passed. It was during the winter of 1914–15 that the fear was strongest, and besides, none of their friends or neighbours felt compelled to leave the sunny South Coast. Most significant of all, there was never any question of returning once the war had ended, not even for a holiday.

Behind the public excuse must have lain a never-acknowledged but more sinister reason. Nancy never discovered the details of her family's disaster: it was just one of the secrets her parents carried for the rest of their lives. 'I am pretty sure,' Nancy wrote, 'that my father got into financial trouble. He'd gambled on the stock exchange, perhaps, or bought shares in a non-existent gold mine. All I know is that there was, from the first, an air of finality about it. Never a hint that we would pull out of it.'

On the day of the move she had a first intimation that their fall from grace was to have far-reaching consequences. She had been promised their new home would come complete with a beautiful garden, like the one they were leaving behind. But when she first saw the grubby little patch of grass at the back, with a narrow border on one side and a few miserable plants struggling to survive in the grey soil at the foot of a high brick wall, she burst out in bewilderment, 'It's a horrid garden – not nice at all!'

Her mother struck back at once. 'You're a wicked girl to say such things! It is a very nice garden indeed!'

Nancy was shocked. She was still grieving for Nurse Peacock, and her mother's words filled her with guilt and confusion. So much of her future relationship with her parents was mapped out in those two sentences: the accusation of wickedness and the absolute negation of her own reality. In their new life at 23 Spring Gardens, the fault lines in her family were to be mercilessly exposed.

Two months after Nancy's death, my father and I drove up to Bamburgh on the Northumberland coast, where he had spent his childhood summers. Bamburgh, with its huge white beach and its magical sand dunes and castle, meant a lot to him, not least because it was where his adored sister Betty, who died when he was twelve, is buried. On our visit in 1983 he planted crocus and snowdrop bulbs over her grave. At a time of bereavement, old griefs come back into focus.

From time to time when I walked past his room in the cottage near the beach which we had borrowed from one of his cousins, I could hear my parents talking to each other. I knew he was transcribing the tapes that they had made together, but even so it was a jolt each time, to hear the quiet murmur of their conversation from behind the closed door.

On the journey north we had made a detour to Gainsborough, and found the house in Spring Gardens that we had heard so much about. We had been prepared by all that Nancy had said and written on the subject, but still we were taken aback. When the cottages were built they must have had a certain charm, but the vast factory wall of the Marshall family's Britannia Iron Works completely overshadowed them. High and black and windowless, the brick wall loomed over the little cottages. It was oppressive, soul-destroying. We drove away in silence.

A sign of changing times, Marshall's Yard is now a shopping centre, but in 1917 the factory dominated the town. It covered sixteen acres of land and employed five thousand workers building tanks, guns and planes. The grind of huge machines and the hooters that sounded at the end of each shift formed the constant soundtrack to life in Spring Gardens.

For Thomas and Louise the immediate problem was how to fit their grand Eastbourne furniture into such a small space. On each side of the front door was a room with a bay window. The one on the left became their drawing room, while the right-hand room served as both dining room and patients' waiting room. Each morning after breakfast the dishes were cleared away and piles of much-thumbed magazines, *Punch* and the *Sphere*, spread over the billiard table with heavy oak leaves which, for some reason, they used as a dining table. At the back of the house was the consulting room, with French windows overlooking the garden, and, next to that, the kitchen.

Stairs with heavy dark green paint led up to the first floor. The two tiny rooms at the front had been knocked into one to accommodate her parents' enormous bedroom suite and massive brass bed. A small room, also crammed full of cupboards, led from this and was Thomas's dressing room, where he kept and cleaned his gun and his golf clubs. Nancy's room, which doubled as the nursery until she went away to school, was at the back, and the sun never reached it. The large doll's house, her rocking horse, toy cupboard, chest of drawers, table and cabinet for her treasures all had to be squashed in somehow. A second door led to a tiny upstairs landing and the bleak cubby hole where their maid slept. This room was above the larder, and always chilly. It gave off a musty, sour smell, as did the little uncarpeted back stairway which tumbled down to the kitchen through a doorway painted dark brown, which looked, when it was closed, like a cupboard. However small the house, there had to be two staircases, since it would never do for the maid to use the same one as the family. There was a lavatory upstairs, but no bathroom. A cupboard off Nancy's parents' room exactly fitted a painted bath with a boiler above it, which was heated by a roaring gas fire. Presumably the maid never got to have a bath.

In later years Nancy realised that 23 Spring Gardens had the potential to make a perfectly decent home, and reflected that even the garden must have been loved once. The problem was not so much the house itself, more her parents' absolute refusal to be reconciled to it. The massive furniture, out of all proportion to the rooms, symbolised their determination never to adapt to their new life. They were too grand for their little house and they considered themselves much superior to their neighbours, who were of the dreaded 'excursionist' class.

Most galling of all, the social inferiors they were forced to rub shoulders with were often more affluent than they were. From the moment they exchanged their gracious Eastbourne existence for the demeaning struggle in Gainsborough, Thomas and Louise's lives were blighted by poverty. 'One long scrimp and save', as Nancy put it. Saving not so they might recapture their former glory but simply to survive from month to month.

Of course, theirs was never the poverty of the kind that so many families experienced in the 1920s. Nancy didn't go barefoot and they weren't hungry or cold. This was genteel poverty, margarine instead of butter but a maid at all times, and a gruelling struggle to maintain appearances. 'This cast a pall over everything,' Nancy wrote, 'and yet I say, why? Why couldn't a competent dentist, in a town of twenty thousand people and no competition, make a decent living and keep up with the Joneses? The man he replaced had done extremely well and after my father retired, his successor lived very well and sped around in a Jaguar.'

If they had been able to remain in affluence in Gildredge Road, with Louise holding tea parties while Thomas strolled with his chums round Willingdon Golf Club, their fundamental incompatibility might never have been exposed. As it was, the couple had no resources to meet the disaster. The move to Gainsborough soured their marriage and broke their spirit. This was never how their marriage was supposed to turn out.

My grandfather Thomas Cyril Myers remains an enigma. His background was solidly respectable, with most of his forebears country parsons. His father had a first class degree in moral sciences from Trinity College, Cambridge, and was rector of Twinstead for over thirty years: Thomas spent his childhood in a spacious rectory with large gardens.

An only child, he was sent to Haileybury in Hertfordshire from thirteen to eighteen. He was not particularly academic. As soon as he left school he meticulously cut out jokey heads from comics and pasted them over the illustrious figures in his history book: Julius Caesar complete with toga, handlebar moustache and a cheroot; King Alfred in a boater. The effect is genuinely funny. Entertainment was always his strongest suit. With no interest in the Church, he chose instead the relatively new profession of dentistry and worked at Charing Cross Hospital and the Royal Dental Hospital in London. He was licensed by the Royal College of Surgeons in 1896. During his London years, shortage of funds never stopped him from having a good time. He went to all the popular musical entertainments of the day and, always methodical except in matters of work, kept all the programmes. In the summer he went to Le Touquet for golfing holidays with his friends. In winter they tobogganed and skated in Switzerland.

Nancy's father during his more carefree bachelor days

He was considered handsome, and photographs show him to have been very much the *fin de siècle* man about town, though to my mind he looks a bit of a chump, with something weak, almost evasive in his expression. Still, he was gregarious and even in old age, white-haired and frail, he had the bluest of blue eyes, hyacinth blue, which actually did twinkle in just the way an elderly grandfather's eyes should. He was always friendly, cheerful and affectionate, with a rippling laugh that seemed to bubble through his speech.

After working for a short while in Guildford he made a tactical move to Eastbourne, where his mother's wealthy and childless sister lived at 11 The Avenue, one of the largest and most gracious of the houses on a wide street overlooking a park. As favourite nephew he lived with her for several years, and was able to set up his own dental practice. While he was treating another elderly lady he met her companion, Louise Shaw, and fell in love. Aunt Charlotte died in 1910, naming Thomas as her executor and sharing her estate between him and four unmarried nieces. With the money, he was able to propose marriage and buy the large house on Gildredge Road. For seven years all was well.

What went wrong? The other recipients of Aunt Charlotte's money seem to have lived comfortably on the proceeds for the rest of their lives. Thomas, who had an additional income from his work, should have been better off than they were. And as Nancy herself said, both his predecessor in Gainsborough and the man who took over from him did very well from their dental practices. But not Thomas. He had a magnetic repulsion relationship with money; whatever he received or earned slipped through his fingers almost at once. The crime writer in me conjures up lurid scenarios of dark deeds and blackmail. But the most likely explanation for the steady haemorrhaging of cash is that he was a gambler: not racetracks or betting shops but a lifelong belief that luck and chance were better stars to navigate by than clarity and planning. He was obsessed with the competitions in magazines, and not at all interested in keeping accounts or sending invoices to patients. But even so, there remains an element of mystery in his disgrace.

And so they moved north, to a new life in the shadow of the factory in Gainsborough. For a little longer, his five-year-old daughter still idolised her father. At the end of her life she wrote: 'My father was everything that was warm and welcoming and comforting. And I was his relaxation, getting away from all the anxieties of money and work.' Thomas read to her every night and together they escaped from their dingy reality into the adventures of Jack London and the Man Eaters of Tsavo, the magical fantasy of the Alice books and Kipling's India, Henty and Buchan. And when his work was finished and the weather allowed it, father and daughter walked together through the Lincolnshire lanes and he inspired her with scarcely understood wonder for the stars. He told her the names of the constellations, and about the incredible distances between them, how small our Earth is in comparison with the Sun, which in its turn is just a tiny speck in the vastness of the Milky Way – heady stuff for a small child. He also told her about money, and explained the gold bars that were held in the vaults of the Bank of England to back the paper notes that were in circulation. As the First World War ended and the grim post-war years commenced, his little daughter must have been the only person left whom Thomas could impress with his expertise on matters pecuniary.

These walks with her father on mellow summer evenings would have been treasured anyway, but they served a dual purpose: not just the pleasure of each other's company and the unspoiled countryside, but an escape from their claustrophobic and unhappy home. Escape, above all, from Louise.

The disaster that sent the Myers family into Gainsborough exile was only too familiar to Louise. All that Nancy remembered about her maternal grandfather was that he had been a tea importer in Liverpool with three daughters. Louise told her the girls had been brought up to expect marriage to a suitable man of their own class, and trained in the delicate arts of being ladylike;

there was no expectation they might ever have to work. But when they were in their late teens their father went bust and their prospects were shattered. The youngest, May, married anyway and disappeared to Australia – one can speculate that her husband was not of the right class. The only option for impecunious young ladies of good family was to become 'companions' and this is what Louise and her older sister Emmeline duly did. In that role they received their board and lodging, but they had no security, hardly any income and no freedom. Trapped in someone else's home, they passed the days and years of their youth shackled to an employer, who might be kindly or tyrannical. Almost worse than the lack of freedom was the lack of responsibility. Louise reached the age of almost forty without ever having had to manage a household budget, to plan or make decisions. All that was required of her was that she be available and genteel. Pour the tea and keep up appearances.

Nancy's mother during her time as a lady's companion in Leamington Spa

Another disadvantage for the lady's companion was the lack of opportunity for meeting eligible young men; Emmeline never did. Her fair beauty grew more faded and dusty and she ended up, in Nancy's chilling phrase, 'rather peculiar' and helping in a run-down boarding house in North London, her life one of those silent tragedies of an era when it was almost impossible for women to forge their own destiny.

So for Louise it was a wonderful dream come true when the debonair dentist made a home visit to her current elderly lady, and fell in love with her. The dashing Thomas Myers was drawn to this modest, serious, rather sadly beautiful woman. His aunt conveniently died, he proposed, she accepted. After all the disappointments of her life so far, the fairy-tale ending had come at last.

Poor Louise, her window of recovery and esteem was all too brief. In 1917, for the second time in her life, her world was turned upside down by the incompetence or bad luck – from her point of view it hardly mattered which – of the man on whom her happiness depended. She had no resources to deal with the catastrophe. Looking back, Nancy always felt that her father had needed a very different kind of wife (though, in fairness, Louise could probably have done with a different kind of husband) – a woman who could take control of their finances, who could budget and balance the books. As the wife of a feckless dentist in a small Lincolnshire town, Louise was out of her depth. She saw what was happening, and hated it, but she had no more control over her fate than she had over the weather.

In her misery, Louise channelled her ambitions into her only child. Nancy must compensate for everything she had lost. Nancy must demonstrate that in one area of her life she had succeeded. Louise needed her daughter to be a beautiful doll, living proof that she was a wonderful mother. But Louise's devotion to her child was fraught with ambivalence, so as her daughter changed from a plump and pretty infant into a skinny and obstinate child, maternal pride turned to exasperation and Louise's frantic efforts to insist on her child's love only drove Nancy slowly, inexorably, away.

During the first year in Spring Gardens, Nancy had a buffer from her parents' disappointments: Margaret, just out of school herself, was employed as nursemaid and governess. They had lessons in her sunless back bedroom – reading, writing and a few sums. They made strings of paper people joined together by fingers and toes and coloured them in. They went for walks.

After a year Margaret departed, the rocking horse was taken away, and soon after that, the doll's house went too. A washstand with a large china jug and basin took its place, and from now on Nancy was expected to put herself to bed. On dark winter nights that was a chilly and frightening thing to do. She imagined devils lurking over the back stairs, and the ghostly figure of Jesus stood white and condemning in the shadows cast by the gas jet on the main landing. In her mind 'gentle Jesus' had become mixed up with her mother and the confusion put her in mortal terror of both God and the devil at the same time.

Every evening her parents climbed the stairs to kiss her goodnight and put out her light. As part of the daily ritual, her mother unlocked the store cupboard in their bedroom and took out two chocolates or sweets to give her after she had cleaned her teeth. (This, for the daughter of a dentist.) The goodnight kiss was fraught with peril. It was a matter of terrible importance for Nancy that her mother should say goodnight first, 'so that I could settle off to daydream my way into sleep soothed by my father's loving embrace'. Her mother's kiss was like medicine, to be swallowed quickly, its bitter taste to be obliterated by the following sweet. Louise was only too aware of the contrast. 'I'm your mother, kiss me like you kiss your father!' she insisted, but of course it was no good. Nancy wrote, 'I just congealed and waited till it was over, with outrage screaming inside me. Later, the words came, and I would repeat them inside myself. *You can't demand love; love is a gift.*'

When Margaret left, Nancy graduated to a proper governess. On weekday mornings, perched on Thomas's bicycle, she went across the town to study with Miss Ancoats, who lived with her elderly mother and sister in a mellowly beautiful old house on the River Trent. At noon, Nancy sat down to lunch with the old lady, who wore an old-fashioned cap, and her daughters, and each afternoon Miss Ancoats walked her home. Her teacher was not exactly encouraging. Even then Nancy was proud of her drawing – 'I did lovely fairies' – but Miss Ancoats gave her cotton reels and scissors to draw, and then compared the finished result with the work of her previous pupil, Mary Kelsey. Nancy grew to loathe the unseen Mary Kelsey, who had surpassed her in every way, though in fact when she was nine and went away to school she was far in advance of her peers.

Nancy enjoyed staying with her grandfather, who gave her a Schipperke puppy

They had no contact at all with any of Louise's family, but Thomas's father, the retired rector of Twinstead, was a benign influence in Nancy's life, one of the two old gentlemen who had such a dramatic impact in the future. At least once, when she was seven or eight, she went to stay with him and his second wife at their home in the Clifton district of Bristol. There, her grandfather attempted to teach her how to play chess and gave her a Schipperke puppy, the first of the dogs that were to be her favourite childhood companions. The two best holidays of her childhood were spent at their shingled bungalow above the river near Bradford on Avon. The cottage was sunny and brightly furnished. Outside there were flowers in abundance and steps that twisted down to the rowing boat moored on the river. 'Unmitigated bliss' was how she described these summer moments. Happiness for Nancy was always associated with sunshine and fresh air, gardens and colours.

She had to work hard to seize her moments of happiness, because at Spring Gardens the family was coming apart. To begin with, her father tried to keep up his sporting life and joined the golf club at Thonnock, but gradually he lost heart. He missed his old companions at Willingdon and claimed he had nothing in common with the socially inferior members of the local club. Nor did he find anyone congenial to shoot with.

The family's social dislocation was as much a part of daily life as the thump and whine of machinery from the factory across the road and the melancholy whistle of the hooters. Thomas and Louise knew they were a cut above the professional people they mixed with in Gainsborough, but the galling truth was that their social inferiors enjoyed larger houses, more servants and a more gracious lifestyle. While Thomas could escape into books and games, Louise had no defence against the humiliations she endured. More and more, her bitterness found expression in rows, books thrown across the room, doors slammed, vengeful accusations.

Years as a lady's companion had made her acutely aware of the importance of social distinctions. She fought a constant rearguard action to get the servant girls to address her with appropriate deference. For some reason, they all had enormous trouble with calling her 'mum', the version of 'ma'am' she for some reason felt was appropriate.

'Elsie' (or Annie, or Mabel, or whatever the name was of the current occupant of the cold room above the larder), she would demand in her querulous voice, 'what do you say when you speak to me? Yes – what?'

'Yes – um.'

Louise's expression showed she felt the girl was cheeking her deliberately. 'No, Elsie, how many times do I have to tell you? It's *Mum* not *Um*. If you want to get on you must learn to speak to your mistress properly. Now, try to say it right this time.'

Nancy felt sorry for these girls, who never lasted long enough to make any real impression. 'Poor things,' she remembered, 'they had a wretched life. They were country girls whose parents couldn't afford to keep them at home after they grew up.' Lonely and homesick, they had to get up early, clean out four grates and lay the fires in winter, bring in coal, carry washing water up to the bedrooms, make breakfast, then do bedrooms out and empty slops. One room was to be done out thoroughly each day and the rest 'gone over'. Meanwhile they must be ready at all times to answer the door and usher patients in – for which task they must always appear immaculate, no matter what they'd been doing. They were allowed no visitors and must never talk to tradesmen. Their only time off was Wednesday evening from six to ten and alternate Sunday afternoons. This was their only chance to go back home to see their families. Some, Nancy remembered, were hardier than others, 'but all had swollen knees, and red, chapped hands – except one, who had grown up on a farm. I remember coming home one holiday and remarking on her soft, white hands. "It comes from the milking," she said. "I can do anything, my hands is always soft and white. The milk sunk in."'

The hapless Elsies and Annies never lasted long, but for Nancy there was no escape. She tried to find a hideaway in the garden. For a while she crouched under the staging in the greenhouse, among spiders and rubble and broken woodwork, and when that proved too uncomfortable she hid in a corner filled with garden rubbish at the far end of the ivy hedge, but that was even less satisfactory than the greenhouse.

Her mother's dissatisfaction with her daughter increased. The accusation of 'wickedness' became a constant refrain. Louise told her she was wicked for wanting to read rather than do something useful like dusting the trinkets in the front room, or going to the shop for raisins or lard; she was wicked when she chirruped a popular song about Felix the Cat, the most popular cartoon character until the arrival of Mickey Mouse, 'Felix Kept on Walking':

By a train at Dover, had his tail run over,
On the rail he left his tail, it gave the folks a thrill,
Still for that he didn't care.
Though he had no rudder there,
Wagged his 'nothing' in the air, and kept on walking still.

According to Louise, a good child would have sung something more suitable, like 'The Lost Chord' or 'Silver Threads among the Gold':

Darling, I am growing old,
Silver threads among the gold,
Shine upon my brow today;
Life is fading fast away.

It's not hard to see why the anarchic and resilient little Felix the Cat appealed to a lively child more than morbid Victorian sentimentality, but for Louise it was all a sign of Nancy's incorrigible wickedness.

There is a terrible desperation in Louise's self-defeating battle to turn Nancy into the ideal daughter who would compensate for all her disappointments. Endlessly Louise washed and scrubbed the child, spent hours doing her hair each day, culminating in the hated evening ritual of winding Nancy's long, thick hair up with curling rags into the great awkward knobs that made sleeping so uncomfortable.

To achieve Nancy's dramatic ringlets, her mother curled her hair
into painful knobs every evening

Nancy must demonstrate and acknowledge that her mother was not just good, but perfect. Often – but always when her father was out of earshot – Louise told Nancy she was wicked because she didn't honour and love her mother as she should. This was all the more unforgivable because Louise was, in fact, 'the best woman in the world'. Nancy came to dread this much-repeated phrase which haunted her for years, well into adult life and even after she had become a mother herself. The woman that she was growing to love less and less, even to dislike intensely, was apparently 'the best woman in the world'. Her guilt and confusion became a torment. Her inability to love this maternal paragon made her feel, in her words, like a pariah, utterly cast out from the human race.

Of course, it is obvious now that Louise must have been crippled with insecurity: her constant insistence that Nancy provide the affirmation she craved was fuelled by her terrible fear that she was anything but a good mother. She saw her daughter's love draining away, was so threatened by Nancy's 'Daddy's girl' devotion that she tried to compel her to kiss her in the same way. But it is easy to feel sorry for a woman you have never met. For Louise's daughter this judicious view was never an option. When she was writing about her childhood in the months before her death, Nancy kept coming back to the toxic emotional atmosphere of her family. Why had she been unable to see through her mother's demands? Why had she not rejected her ridiculous claim to be the best woman in the world? Nancy came to the conclusion that the lie had been drummed into her when she was too young to put up any resistance.

And then there was the ultimate weapon in Louise's verbal armoury. If Nancy was slow to do what was required, her mother declared with terrible finality, 'You can never make up to me for the pain you caused me when you were born.' Sometimes she added that Nancy had almost killed her, had nearly been responsible for the death of the best woman in the world. It's a shocking crime to lay at the feet of a child, especially one who is struggling with negative feelings towards her mother. A tangle of guilt and confusion and shame from which it seemed impossible to escape.

About a year before she died, when my parents were living in the last home they made together, a large thatched cottage in the Dorset village of Milton Abbas, she was sitting beside the fire. She had been knitting for a while, and was more than usually pensive, with that turned-in expression that all those close to her knew so well. 'I've been thinking a lot about my mother recently,' she said. 'And I think I've come to understand her better.'

'How?' I wanted to know. After all these years, had she found a way to be reconciled to the woman whose crabbed misery had cast a blight over her childhood and far beyond?

'I realise,' she said, 'that she was just a rather silly and unhappy woman.'

It's the last thing I remember her ever saying on the subject.

2

A HARUM-SCARUM SCHOOLGIRL

Escape beckoned as the day approached for Nancy to go as a boarder to Lincoln High School for Girls. She had devoured Angela Brazil's school stories, such titles as *The Jolliest Term on Record* and *A Harum-Scarum Schoolgirl*. One in particular filled her with enthusiasm: she remembered it – significantly, as it turned out – as *The Most Popular Girl in the School*, but it was probably *A Popular Schoolgirl* which came out in 1920, the year before Nancy put on her new uniform and travelled the twenty miles from Gainsborough to Lincoln. The message of all these books was the same: there might be ups and downs at a girls' boarding school but essentially they were places of fun and excitement and jolly friendships.

Lincoln Christ's Hospital Girls' High School, to give it its full title, had been founded in 1893. It occupied a large red-brick Gothic building on the side of the hill going from the town up to the cathedral. Most of the 450 pupils were day girls. The 50 boarders were put up in two houses, one on the edge of the cathedral close and the other on the far side of the cathedral, through the imposing arch known as the Bail Gate. It was to this bleak-looking house of grey brick with all its pipes on the outside that Nancy came on that first afternoon, her hair in a long plait with a black bow at the end of it. Bidding farewell to the hated ringlets was a further cause for celebration: no more torment of having her hair yanked back into tight painful knobs each evening.

Nancy and her parents were shown into the dormitory on the ground floor next to the dining room, where the youngest girls were kept under the eye of Miss Wynch, the matron whose little room was just across the hall. Most of the other boarders were the daughters of Lincolnshire farmers, though one girl came from Alberta in Canada. Eagerly, Nancy waited for her parents to leave so her new life, the life of dorm fun and madcap schoolgirls, friendship and larks, might begin.

It always struck me as strange that my mother never reminisced about her schooldays. She did not seem to have made any particular friends. I assumed that she had already retreated into a self-sufficient reserve and kept to herself, that she had failed to find anyone congenial with whom to share her schooldays. Reading the memoir she began just before she died, I now realise how wrong my assumption was.

She was an only child whose parents were isolated by their sense of social superiority and financial inferiority to those around them. Her lessons had taken place alone with a governess. As a result, Nancy was woefully ill-equipped to survive in the rough and tumble of school life. By the end of her first week the Angela Brazil fantasy had been well and truly shattered and her last vestiges of 'Eastbourne confidence' had been knocked out of her. From then until her last year in the sixth form it was all 'misery and boredom', so that even in the final months of her life she didn't like to look back on it.

People's unhappy boarding school experiences can be a common topic of conversation. Nancy never joined in. Her silence on the subject was simply because it had been too hard to talk about. Not just the wretchedness that comprises so many boarding school memories, but deep shame as well.

In the boarding house she was youngest and smallest, at the very bottom of the pecking order; right away she became the butt of the other girls' jokes. When she was writing her memoir, she forced herself to address this: 'For various reasons I appeared so different that I just couldn't be assimilated as a natural human companion – couldn't be a part of we and so, of course, became the enemy.' Her parents had taken endless pains to make sure her voice carried no trace of a Lincolnshire accent, which they regarded as horribly common, so from the very outset she was set apart from the stolid daughters of the local farmers. She tried to win friends by sharing with them all the knowledge about such topics as the cosmos and the gold bars in the vaults of the Bank of England, which her father had told her about on their walks together. To begin with this just irritated her school-fellows, but soon the tide was firmly against her. They called her a witch, a nine-year-old witch. The cruel name-calling of young girls is bad enough for someone who has been affirmed by their parents; for Nancy, already struggling with her mother's accusations of wickedness and worse, the taunts only confirmed her deepest fears about herself. Far from being a popular schoolgirl, she soon found herself the most unpopular girl in the school.

At night she lay in the dormitory with the blankets pulled tightly round her head to block out the sound of the other girls talking about her; she comforted herself with the thought that no misery in adult life could ever be worse than this, and if it was, she could commit suicide.

The misery took its toll, both mentally and physically. She became secretive and stubborn. She developed what she called a 'nervous stomach' which meant that she was either constipated or afflicted with violent stomach pains and, even worse, uncontrollable bowels. Once she discovered yellow splashes on a petticoat and, too ashamed to ask for help, she bundled it up and hid it in a drawer. The offending garment was soon found. The response of Miss Wynch is hard to credit nowadays. She already regarded Nancy's constipation as wilful disobedience – those were the days when well-trained nannies expected their charges to produce a healthy bowel movement every day after breakfast, so she was probably just in tune with current thinking – but the soiled petticoat was evidence of 'truly awful wickedness' (Nancy's words) and was exhibited to the other girls. Not surprisingly, it became the object of much pointing, chanting and whispering, and remained a useful weapon for her tormentors for a long time.

In the classroom things weren't much better. She started off in the second form well ahead of most of her classmates. Miss Ancoats had given her a thorough grounding, so she had neat writing, could spell and do simple arithmetic. She had a smattering of geography and history as well, but was soon bored by the unimaginative way the lessons were taught. Those early walks with her father had inculcated in her a habit of question and answer, of following a line of thought, that was conducive to real learning, and all her life Nancy was to be passionate about anything that interested her. She was dissatisfied with the dry bits of information that were doled out, to be memorised and repeated as required. 'Learn it, keep it, and give it back without alteration on command' was what they demanded. She fluctuated between long periods of dreaming inattention and bouts of intense and challenging interest. Her teachers regarded each state as equally irritating and their scolding veered from 'Nancy Myers, not paying attention again, I see!' to 'Don't argue, don't ask questions! Just get on and do as I say.'

She developed into one of those girls who are always untidy, always losing things and who never know what time of day it is. Morning break-times, which in fine weather were spent getting fresh air in the school grounds, most often found her lurking in the lavatories because once again she had failed to muster two galoshes. Not having galoshes meant a bad mark, and three bad marks would have counted against her house. As she was unable to win house points at sport, she was anxious not to drag the house down by her loose grip on her galoshes. And it wasn't just galoshes. Rulers, pencils, set squares all vanished from her desk, though whether because she was careless or the other girls stole them, she does not say.

When Nancy was writing about this period of her life she struggled to find something to lighten the picture. She described two experiences. From the age of eleven, she looked forward passionately to the twice-yearly concerts in the cathedral. She never sang or played an instrument, but the music provided a much-needed emotional release, the only outlet for her feelings that was available at this time.

The second memory of a snatched moment of happiness only highlights how bleak those first years were. On summer evenings she leant out of the lavatory window and a soft breeze brought the scent of lilac from the nearby garden. With it came a sense of peace and a promise of happiness. Like a prisoner in a cell, she breathed in the scents from the outside world and dreamed of freedom.

At first, it had seemed the ordeal might soon be over. Her grandfather, that kindly former rector who had given her her first dog and who perhaps was more perceptive than her parents, came up with the suggestion that she move to a small school for the daughters of clergy in East Anglia. Nancy saw this as a wonderful chance to make a new start, but her hopes were soon dashed. When she broached the subject to her mother, and even confessed that she was unhappy at Lincoln and begged to be moved, Louise told her she was ungrateful to talk that way when her father was making such sacrifices for her education. Nancy was forbidden to burden her father with these complaints.

So she never told Thomas how unhappy she was. He was to be protected from the truth at all costs. She blamed herself and was ashamed of her misery and of not being the success of whom he could be proud. 'But it was a bad thing,' she wrote later, 'too big a burden for a ten-year-old and it marked the beginning of the end of my wonderful relationship with my father. Or had comfort already begun to be withheld? Otherwise why hadn't I hurled myself into his waistcoat and sobbed out my misery?' Now a sort of inner bitterness began to build up. Thomas's love was not absolute; it was conditional on maintaining the fiction that she was happy at the school where the girls called her a witch and the matron held up her soiled petticoat for general ridicule.

Holidays were eagerly anticipated. At home, there was always a dog to be companion and playmate. The little Schipperke her grandfather had given her did not live long, but he was followed a year or so later by the first of the Micks, a smooth-haired reddish-gold ball of fire. After a year or so, he got distemper. She crouched beside his basket in the kitchen, resisting her mother's instructions to leave him. 'He's dying,' said Louise. 'There's nothing you can do.' But Nancy stayed. 'Not heart-broken,' as she said, 'but feeling I must participate in what I felt to be a moment of great significance and wonder. I can't remember in detail the thoughts that went through my mind as I crouched there, but I was quite calm and entered into a sort of mystical state and had my hand on Mick as he shuddered into death.' Once he had died, she was of course sorry, but matter-of-fact, and he was buried without ceremony at the end of the garden.

The second Mick was a red setter and became the adored companion of Nancy's early teens. He had a kennel by the pump just outside the kitchen door. Every morning when the maid came down at half-past six she undid his chain and he rushed inside, bounding up the stairs into Nancy's room, mud and all. At first they could go no further than the garden, where Nancy practised somersaults and played ball, and then when she was given an old stocking she and Mick had long tugs of war, Mick twisting, turning and jerking until she whirled him off his feet and swung him round in mid-air, until finally they collapsed in an exhausted heap together and got their breath back. These games stopped when it was discovered that Mick's teeth had worked loose; thereafter he had trouble with bones and tough meat.

Mick was not the only companion to be found in the garden. A long, ivy-clad workshop next to the coal shed was where Herman, her father's mechanic, worked all day at his bench. Nowadays he would be called a technician; he made the dentures, plates and bridges her father's patients needed. And, when required, he rolled down his sleeves, adjusted his tie, took his jacket down from the peg behind the door and went through the kitchen to the consulting room, where he performed the duties of an anaesthetist. He had no particular qualifications for this role, but that seems never to have caused a problem.

Herman's workshop was a popular port of call and Nancy's mother expended a lot of energy stopping the maid from chatting to him as she passed his door on the way to the rubbish dump or the coal shed. Nancy learned to approach from the far end of the garden, since her mother of course disapproved of her visits. 'Hanging about in there and stopping Herman getting on with his work,' she called it. And if her father found her in there he would frown and say, 'Haven't you anything better to do?' Herman would tip her off if he expected a visit.

She was drawn to the workshop, especially in those early holidays from school, before her first bicycle opened up a larger world. She loved the apparatus and the materials and the shapes of the tools, loved the mingled smells, hot wax and plaster, but above all she loved the order and the clear imperatives of the craftsman's task. So much of the adult world was incomprehensible and beset with unexplained pitfalls and taboos, but in Herman's domain problems were clear and they could be solved.

She felt the calm young mechanic was an ally. 'I'm sure there wasn't much about the Myers family he didn't know,' she said, and she was aware that he was 'not uncritical' of her mother. From his workshop they could hear Louise scolding the maid and arguing with the tradesmen who trekked under the arch to the kitchen door with regular supplies of milk and meat and coal. 'I now think that he hadn't all that much respect for my father either and I wonder if he sometimes had to wait for his wages.' Like Nancy, Herman was powerless to leave; jobs were few and far between in the 1920s.

He was a man of few words. Nancy boasted, 'I swam a quarter of a mile. None of the other girls in my form can.' (If this was typical of Nancy's conversational style, it goes some way to explain her unpopularity.)

'Did you really?' was his laconic reply.

She tried out gossip and ideas. 'Is it true you can die from eating mackerel but not herring?' (His answer is not recorded.)

All the while, Herman was hunched over his bench, absorbed in his current task; she watched him, asking every now and then, 'Why are you doing that?' before moving to another boast: 'Daddy took me up in an aeroplane. It was five shillings. It was awfully windy. I wish it had been longer.'

Herman could not let her touch any of the equipment on his bench, but just occasionally, when there was a rush of work, her father had to finish a job in the evening after Herman had gone home. Then Nancy was free to mess around, pushing soft wax into old plaster casts, or filing and sanding broken bits of dental plate. She asked questions and learned that nothing short of perfection would do. Her father, tired after his long day, was impatient to get the job done, but Nancy could have happily stayed there for hours.

The highlight of each year came in August: a fortnight by the sea. They went first to Norfolk, then further afield to the Yorkshire resorts of Scarborough and Whitby. In Scarborough, where they went for two years running, Nancy made friends with a girl who was staying in the same boarding house. They quickly became inseparable, curled up next to each other in an armchair reading the same book. They played dares: 'Dare you to ring that door-bell,' or 'Dare you to ask that man the time,' 'Dare you to walk on the edge of that wall.' Two weeks of bliss.

A rare moment of friendship during their annual fortnight at the seaside

But even here there was a problem. The friendship which must have meant so much to Nancy, the 'least popular girl in the school', was a mighty inconvenience to her father. The whole point of the holiday for him was to play as much golf as possible, but if he was playing golf and Nancy was with a friend, what was her mother supposed to do? Louise never seems to have made any friends, and was unable to amuse herself, but if Thomas had to keep her company he could not play golf. So Nancy was discouraged from making friends when they went away.

The family finances remained precarious, and there came a time when even their annual holiday was uncertain. Nancy was terrified that one year this longed-for event might prove beyond their means, because every August, just before they set off, her mother would produce from a secret hiding place a few pounds saved from her housekeeping money. Without this hoard of cash, Louise announced, they would not have been able to go. Then she would stuff the precious bundle of notes into a special pocket sewn inside her whalebone corset and they were free to depart.

But not to the kind of place they felt they belonged in. They always stayed in dingy boarding houses that smelled of cabbage, cats and disinfectant, and never on the seafront. They never went out for a meal. The worst aspect, from Thomas and Louise's point of view, was that their fellow guests were socially unacceptable. At the end of the holiday Thomas would mimic their farewells: 'Pleased to have met you, Mr Myers.' Nancy thought it was a pleasant thing to say, but no, it was common, and dreadful that they were forced to mix with such inferior types.

Each year they made a point of visiting the kind of small hotels in which they felt they belonged. They were shown around elegant places with spacious bedrooms overlooking the sea and sometimes even a basin in the room, with a mirror over it. The lounge might be furnished with chintz-covered chairs and small tables with flowers and magazines on them. Sometimes they were treated to a glimpse of a 'superior guest'. Nancy longed to stay in such a place, where they belonged and where they could hold up their heads. But they never did.

*

In her imagination, Nancy was already exploring worlds that were different from the narrow space her parents inhabited. She was always able to lose herself in books, and two books in particular made a deep impression on her, not least because they were written by relatives and spoke to her of values and experiences she could respect and identify with.

F. W. H. – Frederick – Myers was the first cousin of her Twinstead grandfather, but an altogether more exotic specimen. The son of yet another country parson, F. W. H. also went to Trinity College, Cambridge, where he gained a reputation as a brilliant classicist. He gave up his academic career and worked for thirty years as a schools inspector, but his real life's work was the exploration of what is now called paranormal phenomena. He tried to bring the empirical rigour of science to its study and in 1882 he was one of the founders of the Society for Psychical Research. His magnum opus was *Human Personality: And Its Survival of Bodily Death* and he coined the word 'telepathy'.

The other relative whose books were a lifeline to the teenage Nancy was to be even more significant later in her life, though she had no idea then. Harold Fielding Hall was her father's first cousin and, almost inevitably, the son of a country parson. His break with tradition was even more radical than F. W. H.'s. In the early 1880s he went to Burma; at first he worked for a teak company, but during the war of annexation he worked for the government and after that spent many years as a rural magistrate. Most Englishmen found the climate of Upper Burma impossible; their health collapsed within months. But not Fielding Hall. He fell in love with the country, with its people and with their religion, with everything about it. His finest book, *The Soul of a People*, paints a portrait of the inner life of 'this people whom I love so well'.

It is a remarkable work, still in print more than a hundred years later, and every page shines with his admiration and love for Burma and its people. I did not read it until after Nancy's death, and I realised at once that so much of what I had always thought of as 'Mum's wisdom' was derived from his description of traditional Burmese Buddhism. Read from the perspective of a young teenager trapped in a narrow and dreary existence both at home and at school, the words are dynamite.

He talks of learning Buddhism from the monks:

> To sit in the monastery garden in the dusk, in just such a tropic dusk as [the Buddha] taught in so many years ago, and hear the yellow-robed monk tell of that life, and repeat his teaching of love, and charity, and compassion – eternal love, perfect charity, endless compassion – until the stars come out in the purple sky, and the silver-voiced gongs ring for evening prayers, is a thing never to be forgotten. As you watch the starlight die and the far-off hills fade into the night, as the sounds about you become still, and the calm silence of the summer night falls over the whole earth, you know and understand the teacher of the Great Peace as no words can tell you.

For the girl who had to lean out of the lavatory window to catch the scent of lilac on the summer air, this evocation of a distant Burmese world brought the promise that there was a better way to live.

It is tempting to imagine that there was one Burmese whom Fielding Hall loved in particular. He writes of a woman who gave him insights into Buddhism from a female perspective. And he states that 'To have loved once is more than to have read all the poets that ever sang. So a Burman thinks. To see the moon rise on the river as you float along, while the boat rocks to and fro and someone talks to you, is not that better than any tale?' It was for Fielding Hall. He came back to England and tried to live as an

Englishman again, married an English rose and promptly had a breakdown. His marriage collapsed; he went back to Burma but no longer fitted that world either. He wrote more books, some of them deeply weird. He died in 1917.

At some stage this wise and tortured man must have had some contact with Nancy's family, because his story touches her life later on; during her teenage years, however, she knew him only as the relative whose writing gave her a different way to find answers to the big questions that she was struggling with. She wrote later, 'The family link with Fielding Hall and with F. W. H. Myers greatly encouraged me and helped to strengthen my feeling of really belonging to this other, freer world, and I believed that through me this creative line would be carried on.'

An incident in early life seemed to justify her belief in her artistic destiny. When Nancy was three, and still living in Eastbourne, she fell on a sharp flint, cutting the palm of her right hand and severing the tendons of two fingers, which made it impossible to open and shut the hand. In 1915 the only surgeon considered capable of fitting the tendons together again was at a base hospital in France. It was nine months before he could return and operate on her at Great Ormond Street Hospital. The operation went on for four hours as, by this time, the tendons had shrunk a good deal. The very fact that they could be joined up at all was considered a miracle. Nancy's childish mind took this literally; when later she discovered a talent for drawing she assumed God had worked the miracle so that she could become an artist. As she said, 'This thought was a great steadier and secret source of comfort during my miserable early years at school.'

By the time she was fifteen school had become more boredom than misery and by now her artistic confidence extended to the appreciation of contemporary works. In May 1927 Nancy was part of a guard of honour formed of enthusiastic girl guides on the

Lincoln streets. They were welcoming the Prince of Wales who was to open the new Usher Gallery. Like most young women at that time, she was in love with the handsome and unorthodox heir to the throne, but unlike her fellow flag-wavers, she had firm opinions about contemporary art. She championed a painting by Dod Procter which showed a grey- and purple-fleshed woman lying on a bed among crumpled grey sheets. She praised its strength and realism and disdained those who could see in it only 'dirty feet' and squalor. She also admired the work of Dame Laura Knight as 'robust, meaty and real, as opposed to airy-fairy and idealised confections or the sentimental story pictures still in vogue with my parents. I responded to what I felt was a sweeping away of veils, and of sham and pretence.'

To sweep away the veils of sham and pretence was what she longed for, what she desperately hoped art school would bring. Her greatest fear during these last years at school was that a lack of funds would stop her achieving her dream. Money troubles continued to dog their lives. Her father resented his work and patients, wishing that they would leave him alone and not bother him; accounts were not sent out and his equipment became more and more run down. It was a gradual, relentless deterioration, and the low point came when Nancy was about twelve or thirteen.

One night, after she had gone to bed, her father came to her room and, without putting on the light, he mumbled awkwardly that he needed to borrow the money she had saved. This had mostly been accumulated from Christmas and birthday gifts from her grandfather, and came to about fourteen pounds. The incident was both embarrassing and frightening. Were her meagre savings all that stood between her family and some unspecified but terrible fate?

It was the nadir of their fortunes, and Nancy's faith in the father she had once adored ebbed away.

And then, things started to improve. When she was fourteen, her kindly grandfather died. Thomas went to Bath for the funeral and then straight to London, to the Rootes car showroom which had just opened in Devonshire House in Piccadilly. There he bought a two-cylinder Jowett and, without having ever been behind a steering wheel in his life, drove it back up to Lincolnshire.

The car transformed their lives. On Saturday afternoons they went on expeditions, often taking picnics to the rolling stretch of countryside near Gainsborough known as the Dukeries. Thomas was inspired to take up golf again, and now he wanted Nancy to learn too. He bought her golf clubs and a bag, and 'a new era began'. For a while Nancy was full of enthusiasm and devoted hours to practising her swing in the back garden and poring over her father's old golf books, analysing Harry Vardon's technique. Of course, Louise resented their shared interest. On one occasion she came into the room, snatched the book they were studying and threw it out of the window.

A rare photograph of Nancy and her father survives from this summer of 1926. She had been angling for some time to have her hair cut short, and the opportunity came after several bouts of flu the previous winter. 'Outgrowing your strength' is one of those ailments, like green sickness, that is no longer diagnosed, but in the 1920s too much hair was thought to be a contributory factor. Anyway, her outgrown strength was enough to override her mother's objections and in this photograph Nancy sports a bingle, a modified version of the fashionable shingle. She was delighted with the picture, seeing 'an immaculate couple in an elegant, rather nonchalant attitude. A handsome man and his – not beautiful – but modish daughter, who looked almost grown up' in silk stockings, long, pointy-toed shoes and the dress her mother had sewn for her in the very latest drop-waisted flapper style.

A debonair couple: Nancy, her hair cut in a 'bingle', with her father

And she made her first independent adult friend. Betty Robinson lived with her husband Clem in a bungalow on a council estate within cycling distance of Spring Gardens. Nancy describes her as uncomplicated, stubborn, loyal and forthright. She longed for children but had given up hopes of having any as Clem's first wife had died in childbirth and he couldn't face the chance of it happening again. So Betty took it on herself to run a kind of day centre in her home for severely handicapped children. Nancy was both repelled by these children and drawn to them, and on most mornings in the holidays she cycled over to help out. Nancy said that until Betty took them on, 'the children had mostly been just fed and left to sit around in corners, no attempts having been made to help them develop the few wits they had. What flash of inspiration had first started Betty thinking they might be helpable and that she would set about doing it I just don't know – but she did. With great patience and gentleness she managed to increase their ability to not only do small things for themselves, but get some enjoyment out of life and in doing things together.' Nancy was discovering in herself a rapport with society's rejects which was to play a large part in her life in later years. She wrote, 'They called me "Mitmyer" – the nearest they could get to my name. One little girl, I remember, had a tiny, pointed head, and there was one rather feeble, frail boy. Another boy who was big and clumsy and noisy, would, during walking exercise, move up beside the small frail one when he got tired and gently take his arm. This I found wonderful and moving.'

Life at school was at last starting to improve. During her last two years in Lincoln she became a fairly well-respected member of the community. She also had a brief, passionate friendship with a girl called Ena Bartholemew, who was a year or two older than her. Barty, as she was known, was already in the sixth form and about to leave to read English literature at college. She had not been a boarder for long. Small, round and very emotional, she was phenomenally unpopular, for reasons Nancy found hard to fathom since she was gentle, quiet and kind. But she was different – a fatal mistake. Barty was miserable and kept threatening suicide. Nancy begged her not to. When she left, they exchanged a few letters before their friendship fizzled out, but the memory of intense emotions lingered for a long time.

Apart from this brief period of drama, school life was uneventful. Having stayed always somewhere in the middle of the form academically, she suddenly did much better than expected in her school certificate, for the simple reason that she had a goal: success would mean only one year in the sixth form instead of two.

In her final year she was even made head of house and she relished the responsibilities and privileges that went with it, especially the freedom to go out alone. It was bliss to be able to walk at her own speed, to dawdle or hurry or even to stand still if she wanted. Added to this, she spent as much of her last year as she wanted drawing and painting: her drawing of a figure in a niche in the cathedral was reproduced in the school magazine. She was left alone, the staff were courteous and chatted to her occasionally, and she felt tolerated, finally. Not accepted, exactly, but tolerated, and that made all the difference. Her housemistress and old enemy, Miss Penny, told her when she left that she had been an excellent head of house, adding, 'I didn't think you could do it.'

For years Nancy had been dreaming of art school, and the new life ahead. She knew that she was woefully unprepared to cope with the world; as usual, she turned to books for the information she needed. In her final term in the lower sixth, a new young matron in her boarding house had lent her a copy of *The Constant Nymph*. Margaret Kennedy's bestselling novel focused on the bohemian Sanger family, especially fifteen-year-old Teresa. The Sanger household was a portrait of an upbringing in every way the opposite of Nancy's. The children 'had received no sort of regular education, but in the course of their travels they had picked up a good deal of mental furniture and could abuse each other most profanely in the *argot* of four languages'. When they were finally sent to boarding school, they hated it and quite sensibly ran away. Teresa's passions and fears are treated with as much seriousness as those of the adults, heady stuff for a girl of nearly the same age whose feelings had been endlessly negated. Predictably, the book was discovered by Miss Penny and confiscated, and the enlightened matron was given a ticking off. Nancy was furious: in her opinion *The Constant Nymph*, with its description of creative artists and their bohemian way of life, was exactly the kind of thing she should be reading: she should be prepared, 'not just shot out like a greyhound from a trap'.

But before the greyhound was sent off into the world, Lincoln High School had a final surprise for her.

The only member of staff Nancy respected was the head-mistress, Miss Savill. Small and intimidating, she had a profile like

Savonarola: a firm mouth below a beaked nose. With her beautiful voice and a slow, deliberate way of speaking, she had the air of an abbess and everyone feared as well as liked her – staff as much as pupils. On the whole, the girls had very little contact with her. If guilty of any misdemeanour so terrible that the staff were unable to deal with it, they were sent to quake outside her office until summoned inside. 'Her quiet, brief scoldings reduced the most mutinous of us to wormhood.' Nancy regarded her with veneration, but in her nine years at Lincoln High she had only ever visited her in the role of culprit.

Filled with a certain trepidation, Nancy knocked on her door to pay her a final visit. They exchanged a few words about what Nancy planned to do when she left. Then, out of the blue, Miss Savill pronounced her verdict: 'You know, Nancy,' she said with just a hint of reproach, 'you are a very attractive girl.'

Nancy was stunned. She managed to mumble a few words in reply, before leaving Miss Savill's room for the last time.

Attractive? Her? She'd had no idea.

'You are a very attractive girl,' said her headmistress, with just a touch of reproach

3

SEEING LIFE

Nancy was beautiful. A story illustrating this existed in various versions. The one she told me was that when she and Larry had arrived in a Greek town before the war, the local paper excitedly told its readers that Greta Garbo had been sighted. Larry's sister Margo told me it was a Bournemouth paper that filed the mistaken identity story. Wherever it took place, the significance of the story was that her beauty was of film-star quality.

Like Garbo, she was tall and slender, with long slim legs, a flat chest and stomach and wide shoulders. She had clear blue eyes and fine cheekbones, and I think she possessed some inner quality – a kind of innocence or unworldliness – that shone through and gave a radiance to her classic features. There was even something androgynous about her: she recalled with some pride that homosexual men had often found her attractive.

In later life she was striking rather than elegant. Perhaps it was different when she was in her twenties, when she saw her beauty reflected in the admiring gaze of even unknown newspapermen, but she never had the poise usually associated with beautiful women. She didn't give the impression of being what the French call *bien dans sa peau* – comfortable in her skin. A friend of mine visiting the cottage near Great Missenden that she and my father built in the 1960s, which she loved and where she was as much at ease as she was anywhere, described us all seated at the round table in the kitchen relaxing over the evening meal. He ended with my mother, who 'resembled a beautifully tied knot'. The beautiful and the knot were of equal importance – and maybe that was part of her attraction.

'I was beautiful.' 'Men found me attractive.' It smacks of boasting, like the fading Norma Desmond in *Sunset Boulevard*, and there may have been an element of that, I suppose. When she talked to me about it she was in her late forties and early fifties, and she no longer turned heads. But the matter-of-fact way she said it never seemed like bragging, more like the statement of a simple truth. Her appearance, and the impact that had on people, was important, and it would have been dishonest to have pretended otherwise.

However, Miss Savill's final observation on the awkward pupil who'd had such trouble fitting in at her school did not become immediately apparent, and the story of Nancy's first eighteen months in London is that of an unappealing Lincolnshire duckling who was transformed into a stunning bohemian swan.

Her reading – *The Constant Nymph* in particular – had taught her where she wanted to be, but to begin with, Nancy remained firmly anchored in her parents' world of Edwardian respectability. It was arranged that she follow in the footsteps of Miss Fisher, who had been her art teacher at school, and thus she enrolled at Westminster Art School, and like Miss Fisher she lodged at an establishment for young ladies in Redcliffe Gardens, near Earl's Court.

In this select boarding house, proprieties were upheld by the imposing Miss Mackintosh who wore dresses of long, heavy black silk. The eight young ladies in her care were required to change into evening clothes for dinner. Nancy's evening dress was made of artificial silk in a dull green embellished with muddy pink flowers, and she was conscious that it was dowdy compared with the other girls'. She had two day dresses. Before leaving home she was photographed in the one which was bought: also green, this had buttons down the front and a fawn binding round the collar. Her other dress, dark blue tweed with a white cotton collar, was made for her by her mother.

A professional photograph taken just before Nancy left Gainsborough
for art school in London

Nancy made no particular friends at Miss Mackintosh's and from the moment she set foot in it her sole aim was to escape; she had no wish to be a young lady of the kind Miss Mackintosh desired and the whole set-up represented everything she was trying to get away from. But she knew she had to stay there for a year at least. And at art school, she was beginning to dip her toe in the world she had dreamed of for so long.

Westminster Technical Institute and School of Art no longer exists. In 1929 it was a small but prestigious institution in

Vincent Square headed by Walter Bayes, a follower of Walter Sickert. Chunky and white-haired, he was quite without patience. He treated all his pupils the same, and if he thought a student was doing something bloody silly, he said so. A couple of elderly women who came to his painting class once a week were regularly reduced to tears. Now sixty, he had been head of Westminster for ten years and had developed a one-track-mind teaching method based on what he called 'transposing the colours'.

'Just make that yellow background purple,' he would tell the student. 'Now, what colour will the flesh be?' To demonstrate his point he blobbed big splashes of yellow or green or whatever he had decided the flesh should be on the canvas, much to the distress of the old ladies, who never cottoned on to what he was doing and kept trying to paint what they saw in an increasingly puzzled way.

The first-year students were taught drawing by 'Daddy' Lawrence, a patriarch with a long grey beard; Nancy found him an uninspiring teacher. Westminster threatened to be a terrible let-down, but Nancy quickly discovered that all the excitement occurred on the courses taught in the evenings. As excitement, artistic and social, was what she longed for, she signed up for two classes and got something of value from each.

Both classes were taught by men who had been scarred by the Great War. Frank Medworth taught wood-engraving, and though Nancy never got very far with the subject she fell in love with her teacher; not, as she said herself, in an adult way, but more from a yearning for a father figure. Medworth was in his late thirties, fairly handsome with a small beard and a hole in his head. This was a large depression in his left temple which pulsed in and out like the throat of a frog, legacy of a wound sustained on the Western Front. Nancy fantasised that he would invite her home for tea with his wife, and that the newly married pair would 'sort of adopt' her. It did not happen, but during their weekly classes he always made a point of stopping by the 'donkey' her work rested on, and giving her praise and encouragement.

The second evening class was life drawing, taught by Bernard Meninsky. Also in his late thirties, Meninsky had been born in the Ukraine, studied at the Royal College of Art and in Paris, and had fought with Allenby in Palestine. At the end of the war he'd had a breakdown and been discharged. During the day he taught at the Central School of Art and was building a reputation as a strong, bold draughtsman and painter. Like Medworth, he singled Nancy out for special praise, once even comparing her 'short pose' figure drawings to the work of Matisse, which understandably sent her into raptures.

London in 1929, the year of the Wall Street Crash, was still a city of the walking wounded, the legacy of the Great War lingering everywhere. The two teachers who gave Nancy much-needed encouragement typified this – Medworth with the pulsing hole in his head and Meninsky with recurrent mental problems – and it is telling that both men committed suicide after the Second World War. Nancy was deeply troubled by the amputees and beggars who were everywhere to be seen, but though she sometimes tried to help individuals she never developed any coherent political response to the problems that were so much in evidence during her years in London. At a time when so many young people were finding solutions through communism or fascism, her only loyalty was to bohemianism, the belief that she belonged to a distinct elite for whom all that mattered was dedication to the creation of artistic excellence.

The evening classes provided stimulus and encouragement. They also introduced her to three Portuguese siblings, the Amarals, who had an unmistakable aura of artistic glamour and who welcomed her into their circle. Luciano, the boy, was especially attractive. Tall and extremely thin, he had dark, curly hair and was witty and charming. His hands had a perpetual tremor from excessive smoking and coffee, but this in no way affected his engravings, which Nancy considered to be exquisite. She thought him wonderful and the high point of the week was going with him and his sisters, as well as a handful of other friends, for a coffee after their class at the Lyons Corner House near Victoria Station.

Coffee in a Lyons Corner House might not seem the height of wild behaviour, but it was enough to cause trouble back at Redcliffe Gardens. After a couple of warnings the redoubtable Miss Mackintosh put her foot down: in future, Nancy must return home as soon as the class finished at nine o'clock. Nancy protested that on this occasion her lateness was due to one of her frequent guilty tangles with beggars and flower-sellers, as she'd given money to a shrivelled old man with a couple of bunches of wilted snowdrops on his tray and a pathetic notice asking for help – another destitute 'hero' from the Great War. She felt morally obliged to buy one of the bunches, which left her with not enough money for the Tube and she had to walk part of the way home. A compromise was reached: Miss Mackintosh agreed to let her stay late on one evening only, but after the second class she had to return straight away.

By this time Nancy had chummed up with a fellow student at Westminster called Cecily Rawson. Small, neat and dark, Cecily had beautiful eyes and hair cut in an Eton crop. She tried to minimise her breasts so as to have a boyish figure. After classes the two girls visited teashops together and discussed the kind of furniture they'd buy when they set up house. Cecily was something of a Puritan, and later that caused a serious rift between them. Towards the end of that first year there was a hint of future troubles when they were both attendants on the Westminster float at the Chelsea Arts Ball. Before they set off, Nancy recklessly took off her flesh-coloured vest, exposing a small area of skin between the top and bottom portions of her costume. Cecily, who kept her vest firmly in place, took a dim view of this and said Nancy had let her down. For Nancy, the incident of the vest was a tiny landmark on the way to emancipation.

At the weekend she and Cecily sometimes went skating together: either ice-skating at Queens in Bayswater, or the cheaper roller-skating in Brixton. There they circled round and round, munching on chocolate bars, and the noise of the roller-skates on wooden floorboards was thunderous. But all in all, weekends were something of a problem, and Nancy was often lonely. She went to museums and for walks in the parks. Sometimes on Sunday afternoons she went to visit her grandfather's widow who had moved from Bath to Richmond.

Nancy was fond of the woman she always referred to as her grandmother, and cherished the sense of familiarity and the echoes of the happy memories of holiday visits. Her childhood had been singularly lacking in relatives or old family friends. Her grandparents were the only people with whom there had been regular contact, so during this often lonely and confusing first year in London the visits to her grandmother were important. Looking back, she considered that they probably meant a lot to her grandmother as well. Her husband had died only four years earlier and her adored son Edward, who had been a genuine hero in the Great War and received a VC for his part in the landing at Zeebrugge, had recently died. After his death, Mrs Myers had become a Christian Scientist. According to Nancy, she had come to resemble the Red Queen in *Alice in Wonderland*, with the same dramatic hair and profile. She welcomed Nancy's visits and plied her with delicious scones and cakes.

But even here, the welcome was mixed. Aunt Rachel, Mrs Myers's only daughter, hated Nancy's visits. When she was younger, Rachel had been the artist of the family and painted a good deal, but by the time Nancy appeared on the scene her artistic output had dwindled to the manufacture of men's grey socks on a knitting machine – presumably to make a little money for herself – and she bitterly resented her young relative. At some stage her resentment built up to such a pitch that she wrote to Nancy, ordering her not to visit any more. Nancy was deeply distressed and managed with difficulty to write a placatory letter back. Grudgingly, Rachel permitted her to return. Mrs Myers never knew about the letters, but for Nancy the damage was done; in spite of the old lady's continuing welcome, Rachel's hostility made Nancy so uncomfortable that she visited less and less often, and eventually the visits stopped altogether.

It was a great pity, she reflected later. Relations with her parents were abysmal, and she was quite without other relatives or family

Nancy was 'in a bit of funk' when she went to be interviewed
by the outgoing head of the Slade

friends. A wise and loving grandmother would have helped a lot. As it was, the spat with Rachel provided Nancy with yet more proof that she was never going to be acceptable to the 'straight' world.

It was during her second year in London that, outwardly at least, Nancy made the leap into the kind of world she had only ever glimpsed in books and pictures. She began by striking out from the path trodden by her school art teacher. Miss Fisher had gone to the Royal College of Art; very well then, Nancy would go to the Slade. She arranged it herself before going back to Gains-borough for the summer holidays. In 1930 Henry Tonks, the legendary head of the Slade, was in his late sixties and on the verge of retirement; he had been teaching there for nearly forty years and had a reputation for being irascible, so Nancy was 'in a bit of a funk' when she set off to see him. To her surprise he was mild and pleasant as he looked through her sheaf of drawings and enrolled her at the school for the coming autumn.

Nor was she returning to Miss Mackintosh's sedate establish-ment in Redcliffe Gardens. She found herself a room near Eccleston Square, in a house which was mainly inhabited by medical students, though she wasn't to stay there for long.

Eighteen-year-old Nancy took her place among the many women students at the Slade – 222, compared to just 73 men – and immediately entered a different world, far more impersonal than the cosy regime under old Daddy Lawrence at Westminster. No one paid much attention to the rules. The classes were very large and the masters wandered round looking at students' work, but without any great interest. New students were expected to spend a lot of time drawing marble busts and statues in the antiques room. Nancy found this boring and signed up for life drawing as soon as she could.

But even the life-drawing classes were a disappointment, with their heavy emphasis on clinical anatomy. Students were expected to attend weekly anatomy lectures, and practical sessions as well. Nancy did not stick with anatomy for long. She wanted to paint like Gauguin, not cut up bits of pickled flesh fished out of jars.

Sometimes during those first months at the Slade she returned to her evening classes with Meninsky at Westminster, but mostly she learned from her fellow students. Her taste was developing too. As a schoolgirl she had been thrilled by the bold paintings of Dod Procter and Laura Knight, but now she saw them as dull and unsubtle in comparison with the excitement, colour and freedom of the French Impressionists and Post-Impressionists.

University Rag Week took place in early October, a month after the beginning of term. Dressed in turquoise pyjama trousers, a pullover and a black beret, Nancy armed herself with a collecting tin and took to the street. She had a plum pitch in Oxford Street and did a roaring trade. 'For the first time in my life,' she said, 'I really let myself go, rushing up to people and rattling my tin and grinning until I almost bust my face.' At midday her success was measured in a tin full of half crowns – a most impressive haul. The afternoon was equally energetic. Running up and down beside her as she grinned ecstatically and shook the tin at bemused shoppers was a stocky, rather short Jewish fellow student called Archie.

A passer-by invited them to a party which was to be given by a well-known illustrator that evening. Nancy and Archie had something to eat, then set off, still clutching their collecting tins, for an address in Bloomsbury. They climbed a dark staircase and found themselves in a couple of rooms filled with noise and smoke and older people in varying stages of drunkenness. It was a proper bohemian party, the first Nancy had ever been to. Everyone was tipsy – even the resident Alsatian and the parrot.

Someone thrust a drink into her hand; she sipped it and thought it rather nasty. She and Archie stumbled around through the tangled legs and feet, and people were friendly and fumbled for money to shove into their tins. This, thought Nancy, was seeing life, just like she'd read about in novels.

Equally important, her friendship with Archie meant that she had broken through the invisible barrier which separated the mass of women students from the relatively few men. Another consequence was that she found somewhere better to live than the dismal room near Eccleston Square. Archie was about to move out of a room in Euston Square and he passed it on. For thirty shillings a week Nancy had a room to herself with a view over trees; she got a bed, service and a good breakfast. The flat belonged to a family called Laing.

Her first night at the Laings' was almost her last. Archie had suggested that she should have a house-warming party, and brought a celebratory bottle of Chianti. At most there were two other guests. They sat in a half circle on the floor in front of the fire and drank the Chianti. Nancy found it sour, but revelled in the feeling that she was being a proper bohemian hostess. In the morning she discovered their modest celebration had kept the Laings from their sleep and she had to reassure them she did not usually spend her evenings in such wild debauch. She was allowed to stay.

Mr Laing was burly and taciturn, with a bushy moustache. He was a freemason, and once on the sly he treated Nancy to a glimpse of his masonic apron, which no woman was supposed to see. His wife was a fussy little woman who tended to give in to her husband rather than put up with his sulks and bad temper. Their daughter Janet was a few years older than Nancy and her face was disfigured by a protruding lower lip which was purple and blotched. She and her mother were both Christian Scientists, like old Mrs Myers, and Nancy once accompanied them to their church. After the debacle of that first evening, Nancy and the Laings got along pretty well.

Her friend from Westminster, Cecily Rawson, was unwittingly responsible for Nancy's dramatic leap from timid schoolgirl to someone who was, outwardly at least, a wild and sexy bohemian. Cecily suggested that the two of them should go to see the Procession of the Holy Blood in Bruges. The trip, including travel and hotel, would cost them four pounds and ten shillings. When she wrote to her parents asking for the money, Nancy stressed the educational aspects of the expedition, and they duly gave their permission. During a life class at the Slade, Nancy mentioned their plans to a fellow student, Bee Falkener, who said she would like to come along too.

Nancy had admired Bee for some time, but had only ever spoken to her casually. Tall, with masses of thick dark hair, Bee possessed dash and flair. 'Great, big, blooming, easy-going Bee,' Nancy recalled with affection, 'always smiling and making funny, floppy, self-derogatory gestures, with an all-embracing, generous sort of assurance.' Her Australian parents were extremely rich, owning a huge chunk of sheep-farming Australia – 'about the size of the British Isles', according to Bee. In 1931 the whole family were living in England while the children were educated. Nancy was delighted: of course Bee could come.

Strait-laced Cecily was less pleased, and as soon as Bee was included in the expedition, culture ceased to be its only purpose: Bee wanted to have a good time. Nancy was torn between loyalty towards Cecily and her admiration for Bee.

For the first couple of days, Cecily kept a firm grip on activities. They visited museums and galleries and stood among the huge crowds lining the streets to watch the great Procession of the Holy Blood. They explored the ancient town, wandered beside tree-lined canals and enjoyed the general air of festive gaiety.

On the fourth day heavy rain set in and they were confined to their hotel room. They grew bored. Bee suggested cutting Nancy's hair. Nancy agreed. When she left school she had been given a permanent wave, but as soon as she got to London she felt it was far too conventional and let it grow out. Now she wore her hair in the style known as 'earphones': a centre parting with two plaits wound around her ears; it was severe, but more suitable, in her opinion, for the look of an art student.

In their large shared bedroom, with the rain pouring down outside and the disapproving Cecily looking on, Bee took up the scissors and set about chopping off Nancy's long, thick hair. She cut it short and straight around the back and with a thick fringe at the front. To complete the effect, Nancy borrowed Bee's lipstick.

The rain stopped and the three girls set off for the fairground with its rifle ranges, hurdy-gurdies and roundabouts. Before long they had fallen in with a couple of young Belgian men who spoke hardly any English, but who suggested they should head off to the nearby resort of Blankenberge for the rest of the evening. Cecily was appalled and stomped back alone to their room while Bee and Nancy set off for the coast.

Nancy found the evening traumatic, but also thrilling. Her main memory of Blankenberge was of sitting in the harsh glare of a brasserie-type chromium bar. On the return journey there was a great deal of fumbling and embracing, which Nancy found both sinister and uncomfortable. 'Although I was just nineteen,' she said, 'I'd had *no* direct experience of the touch of sex.' Those cramped gropings in the back of the taxi were hardly enjoyable, but she wouldn't have missed it for the world. As they headed back to Bruges she looked out of the window at the lights, and a voice inside her was saying, 'This is it. This is real life!'

Afterwards she was terrified that she might be pregnant, even though she had enough theoretical information to know it was impossible. But still, the fear persisted: some deep-rooted conviction to do with guilt and the certainty that pleasure – any kind of contact with the male sex – must be punished.

Once back at the Slade, her life was turned upside down. It was as if those few days in Bruges had made her visible for the very first time. She sat on the steps outside the main entrance to the school in the warm summer sunshine and people came up to her and wanted to know where she'd come from. It was unusual for a new student to appear in the last term of the year and Nancy, quite literally unrecognisable with her straight bob, thick fringe and generously applied lipstick, was thought to be a newly arrived stranger. It's the classic story of female transformation, so often seen in films – 'Miss Snooks, you look so different without your glasses' – and fairy stories – 'You *shall* go to the ball!' – but rare in real life. Nancy was taken entirely by surprise. Until that moment the only person who had told her she was attractive was her elderly headmistress. Now she had proof of it daily.

At Bee's side she joined the small elite of women students who hung out with the men. From the moment she returned from Bruges she was surrounded by men who wanted to know her. She was bowled over by this transformation, as she said, 'seemingly achieved with just a haircut and a dash of lipstick'. In her dreams of bohemian life she had never imagined this kind of attention. The height of her fantasy had been that she would eventually meet a man, fall in love and settle down with him. Nothing in her previous experience as lonely child, school outcast and solitary student had prepared her for this. For the first time in her life, she was in demand.

Two men in particular stood out in her memory of that summer term, with its first sweet taste of popularity. The painter William Townsend was three years older than Nancy; he had already left the Slade and was living in Canterbury. Tall and good-looking, 'he appeared almost godlike' when he turned up one day and invited her to lunch. They went to Antoine's, a small French place in Charlotte Street – definitely not a student haunt. The details of that meal never faded. They ate upstairs: there were stiff white tablecloths and flowers, an enormous handwritten menu and a bottle of wine. For Nancy it was a truly magical experience. And for him? 'I fear,' she said, 'he must have found me both gauche and boring.' Afterwards he wrote once or twice but seldom came to London, and she had no memory of them ever meeting again.

The other man was completely different. Vladimir Glass was a Russian medical student and also an artist. He was dark and stocky, with straight black hair, enormous Byzantine eyes, a dramatic nose in a white face and full, fleshy lips. He could be seen walking the Bloomsbury streets with his long college scarf flowing behind. 'A purposive walker,' Nancy called him, 'and a purposive would-be lover.' He literally pounced on her, and for a couple of weeks he took over her life. She went with him to his basement lodgings, which he had decorated with blood-red walls covered in skulls and bones. He lent her books, including the *Kama Sutra*, and gave her information he thought she needed, albeit 'with rather more medical detail than I cared for'. Vladimir's instruction included practical demonstrations, with a lot of aggressive smothering and kissing which she found unpleasant – his breath smelled – but felt she ought to be enjoying. After a lot of tongue-kissing, he had a disconcerting tendency to breathe the single word '*Impregnated!*' in her ear.

At the end of term Nancy returned to Gainsborough and the

fear of pregnancy, which had dogged her after the trip to Belgium, returned to haunt her again. Logically, she knew she couldn't be pregnant, but then again – *Impregnated!* – Vladimir was a medical student so maybe he knew something she didn't. Against all reason, the fear and guilt cast a shadow over the summer.

When Nancy returned to London in September 1931, a new phase began, one in which she developed into a different kind of person – outwardly, at least. 'A leopard cannot change his spots,' she said, 'but a person can, easily, and this I did.' Inside, the change was much slower, and perhaps never completed.

Still, for the time being, she was understandably entranced by her new persona. She had become *someone*. There were practical as well as social reasons for relishing her departure from what she called 'the indistinguishable mass of girl proles'. At the Slade, male and female students were separated for life-drawing classes in the interests of decorum. As women students outnumbered the men by more than three to one, this meant they were squeezed together, sometimes three deep, around the model, while men were able to spread out in a more informal manner, thus receiving far more individual attention from the teachers. Nancy got round this problem by following Bee into the sculpture school. In the days before Henry Moore and Barbara Hepworth fired the imagination of a new generation, hardly any students chose sculpture; just a small number worked 'like troglodytes in the basement, getting happily covered in clay and spattered with plaster'. Only two of the other students were women. Carmen was as Spanish-looking as her name suggested, with a thick mop of hair which frizzed out. The other was called Diana. Small, fair and delicate, she had the quiet self-confidence and the bored drawl of the sophisticated upper classes. She dressed more stylishly than the other students and Nancy imagined for her a 'home life of country house party style somewhere in the shires'. Diana didn't seem to take her art very seriously, but for Nancy and Bee, even if they didn't achieve much, the Slade was 'the centre of our lives and hopes'.

And a thoroughly enjoyable centre it was. The four women formed a loose group, meeting for meals in the main college dining room. In good weather they perched smoking and chatting on the balustrade outside, to be joined by their friends among the male students, 'which meant most of them, at one time or another'. All this Nancy found delectable. Swinging her long legs over the balustrade, she tossed her hair and chain-smoked and worked hard to appear effortlessly sophisticated. Since she alternated still between boldness and timidity, she thought hers was probably a somewhat uneven performance. They gossiped and discussed galleries and films and books; always an avid reader, she was now discovering the work of Aldous Huxley, D. H. Lawrence, Evelyn Waugh and Wyndham Lewis.

Attractive and in demand, Nancy was not lacking men eager to unburden her of her virginity, including one of her teachers. Ralph Nuttall-Smith, who taught sculpture and modelling, pursued her for a while with an ardour that she described as 'particularly repellent'. He was tall, bony, spectacled, red-faced and grizzly, and he attempted to win her sympathy by calling himself 'an emotional casualty of the War'. At first, she was flattered to be taken out to dinner by him, consulted and confided in, but he was not content with that. After dinner they returned to his room for coffee and then, 'to prove that I trusted him', she was persuaded to lie down beside him on his rather grotty couch and demonstrate 'that I wasn't disgusted by him'. For a while, she dutifully lay beside him, trying to steer a middle course between revulsion and making any movement that might encourage further intimacy. This seemed to her to go on for a very long time, with him lying on his back with his legs crossed, fully dressed except for his shoes and one large toe jutting out from a hole in his grey sock, while he droned on and castigated himself. And that was it.

Beneath her new-found veneer of sophistication, she remained incredibly naive. 'I hadn't really cottoned on to what sex was all about,' she wrote later. Whatever sex education had been on offer in Spring Gardens and Lincoln High, it's a racing certainty that ignorance, shame and 'Don't!' were major components. Men, an essential but hitherto unknown ingredient of the adult world, were a novelty to be explored because each one she met presented some new aspect of maleness that needed to be tested and assimilated. Looking back, she thought she was searching for different things in different men: one to be a father-advisor, another an artistic mentor and a third to be a lover and mate. And perhaps a fourth, the brother she had always longed for.

Meanwhile, her devastating combination of attractiveness and social ineptness made for a series of situations that bordered on farce. And her popularity went to her head – hardly surprising, considering how new it was. Like someone who has been hungry too long, she wasn't about to turn down offers of food, however unappetising. The highlight came when Nancy discovered she had invited seven men to be her partners at the annual Slade dance, all of whom expected exclusive attention. She wore a string vest, with nothing underneath, and spent a lot of time being cornered by determined partners. On the whole, she considered the evening a triumph: 'This was getting back on the most unpopular girl in the school image with a vengeance.'

At the beginning of the academic year Nancy was still living in the Laings' flat, but as her social life took off and she began to go out in Bloomsbury more, to the Yorkshire Grey pub on Langham

Street or Bertorelli's restaurant in Charlotte Street, they grew increasingly disapproving. When she heard that a fellow student was moving out of his studio room, she seized the chance to have a place of her own – a highly unusual step for a nineteen-year-old girl at that time. In January 1932 she moved into a large, bare oblong box at the back of a slum terrace house in Robert Street, just off the Hampstead Road. It was typical of the cheap studios that had been built over the back yards of poor houses to accommodate impecunious artists, and it cost one pound a week.

The Robert Street room was approached through the dark, smelly hall and passageway of a lodging house. It had a small coal fire in the middle of one wall and Nancy inherited a deal table and a couple of kitchen chairs, as well as an old gas cooker. There was a sink against the outside wall of the house, a shred of dusty carpet in front of the fire and some remnants of old brown linoleum that clung like stains to the bare floor. Two iron bedsteads with sagging mattresses and skimpy, 'malevolent-looking' dark pink covers stood on either side of the fireplace. Her first home inspired fear as well as pride. It was bitterly cold and rather spooky, so she persuaded a friend from school called Joyce Winter to keep her company for the first week. After that she was on her own until Bee moved in.

Spooky or not, Nancy had plans for Robert Street. For a few months she organised an informal evening life class for about nine or ten fellow students. This meant she had to get hold of a model and enough coal to keep a roaring fire going for a couple of hours. On the first evening a procession of students arrived bearing bits of equipment, most of it taken from the Slade. One man, Stephen Gilbert, marched boldly out with an easel under his arm and carried it all the way to Robert Street. Life drawing at Robert Street provided a welcome change from the segregated classes at the Slade: in a cloud of smoke from pipes and cigarettes, the two sexes worked side by side from half-past seven until half-past nine, with a quarter of an hour's break in the middle. Afterwards, when everyone had dug in their pockets to contribute to the seven shillings the model was paid, they sat on the two beds in front of the fire talking and drinking beer and cups of tea. The hanging light was switched off, and as Nancy looked around the firelit faces she felt like Madame de Staël, presiding over her artistic salon.

She needed that pride, needed desperately that sense of herself as an independent artist. She was increasingly disillusioned with the teaching at the Slade, but more critically, the tensions between her London life and the Gainsborough world she was desperate to escape were becoming intolerable.

Among Nancy's papers are more than a dozen pages handwritten on blue foolscap, with the words 'Late Holidays Home' scrawled across the top. Reading them, one gets a sense of just how precarious her new persona still was, and how now, just when she was on the brink of breaking free from her parents' world for ever, the terror of never escaping was at its most intense.

It was during these last holidays home, she wrote, that the horror of the Gainsborough house took hold and hardened in her, to reappear in dreams and nightmares for the rest of her life. In these dreams she has returned to Spring Gardens voluntarily, only to find herself trapped. 'This dream, in different forms, still comes back periodically,' she wrote the year before she died, in a passage with far more crossings out and overwriting than usual. 'In the dream I am married and Teddy and I decide to go and live in the house and transform it into a delightful place to live in. In some dreams we are going to find congenial friends living round about. But we're inevitably defeated: the rooms refuse to change. They remain stonily the same. Fires are lit only to go out. Paper falls off walls, friends disappear, people dissolve away from us. We are trapped, alone, in this horrible house for ever.' She has added in pencil, 'And ever.'

It would have been so easy to fail, to get sucked back into the quagmire of her family and end up like her cousin Rachel, caring for her elderly mother, her artistic ambitions reduced to the knitting of men's grey socks. The money for her education might have dried up: this was an ever-present fear. Or one of her parents might have become ill, necessitating her help at home. Pregnancy would have been an unmitigated disaster. In 1932 there were a hundred reasons why an unworldly twenty-year-old with no independent means and no marketable skills might fail to make the break from her family. The wonder is that she achieved it at all.

So long as Nancy remained at the Slade, she was expected to return home for the holidays, and she dreaded them. Her parents' reproaches were unending: Nancy was a bitter disappointment. Her mother's chief topic of conversation was how Nancy had shamed her, how she ought to be doing things for her instead of doing the things Louise hated to see her doing, such as drawing and reading. And she was still obsessed with the idea that Nancy could never make up to her for the pain of her birth, so she nagged and glared at her as though the intensity of her feeling could force her into being the child she needed. But guilt and misery had long since banished any chance of love.

Time and again, Nancy struggled to unravel the snarl of her dismal family. If Thomas had not let his wife down so cruelly, if Louise had enjoyed the lifestyle she had been expecting when she married, things might have been tolerable. He was basically affectionate, but too lazy and cowardly to be of any help either to his wife or to his daughter. Instead, Thomas reinforced the fiction that all was well, that they were 'the world's chosen people', temporarily embarrassed sometimes, but 'wonderful, superior people'. Even when Louise's pettiness and meanness exasperated him to the point of stamping fury, he clung to the mantra that she was 'the most wonderful woman in the world'. During one of those final holidays home, Nancy made one last attempt to find common ground with him. Louise had been particularly outrageous and, as they had done so often when she was a little girl, father and daughter set off for a walk together. Nancy was struggling to make sense of it, 'wanted, I think, to sympathise with him as an adult'. But it was no good. He turned his head away and said in his most testy, don't-bother-me voice, 'Your mother's the best woman in the world.'

Once more, Nancy had been thrown back on herself. This seemingly trivial incident marked a significant step in her separation from her father. She knew that she would never again be able to find comfort in his arms. In her words, 'the rock had become straw'.

After that, she gave up.

Which left the problem of money. So long as she remained at the Slade, she was financially dependent on her parents and vulnerable to their accusations that she was wasting her time, bringing shame on the family and all at their expense. And the uncertainty was crippling. Most of the students were hard up, but at least their hard-upness was reasonably predictable. Nancy's father always left it to the very last minute, when her bags were packed at the end of the holidays and they were waiting to go to the station. Without looking at her he would hand her a cheque, mumbling something like, 'You'd better have twenty pounds – or thirty,' adding that he hoped it would last. And then, even more peevishly, 'Keep an account, can't you? I never know what you spend it on.' These transactions always left her feeling shaken, and she didn't begin to recover until the train was halfway to London. If she had to write home for more during the term, the money was forthcoming, but she always delayed as long as possible before asking.

For the first couple of years this was no more than a recurring unpleasantness, which she only thought about when she had to, but by the end of 1931 the problem had become critical. The Robert Street studio was presented to her parents as part of an economy drive: she would become a part-time student, three days a week instead of five, which would reduce her fees from twelve pounds a term to eight. The idea was that, with a studio of her own, she would be able to work there for the other days. But, as she said, it also meant giving up on her hopes of completing the course. Nancy's fundamental belief in herself as an artist had not changed, but now it was as if there was a 'sheet of glass' (her phrase, a generation before the 'glass ceiling' became a commonplace of women's experience in the workplace) that she could not get through. She believed she would manage it, in time, but meanwhile, what was she to do?

The twelve months before Nancy met Lawrence Durrell were punctuated by a series of attempts to support herself, most of them as tragi-comic as her dating disasters. But during these months she was involved, in a way which she found both rewarding and troubling, with a man to whom she was, for the first time in her life, genuinely attracted.

Roger Pettiward had swung into her life in the previous term. More than six feet, five inches tall, he had red hair, a rangy look and what Nancy described as an exaggerated drawl. He had come to the Slade after taking a degree at Oxford. She had seen him around, always with a man called Reynold with whom he shared a flat. Reynold was extremely good-looking in a conventional way and, despite having been educated at Bedales, it was rumoured that he was unable to read or write.

Nancy was attracted to the red-haired, flamboyant Roger Pettiward from the first

One day, when Nancy was lounging about on the steps of the Slade with a few of her friends, Roger sauntered up and, never having spoken to her before, suggested that she might accompany him to an exhibition at the Redfern Gallery the following afternoon. She agreed. When he had gone, she conferred with her pals, who told her that he had been to Magdalen College, Oxford, and, before that, at Eton. *Oh dear!* she thought. When Roger appeared at the appointed time for the expedition he was wearing his man-about-town outfit, a peacock-blue Harris tweed suit, with a checked shirt, bowler hat and neatly folded umbrella. Walking across the quad beside this apparition she felt extremely self-conscious, rather, she said, 'as if I was going for a stroll with a talking ostrich, or something equally bizarre'.

She began to make conversation. Hadn't he been at Magdalen College?

'*Mord-lin*,' he drawled. 'Magdalen is Mary.'

Oh Lord again, she thought.

And that was all she could remember about that particular expedition. But after that, whenever Roger joined her group of college friends, he would often as not come up beside her, and when she approached the favoured alcove table in the basement cafeteria where they gathered, he would move over, reach out a long, lazy arm and pull a chair up for her next to his.

Right from the first, she never knew where she was with him. To begin with, she was just flattered by the attentions of this striking, strange and supercilious character's attentions. Then she gradually became obsessed by him, and spent a lot of time trying to make sense of his enigmatic behaviour. By now there were a lot of 'eager swains' around who were pressuring her for 'intimacies'. (The language she uses here is interesting: 'eager swains' and 'intimacies' are the kind of euphemisms she never used as an adult. Most probably she was unconsciously reverting to the embarrassed phraseology of the naive and confused nineteen-year-old who did not have the vocabulary to talk or even think about such topics.) However she put it, she was slowly finding ways to deal with her new popularity. Her circle of admirers now extended beyond the narrow world of Slade students (and occasional staff) to the various artists and hangers-on whom she met in pubs and gatherings in Bloomsbury. Roger, uniquely, laid a kind of claim to her without sex ever being part of the equation.

The rooms for the annual Slade dance were traditionally decorated with cartoons drawn by senior students. Roger, with his send-up attitude to the world, was brilliant at this, and Nancy was good at quick, flowing figure sketches. They worked together on the decorations, and Nancy produced a very good cartoon of Roger, with his small, snub-nosed head, elongated body and enormous feet. His outfit completed with a little bow tie, he looked like Koko the Clown on stilts. At the dance itself, the one to which she discovered she had invited seven men, it was Roger who rescued her. Each time one of her would-be partners got hold of her, he sloped up and whisked her away to prance around the floor with him, at top speed and in his highly individual fashion.

After this, they went along to other art-school dances together. Or perhaps, she said, 'it's better to say we raided them, behaving boorishly and childishly'. They considered these dances to be very tame affairs and were soon bored. At the Central School they did a sort of Lancers' side-step gallop at full speed up and down the length of the hall, bumping into any dancers who weren't quick enough to get out of their way and whooping as they went. They only stopped when they were covered in sweat and so out of breath they couldn't go on any longer.

At Westminster, her old school, they varied this behaviour by removing all the light bulbs from the corridor leading to the main life-classes room which had been cleared for the occasion. Daddy Lawrence was annoyed, but no sooner had he replaced the bulbs, with orders that they must not be touched, than Nancy and Roger danced out into the corridor again. Roger stretched out a long arm and the place was plunged back into darkness. 'Liven the place up,' said Roger laconically. Nobody seemed to be having much fun, except them. The old place seemed very dead.

They also jigged around energetically at the Chelsea Arts Club Ball, but even they were unable to disrupt that enormous jamboree, however much they barged about amid the general confusion and noise, the trundling floats, the balloons bursting, the universal hullabaloo. Roger was extremely sick in a corner – but then so were lots of other people.

During this time, Nancy discovered within herself an unexpected fund of energy and stamina, which gave her enormous satisfaction. As she said, 'my relationship with Roger was pure, instinctive, joyous release'. Her partner, the hooligan of the dance halls, seemed to bear little relation to the slow, aloof Roger of the Slade.

The words she uses are chosen carefully. Roger was the only person to whom she was physically attracted. She was obsessed with him. Pure, instinctive, joyous release. The inescapable conclusion is that she had fallen in love for the first time in her life, but she never uses the word itself. In fact, apart from her puppy love for Frank Medworth, one of her first teachers, she hardly ever uses the word when describing her feelings. This is strange, because she was capable of great and abiding love. But the word had been hijacked by her mother, and was poisoned by guilt and coercion. *You can't demand love*, the small child had repeated silently to herself when Louise insisted on her night-time kiss. *Love is a gift*. Love as a feeling she knew well, but the word itself carried too many negative associations. Instead she tried to pin down her precise feelings in a different way.

After the evening life-drawing classes at Robert Street, when the model had departed, one or two people sometimes slept over and stayed for breakfast, Roger and Nancy on one bed, Bee and someone else on the other, and there might be another couple on the mat in front of the fire. When she took over the studio, her landlord had stressed that there were to be no parties – as much because the entire house shared a single lavatory halfway up the stairs as for any moral reasons. During these occasional all-night sessions the men, being fairly tanked up with beer, made frequent journeys up the dark stairs, trying not to fall about too much. For the next few days Nancy would scuttle through the musty hall and corridor to avoid the indignation of the suffering lodgers, who mostly just peered around their doors and muttered about whores who should know better.

Throughout the first five months of 1932, Nancy's anxieties about money and the future were kept at bay by her relationship with Roger, which continued, as she put it, in a casual, offhand way. 'It can hardly have been said to have developed but, certainly for me, it provided a strong, vibrant thread through my life.' But in late May that 'strong, vibrant thread' came under threat from a most unexpected quarter: an English colonel who had gone missing in South America seven years earlier.

In 1925 Colonel Percy Fawcett, mystic and man of action, had set off with his son and another young man to search for a legendary 'lost world' in the Matto Grosso, that huge and uncharted region in the centre of Brazil. They had warned that they might be gone for two years, but by 1928 there was still no word of them and so a relief expedition was raised by an American newspaper syndicate. That had to turn back when only four or five days' march from the place where the Fawcett party was rumoured to have been killed. In 1932 a new expedition was being organised and an advertisement was placed in the personal section of *The Times* for 'two more guns', who were required for an 'exploring and sporting expedition'. Peter Fleming, whose younger brother would later become famous as the creator of James Bond, decided to put his fledgling journalistic career on hold for a few months and sign up. He described what happened next in the book he wrote about the journey, *Brazilian Adventure*.

Roger was walking along Gower Street. He had passed the School of Tropical Hygiene. He had passed the Royal Academy of Dramatic Art ...

By one of those coincidences which ... would hardly pass muster in a work of fiction, I came out in a great hurry from my office on the other side of Gower Street just as Roger passed. At Eton and at Oxford I had known him only by sight. In the last three years I had met him three times. But here was a fine large chap with an eye for comedy: so I called across the street: 'Roger, come to Brazil.'

'What?' said Roger: playing, I dare say, for time.

'You'd better come to Brazil,' I said, getting into a car.

'Why?' said Roger cautiously (or perhaps incautiously), also getting into the car. We set off down Gower Street . . . I talked rapidly. At the end of Gower Street Roger got out.

'I'll let you know for certain on Monday,' he said. But his fate was sealed.

Roger signed on for the Matto Grosso expedition as an extra gun, and also as a surveyor, having already travelled extensively and done some work in this field.

Roger spent his last evening in London with Nancy. They ate at Schmidt's and then went back to Robert Street. It must have been a cold June, because when he departed he was wearing a warm seaman's jacket. The time came for him to leave. He and Nancy embraced on the doorstep, he took a few steps and then turned back. He hugged her tightly, mumbled something and then he was off, loping away down towards the Hampstead Road.

Things began to fall apart after that. 'London was just an expanse of grey, dirty streets, salt lost its savour, etc etc . . . ' she wrote, that etc etc following the salty cliché a wry acknowledgement that she was describing the classic symptoms of heartbreak. Once Roger was gone, she was left 'in a great emptiness' and with a lot to think about. Most important, she had to find a way to support herself and remain in London. She began casting around, though without inspiration or direction, for some way to make enough to survive.

In the summer of 1932, nearly three years after the Wall Street Crash and with no end to the Great Depression in sight, this was no easy task. There were hardly any casual or part-time jobs by which students could eke out a living. During the spring she had fantasised about making money from painting portraits or designing book jackets, neither of which she yet had the skills to do effectively. Painting and decorating, perhaps? Interior design had been made fashionable by Duncan Grant and the Omega Workshops, and only a few years earlier Rex Whistler, at just twenty-two, had painted the murals for the restaurant at the Tate Gallery.

One of the people Nancy and Bee had got to know as their circle widened was a painter called John Armstrong, and he passed on a few days' work to her. He had been commissioned to produce murals in a beautiful flat that belonged to 'some kind of businessman' in one of the Bloomsbury squares. Nancy was to undertake the preliminary work, repainting the windows and doors and applying the pink background on the walls. The flat came complete with manservant, and she was given a couple of lunches, with wine, as well as expenses for paint and brushes. But after a few days she realised sadly that it was her sex and youth, 'not my skills, such as they were', that were being paid for – though whether it was Armstrong or the businessman whose attempts at seduction brought her employment to an end, she does not say.

It was to be a recurrent theme, and illustrates just how tricky it was to survive as a single, unchaperoned and attractive young woman in 1932. Reared in ignorance, the middle-class female was, as a rule, kept under strict surveillance at home until she could be safely handed over to a respectable husband. Nancy, with her pasted-on sophistication, no protectors in sight and a place of her own to go back to, must have seemed like fair game. Friendship between the sexes seemed to be impossible, though Nancy could never understand why. The second wave of feminism was still a generation away.

One or two of the older women students at the Slade were in the process of developing an original style – finding a way to transcend the sheet of glass that was blocking Nancy – and she would have liked to talk to them, but had no idea how to approach them. Women who made their own way were few and far between, and their friendship would have made a significant impact.

At the Slade she had already discovered that women students, although very much in the majority, were second-class citizens, and in the bohemian circle that revolved around Fitzroy Square and the Slade, things were not much better. One of the seven hopefuls who had trailed after her at the annual dance, a 'lugubrious young man', had for some inexplicable reason brought his wife along too. Her presence didn't prevent him from making vigorous efforts to trap Nancy in a corner whenever he could, 'in close and unwelcome embraces'. (That uncharacteristically novelettish turn of phrase again.) After one such tussle his wife suddenly materialised with a long, tear-stained face, red-nosed and desperately dreary-looking. In Nancy's imagination the wife was already sucked dry by childbearing and poverty, a hopeless drudge at – what? – twenty-six or so. No word was spoken, there was nothing to say, but Nancy felt terribly ashamed at the time, a feeling that returned whenever she thought about it afterwards.

She had discovered that she had always to be on the alert and stop being 'a trusting child'. Men were strange beasts, and their seduction techniques were often lacking in finesse, to say the least. One artistic-looking man invited her to see his pictures so she visited him in 'the usual bare, scruffy little rooms'. No sooner was she inside the door than he made a sudden bound and she found herself on her back on the kitchen table. Almost suffocating under his smelly, scratchy beard, her spine ground into the table's surface, she managed to scramble out of the way just as his pale, haggard wife appeared in the doorway with their baby in her arms. Nancy was torn between anger and shame, but this incident confirmed her view that unfairness and degradation were the lot of any woman marrying a poor artist.

It was during this period that the lack of any family or family friends she could talk to, or just spend time with, was most keenly felt. The rupture with Aunt Rachel, which had effectively ended any contact with her kindly grandmother in Richmond, had cut off her only potential link with the past and the world beyond the pubs and lodgings around Gower Street and Fitzrovia. Nancy was at this time scornful of those who still lived at home. Roger Hilton, the son of a Hampstead doctor, who was later to become a leading international avant-garde artist, was one of these homebody students. At that time, Hilton had a keen, serious, analytical attitude and he wanted to spend time with Nancy. Looking back, Nancy realised she could have benefited from getting to know him better, but at the time she was put off by what she considered to be his tameness, hesitatingness and, above all, his 'home-boundness'.

The male student who seems to have come closest to being a friend was Stephen Gilbert. Though a couple of years older than Nancy, he looked and seemed younger; he was the grandson of the celebrated sculptor Sir Alfred Gilbert, who created *Eros* in Piccadilly Circus. For the most part he was utterly broke, even by contemporary standards of student poverty. It was whispered among the students that he sometimes slept in a Rowton House hostel, made famous by George Orwell, along with 'beggars, street riff-raff and the lower type of criminals'. When Nancy asked Stephen about this he said, 'Yes,' he had been to Rowton House sometimes, and 'it wasn't too bad'.

But Stephen never appeared to be cast down or worried by his circumstances. She describes him as 'quite exceptionally unneurotic'. He plodded around in his purposeful way and gained a reputation as a fine strong draughtsman, producing many large, well-modelled drawings. After Nancy moved to Robert Street she saw quite a lot of him, as he frequented her evening life-drawing sessions, and for a while she had hopes that a little of his moral fibre might brush off on her. 'But alas,' she commented ruefully, 'it didn't.'

Nevertheless, he was an important part of her life in these months and often came to Robert Street to chat and work. He had thick brown hair, which was hardly ever cut or washed, broad cheekbones, a beaky nose, heavy-lidded grey eyes and a small mouth, which was often turned down at the corners in wry grimace. He was slight, but strong, always dressed in what must have been his old, black school suit, a frayed striped shirt and a stringy black tie. His wrists and neck showed a grey tidemark at collar and cuff. His unprepossessing appearance meant that his cultivated, throwaway drawl came as a surprise.

When Nancy received a letter from her mother, asking her to send a picture for a charity sale in Gainsborough, she turned to Stephen for help. By this time her relations with her parents were so awful that 'any communication with them pretty well set me in line for a nervous breakdown', and this one was no exception. Her mother pointed out that so far there had been no result from all the sacrifices they had made to send her to art school, so the very least she could do was send a picture. Nancy said she would – but what? She had sheaves of nude drawings, a couple of unfinished still lives and a few perspective exercises, but not much else. What could she send?

She talked it over with Stephen. Oils were out of the question as they wouldn't dry in time. They decided on a pastel study of flowers – surely a safe subject. Nancy bought a bowl of pink hydrangeas and they both set to work. Nancy was quite pleased with her picture, though conceded that Stephen's was marginally

more decisive. Presentation was not something they even considered so, perhaps mounted but certainly not framed, the pink
hydrangea picture was sent north. Disaster. After the charity
event, Louise wrote to inform her that the picture had not even
sold. Once again, Nancy had shamed the best woman in the
world in front of her friends.

This trivial incident set off a terrible domino reaction and
Nancy had to fight her way through all the old battles until she
regained some equanimity. Stephen had no sympathy for her
'neurotic problems' and unintentionally reinforced her crippling
self-doubt. According to his way of thinking she was just a
flibbertigibbet; all she needed to do was work hard like he did.
Once, when she was trying to do an oil painting of a corner of the
studio fireplace, she asked Stephen for advice. He said, 'I won't
look at it till you finish it. You'll never be any good unless you
finish things.'

Most probably he was trying to be helpful, to pass on some of his
moral fibre, in fact. Nancy describes herself at this time as 'a neurotic girl' and her endless self-doubt and need for reassurance must
have been intensely irritating to someone who had no experience
of either. But the combination of financial anxiety and lack of
direction meant that during this period the artistic self-confidence
which had led her to forge a creative life for herself slipped
through her fingers, and she put her artistic ambitions on hold.

What she needed was a mentor – or even a kind auntie. But
neither was available. And the close female friendships which are
the backbone of young women's independent lives today were
less common in the early 1930s. In a male-dominated age, where
the status of even the most accomplished woman still derived
from her relationship with a man, female friendships were rare
and fragile creations. Nancy's disastrous experience with girls at
school made this kind of intimacy harder for her than for most.

The security of Robert Street also came to an end, soon after Roger left. Bee's mother turned up unexpectedly and pronounced the studio unfit for human habitation. Nancy and Bee moved up to a large room somewhere north of Camden Town. It had no charms for either of them and they used it purely as a place to sleep and to keep their few possessions. Her links with Bee – flamboyant, cheerful Bee – began to weaken. They drifted in different directions, finding different groups of friends. By this time Nancy was attending the Slade more for company as it was no longer the centre of her life. 'Come to think of it,' she said, 'there was no centre during this summer after Roger left. I was attracted to no one and drifted about.'

Drift, drifting, drifted . . . the word crops up time and again when she talks of these summer months, when Roger Pettiward was incommunicado in the rainforests of Brazil. In spite of her underlying gloom, Nancy continued to make friends, most significantly three young men who had met while they were at school at Winchester. One in particular was to play a key role in the course of her life.

George Wilkinson had ambitions to be a writer, and had already achieved the look and manner of a mature literary figure. He prided himself on his resemblance to Lytton Strachey. Tall and cadaverous, with spectacles and a beard, he had a mild demeanour and a habit of constantly twirling the ring on one of his long, elegant fingers.

His father had been a domineering figure, insisting on absolute obedience from George and his two siblings. George liked to tell the story of a tea party at his home. One of the guests had no spoon with which to stir his tea and George obligingly leant forward and said, 'Here, have mine.' Whereupon his father fixed him with a disapproving eye and said, 'My spoon, George, not

George Wilkinson prided himself on his likeness to Lytton Strachey

yours. Everything in this house is mine.' Nancy thought his tyrannical father had 'a very strangling effect' on George, and not just emotionally. He always attributed his lack of robustness and generally rather weedy physique to the fact that he never had enough to eat at Winchester. Soon after his arrival at the prestigious but in many ways archaic public school, he wrote home to explain that boys were expected to buy their own evening meal, since only bread was supplied by the school. Please could his father send some money. Certainly not, replied Wilkinson *père*: if the school thought the boys needed more nourishment, it surely would be provided. As a consequence, while his friends were enjoying toasted cheese and eggs, young George had to make do with bread and scrape. However, by 1932 the tyrant had died and George came into a modest legacy, which meant he could plan his life for himself and was in a position to entertain his friends in his small flat in Fitzroy Square.

George and his friends must have been an odd-looking trio.

George was gangling and already had a patriarchal beard. His friend Peter Bull was short, with a disproportionately large head. In time his body filled out and he looked genuinely bull-like, but at twenty he must have looked a bit like one of the caricature figures on the Happy Families cards. Nancy describes Peter's as 'a great head, a beautiful head' with its massive bone structure, great blue eyes and full fleshy lips. Like his old school friends, Peter had the Wykehamist slow drawl and the beginnings of the rich, dark voice which he was to develop later to good effect on the stage and in films. (He is probably best known now for his part as the Russian ambassador in *Dr Strangelove*.) It's an irony that this gentlest of men eventually carved a niche for himself playing bigots and bullies; when Nancy first knew him he was still trying to get onto the stage.

The third friend remains a shadowy figure. Nicholas Phipps – the Honourable Nicholas Phipps – was even taller and skinnier than George, with a 'clipped, rather wooden face' like an elongated Noël Coward. He was elegant and monosyllabic and, like Peter Bull, was trying to get into the theatrical world. He had already had small film parts at Elstree Studios. To Nancy he was an exotic, as though he had stepped off the pages of Evelyn Waugh's *Vile Bodies*.

Nancy was drawn to these three young men. She thought they had a 'certain style about them', which she hadn't come across before, the courtesy and polish of their public-school background; they were gentle and paid her compliments and, unlike the majority of her Bloomsbury friends, they didn't shout and get drunk. Nor did they pounce on her: Peter because he wasn't attracted to women, and George because he already had a girlfriend, Pam Black, whom he was later to marry.

Pam became a close friend, in some ways replacing Bee. She was bright and scatty, an Eton-cropped blonde who also wanted to go on the stage. She and George, so physically unalike, had an unusual bond in that both had parents who never spoke to each other, using their children whenever communication was unavoidable. Pam's parents had separated by this time: her father was running an antiquarian bookshop off Kensington Church Street and her mother had a teashop in Ditchling.

It is significant that Pam and the Wykehamists entered Nancy's world complete with family background. Up till then, in her eagerness to escape her own parents, she had been incapable of seeing her friends in the context of their families. Anyone who 'hung onto' their family – in the way that Roger Hilton seemed to be doing by living at home – was in her view missing the point. Being an artist was a vocation, which made demands on those who chose that life, and bohemianism was much more than just choice of clothes and style. Like a recent convert to a religious cult, or the Communist Party, 'you had to *shed* your family' and everything associated with them in order to become an artist. But for the Wykehamists, especially George with his tyrannical father, the family context was a part of their mythology. Nancy still did not talk of her own parents, but she began to take account of those of her friends.

Another friend she made during this summer of drifting was John Gawsworth. He was an altogether new kind of friend: she was intrigued by him, and he was excited by her. The same age as Nancy – just twenty – he had been phenomenally quick off the literary starting block, and had been published while still at school. By 1932 he already had five books, including poetry and anthologies, to his name and had established himself as a colourful figure on the London scene. Nancy described him as spiderlike, very thin and white, with a pointed nose, sharp little black eyes and freckles. He wore a wide-brimmed black hat and had a moustache that must count as one of the least attractive ever: 'nasty droopy little bit of black stuff – mousy stuff coming either side of his mouth'. (By 1941 he seemed to have developed an uncanny resemblance to Inspector Clouseau, as played by Peter Sellers in the *Pink Panther* films.)

John Gawsworth pictured in Cairo, 1941

Like many physically unappealing men, he made up for his deficiencies by creating himself as 'a character', and modelled his behaviour on that of the Georgian poets of the pre-war period, bustling around, always knowing everybody worth knowing. He was also a fanatical collector of literary memorabilia. He took Nancy out to the suburbs to meet someone she described as 'a very old king of Georgian poets'. This must have been M. P. Sheil (actually a novelist), who styled himself King Felipe, the exiled monarch of the Caribbean island of Redonda – a title that did not cut much ice with the Colonial Office.

For a while, Nancy was John Gawsworth's muse, and to

celebrate his birthday in June that year he published thirty copies of 'Song for Nancy', which begins:

Upon your breast, O nymph, upon your breast
The cares of this war-weary world might lie,
A sleeping boy that lets his dreams go by . . .

And ends:

Upon your mouth, O nymph, upon your mouth
A lover's lips might lie and consummate
The service of the kiss and culminate
The virgin years, the harvest parched with drouth.

As well as writing her poems and impressing her with exiled royalty, Gawsworth took Nancy to the Café Royal where he held forth loudly, and introduced her to Aleister Crowley, the legendary apostle of sex-magic and demonology. Now fifty-seven, Crowley's reputation as 'the wickedest man on earth' had just received a boost from Nina Hamnett's book *Laughing Torso*, in which she called him a 'black magician'. Two years later Crowley was to sue her for libel, with the result that his notoriety was fixed in stone and he was bankrupted. When Nancy met Crowley, his reputation for evil and his dark personal magnetism were enough to frighten her out of her wits, which presumably was the intention.

But still, as always, there was the problem of money. Her first real attempt to support herself came through another of her new non-Slade friends. The same age as Nancy, Peter Proud was fresh-faced and cheerful. He was also well able to look after himself: since leaving school at fifteen, he'd worked at the film studios at Elstree. In the summer of 1932 he was temporarily out of work and so plunged with his usual enthusiasm into the task of working for the Realsilk Hosiery Company. Why didn't Nancy have a go? Nicholas Phipps, whose film career was in the doldrums as well, came along too.

Their training, such as it was, took place at the Realsilk Hosiery headquarters in Soho. Harry, a young-old man with crinkly hair and an over-bright manner, taught them how to demonstrate the superiority of Realsilk over other stockings. In those pre-nylon days, stockings were expensive and horribly liable to ladder. The sales trick was to put one hand right down inside to the toe of the stocking and, with your index fingernail pushing up vertically, draw it back crisply in one swift movement. This showed their resistance to laddering, a sure hit with husbands and lovers who were accustomed to their women's shrieks and moans every time a ladder appeared. Then they were taught to point out how soft they were to the touch, how finely meshed, the subtle range of colours. They were each given a little satchel containing one demonstration stocking, samples showing the colour range and a sheaf of order forms to be filled out by the purchaser. They got a cash deposit with each order, which was theirs to keep; this meant they could earn their next meal as they went along and do just as much selling as was necessary each day.

In case ready cash wasn't incentive enough, head office decreed that the working day should start with a sing-song. At this point the life of the Realsilk Hosiery sales person becomes rather surreal. In the summer of 1932 the craze for hiking was at its height, with eager hordes setting off each weekend with knapsacks on their back. Ever topical, the Realsilk Hosiery Company had adapted the current hit, 'I'm Happy When I'm Hiking', to meet the needs of the merry band of sales personnel. Their song began:

I'm happy when I'm selling
Realsilk hosier-eeeee!

'It was quite a striking song,' said Nancy, and sometimes Nicholas Phipps brought along his ukulele for the early-morning, bleary-eyed, pre-selling pep talk and sing-song.

Their bizarre working practices appeared less amusing when a new salesman joined their ranks. A dark, cloth-capped miner from the north, he had left his family back home and come south in search of a job; he could have come from another planet. Even though they were all accustomed to skip meals from time to time when funds ran out, the gulf between their play-acting and his desperate reality was huge, and besides, how could this unhappy man sell anything to wealthy Londoners, let alone silk stockings? The intrusion of his brutal reality was deeply disturbing, but Nancy at least found it impossible to make any connection with his plight, either politically or personally. For the brief time the out-of-work miner was with them, they were all consumed with discomfort and shame.

Her salesmanship suffered from the inability to see good ideas through that had so exasperated Stephen Gilbert. One morning, she decided to target the young car salesmen who stood around in front of the showrooms in Poland Street. She wandered down the street, picked a couple who were chatting together, went through her act and they readily ordered half a dozen pairs apiece. 'It was all as easy as pie,' she said, 'and I'd made a pound.' But she didn't repeat her success. Having thought of it and done it once, that was enough. Next time, she tried somewhere else and a different technique.

All the while, behind the running around there lurked a persistent worry about the future. She was conscious of the futility of what she was doing and was correspondingly guilty and depressed. Much of her time was spent dreaming about Roger Pettiward. All the people she was going around with were just cardboard figures – a way to pass the time until his return. It was,

Nancy wrote, in one of her most telling passages, 'as though Roger had left me in the middle of a phrase of music, with the last note lingering, waiting for the following note which would complete the phrase. And until the note came I was suspended, waiting, unhearing of anything else.'

She speculated endlessly. What did she mean to him? What would happen when he came back? Should she sleep with him? Should she have slept with him before, and then perhaps he wouldn't have gone? But then, he'd never actually asked her to. She'd heard that he and the other male students slept with some of the models and she thought this was probably true. Should she offer to sleep with him when he returned? But she was scared of sex, as well as not knowing much about it. Another factor, she writes, was Roger's 'enormous size. Everything about him was so large and this added to my apprehensions.' She had no idea what sex offered, how it could change and deepen a relationship. All she knew for certain was that it changed a woman's status, and not always for the better. And in the margin next to these reflections she has written, 'Whatever a woman did, the men had a word for it. Was it better to be a cock-teaser or a tart?' At that moment, no other option seemed to be available.

The determination that had propelled her from the suffocating gloom of Spring Gardens had been slowly eroded by the uninspired teaching at the Slade, uncertainty over Roger and the continuous grinding anxiety about money. *Drift, drifted, drifting.* At some stage during the summer of 1932 Nancy seems to have lost her way. By the end of October, Roger Pettiward had returned from his adventures in Brazil. But by then she had gone on the stage, and by then too she had met Lawrence Durrell, the man who was to share her life for the next ten years.

4

'THIS ODD, SIDEWAYS WAY'

Their first meeting should have been memorable. Almost all couples have a shared founding myth: 'The first time I saw you, you were wearing that purple shirt,' or 'I knew the moment I saw you this was going to be special.' Not so Nancy and Larry; they were both vague about how they met – 'in a pub, or somewhere', according to Nancy. The vagueness is significant. Nancy had spent the previous eighteen months parrying endless sexual advances from the men she encountered – apart, of course, from Roger, who never made any. The fact that Larry, so small and boyish and unthreatening, barely registered on her radar meant she fell into a relationship almost without noticing. From her point of view, the most noteworthy thing about him was that he had a car, a rare asset among her mostly penniless friends.

She remembered this one day when Bee's parents were throwing a party and Nancy needed to get down to the Falkeners' Surrey home with her friends. She roped Larry in, packed as many of her Slade friends into the car as possible and then set off for Reigate. Later, Larry was to make a good story out of this episode. He maintained that he'd been ill in bed, suffering with flu and a high temperature when Nancy made her appeal for help. His mother had come up to London to nurse him; he had

The first thing Nancy noticed about Larry was his (mother's) car

to escape from his Soho flat through an upstairs window so he could drive them all to the party.

After all this subterfuge, the party was a bit of a letdown. Nancy remembered Bee's wealthy sheep-farming father, a large, red-faced Australian, who spent the evening shouting across the room to a lot of other large red-faced men in dinner jackets. Meanwhile Bee's elegant mother was alarmed by what she considered to be the Slade 'rabble'. She appealed to Nancy to 'find my baby girl!' – presumably Bee had disappeared with a male friend – because she was 'afraid something terrible may have happened to her'.

By the time this ill-assorted gathering broke up in the early hours of the morning, none of the Slade gang was capable of driving: 'either couldn't drive, or drunk, or both', according to Nancy. The car's owner was curled up ill and asleep on the back seat, so it fell to her to get them all back to London. She had never driven anything except her father's old two-cylinder Jowett, and barely managed, losing the way and crashing the gears, to get them as far as Covent Garden, where they ground to a halt in the middle of an enormous early-morning snarl-up of market traders. Marooned in a sea of porters and huge loads of fruit and vegetables, she panicked.

At this point, Larry woke up. He uncurled himself, took the wheel and got them all safely back to Soho. If she had never met him again, Nancy said later, only the car would have remained in her memory.

When Nancy looked back on the critical events of late summer and autumn 1932, they fell into separate compartments in her mind: Roger's return, followed by a gap before Larry appeared on the scene. But the external evidence proved this was impossible: Larry had already become a part of her life before the South American adventurers returned, by which time she was already on the stage.

Her confusion, and her reliance on external factors, is significant, because at this stage in Nancy's story the nature of the evidence changes dramatically. For one thing, as soon as her life starts to run in parallel with Larry's, it is much more fully documented, at least as regards externals. Larry's story has been told many times and copious quantities of print exist to chart his progress. From then on, until their bitter parting in Egypt in 1942, Nancy's voice was all but inaudible in the clamour of the (mostly male) voices with which she was surrounded.

But there is a second, more critical change in the nature of the evidence. In the summer of 1982, fifty years after the events she was trying to describe, Nancy was diagnosed with bone cancer. Her second husband, Edward Hodgkin, described what followed:

'The next day was dull and wet, and after tea we sat in the sitting-room unable to think of what to do. I suggested reading aloud, or playing music on the gramophone, but Nancy didn't want either of those. "I'm tired of stuff just flowing over me," she said. She then had the brilliant idea of talking to me, with a tape recorder, about her life before the war.' Inevitably, there is a shift in tone. She still struggles to pinpoint the precise truth, but the leisurely introspection of the written memoir has gone; they were both trying to buoy up the other's spirits during a tough time. And there was the inevitable constraint imposed by discussing her life with Larry with her present husband. She was aware of this and occasional handwritten notes survive, which fill in some of the gaps in her spoken memoir.

At some stage, in July or August, Nancy bumped into Larry in one of the pubs they both frequented, perhaps the Yorkshire Grey or the Plough, and invited him to lunch. There was no particular significance in this invitation. As she said, 'I went around issuing invitations in a vague way to anyone who happened to be around. Rather like filling in the empty spaces in a crossword puzzle with any old letter, not making words, just filling in spaces.' And she had moved house again.

Home was now, albeit briefly, a studio flat belonging to James Holland. Older than her, Holland was already established as a commercial artist when he invited Nancy to go on holiday with him. When she refused his terms (sex), he said, 'Oh well, you can stay in the flat while I'm gone.' As this was the moment when she was at her most broke – selling stockings was obviously not going well – she accepted gratefully.

Afterwards, Larry turned that first lunch into another good story; he claimed that when he arrived at Holland's flat the hoped-for lunch did not materialise. Instead he found nothing remotely edible at all apart from a stale bun in a paper bag and some sour milk on the doorstep. Nancy had no recollection of this incident. In all her first memories of Larry she stresses his youth and sweetness. 'He had a sweet little face, and he was quiet and gentle because he was unhappy.' He was doing things he didn't like – such as working for an estate agent in Leytonstone – and although he was renting two rooms in Marsham Street because he thought Verlaine had lived there, he knew hardly any artists or writers.

Nancy took him under her wing. As Larry wrote poetry, she thought he would like to meet writers, and took him along to meet George Wilkinson and his friends. He was an instant success with the Wykehamists; in their company he blossomed to become witty and interesting, and they thought he was marvellous.

Nancy was pleased with the success of her literary matchmaking, but only in an abstract way. She remained obsessed by her own troubles. Crucially, she never had any idea that Larry might be the kind of person she would ever fall for.

That is, until the day she was forced to take notice of him. She was in his flat and he was 'vaguely making love to me'. (It probably didn't seem so vague to Larry: a few years later he wrote to a friend who was having woman problems with the advice that women were like reels of cotton; you had to work hard to make them undress.) Nancy's phrase – 'vaguely making love' – perfectly expresses the spirit of absent-minded passivity in which she had allowed a succession of men to try their luck: a variation on the theme of princes having to answer a riddle in order to win the princess – in this case the girl with the flashy reputation who was in fact a confused and apprehensive virgin. On this occasion, the suitor, so unlike what she had been expecting in a mate, struck lucky and Nancy started to respond.

Larry was writing poetry, but working for an estate agent

'Heavens,' she said, 'something's happened! Bells are ringing. What's happening?'

He said, 'Good heavens! Can't believe it.'

(It's hard to believe that her account of this exchange is strictly accurate, with its echoed exclamations making them sound like a couple of maiden aunts who have dropped the sugar tongs, but the gist of the story – their mutual surprise and pleasure – is what is important, rather than the precise nature of the verbal squeaks.)

Something was happening ... After all her bleak experimentation, from those first gropings in the back of the taxi in Belgium; the smothering kisses from Vladimir Glass with his bad breath and his whispered '*Impregnated!*' which so alarmed her that first summer of her transformation; the dismal sessions on the couch with her Slade tutor, trying not to let him see her revulsion; the various swains who grabbed her at the Slade ball;

and Roger, to whom she was attracted but who never made any attempt to grab her at all, she suddenly and unexpectedly found herself aroused when she was least expecting it.

That in part explains Larry's success. She wasn't expecting it. Her defences were down. It was impossible to be alarmed by this cherubic-looking young writer for whom she felt an almost motherly affection. And so, what might have been just another session of passive and vaguely distasteful lovemaking that stopped short of actual sex astonished her by becoming a discovery of the pleasures of mutual attraction.

She was forced to take notice of him.

In the early weeks of their relationship, his appeal to her maternal instincts was fairly blatant. Before her evenings were taken up by the theatre, they often used to drive out of London as the light was fading; he told her that he had a bad heart and from time to time, just in case she wasn't convinced, he'd stop the car and clutch at his chest. For a short while he did that frequently, before his heart problem mysteriously cured itself, never to reappear. But it worked. Nancy liked caring for people, and now here was this boy-man who needed her affection. All of her first memories are of feeling sorry for him, because he presented himself as being soulful and misunderstood. Nancy felt that he had suffered when his parents brought him to England from their home in India, and left him there alone.

He gratified her by indulging in a good deal of baby talk (rather like the couple in *Look Back in Anger*, said Nancy) of the 'I'se only ickle baby – I'se only really teeny weeny' variety. Nancy hadn't had anything to mother before, so the pretence, so embarrassing in retrospect, satisfied a need in both of them. That phase didn't last long. The baby talk and the bad heart gave way to what she described as a dominating sort of maturity.

By that time, they were established as a couple. Curiously, their relationship must have become an accepted fact while she was still fretting over the absent Roger. And it had all happened, as she herself said, 'in this odd, sideways way'.

Towards the end of the summer, Nancy went with George's girl-friend Pam Black to an audition, just to keep her company. To her surprise, Nancy was selected, while Pam was not. Nancy had not the slightest interest in the stage as a career but, at that time, any income was better than none so she took the job.

Predictably, her parents were less than thrilled by this career move. Her father sent her a furious letter: 'I'm not going to have you kicking your legs up on the stage!' Nancy wrote back to reassure them that far from being 'a leg show' it was a 'highbrow translation of a tragic German play', which was true, up to a point. Whether Gainsborough would have relished the fact that her acting debut was to be in a groundbreaking tale of passionate lesbian love is highly doubtful.

Mädchen in Uniform had started life as a German novel; the previous year it had been turned into a brilliant film, which has now achieved cult status as a lesbian classic. The film's director, Leontine Sagan, brought it to the London stage, with the young Jessica Tandy playing the doomed heroine Manuela von Meinhardis. The action takes place in a Prussian girls' boarding school; all the girls are infatuated with their charismatic teacher Fräulein von Bernburg. Her increasingly passionate relationship with Manuela leads inevitably to tragedy. Nancy was one of the schoolgirls and, apart from the words 'Pass the butter', she had an entirely non-speaking part. Most of the other schoolgirls were from the Italia Conti stage school and a good deal younger than her. They had ringlets or bows on their hair and Nancy found them giggly and silly. So far as she was concerned the rehearsal time was just one long bore; they had to wait in cramped and draughty corners for hour after hour while the principals rehearsed and then, briefly, people shouted at them while the crowd scenes were blocked out. As she observed, if you were not interested in acting professionally, none of this was exactly rewarding. Worse, the principals never spoke directly to the schoolgirls, which made Nancy feel 'very bolshy'.

Though Nancy herself did not make the connection, the subject matter of the play probably compounded her discontent: the enclosed and torrid world of a girls' boarding school, with its regimentation, cruelties and suffocating emotions, must have stirred up painful echoes of Lincoln High.

It would not have mattered so much if they had been properly paid, but their wages were only thirty shillings a week and however much she economised, it was not possible to survive on so little. At one point Jessica Tandy tried to drum up support for Equity, the new actors' union that had been established two years earlier. She asked them each to contribute a small amount – sixpence or a shilling – each week, but Nancy refused on the grounds that she had no interest in the future of the stage and needed every penny of her wages. After that she was 'a bit unpopular in the upper heirarchies', though her little mates in the crowded dressing room did not hold it against her.

Children in Uniform opened at the Duchess Theatre, just off the Aldwych, on 7 October. Each evening after the performance Larry would be waiting for her in a late-night café near by. They took the bus up Southampton Row and had a meal together. The very pattern of settled coupledom.

And then, two weeks after the play's first night, Roger Pettiward finally came back from South America.

He had been away for four months, four months during which Nancy had endlessly speculated about their relationship. She imagined what it would be like when he returned. Sometimes she thought it might be at a party: he would come up to her as though he'd never been away, they'd join up and the 'musical phrase would be completed'. At other times she imagined that he would phone one day, they would meet alone and she would rush into his outstretched arms.

The reality was very different.

Roger's adventures have been brilliantly described by his companion Peter Fleming, who said that having Roger join them was 'the best thing that happened to the expedition', because he 'always saw the joke'. *Brazil Adventure* is permeated with the vanished spirit of the gentleman adventurer, courageous, foolhardy, arrogant and very funny. The expedition leader, to whom Fleming gave the pseudonym Major Pingle, was less impressed by the *Boy's Own* recklessness and exuberance of the two young men: a few miles from the inaccessible spot where Colonel Fawcett was reputed to have been killed while searching for the Lost World, tensions came to a head and the party split in two. Fleming, Roger and another companion raced the main body of the expedition down five hundred miles of South American river. They revelled in danger, starvation and hardship as only those born to wealth and comfort can; Parody was their muse as they strove to experience the Real Thing (Fleming was much given to capitals when conveying their devotion to the spirit of Parody). Even at moments of intense danger and discomfort, the two Old Etonians maintained their own ironic language, so that water was always the 'Precious Fluid' and a gunshot was 'the well-known bark of a Mauser'. References to their world of privilege crop up in the most unexpected places: for instance, two young otters they adopted are described as uttering 'continuously a fretful whiffling sound, exactly reproducing the tone in which very old men in clubs reprimand the waiter for bringing them the wrong liqueur'.

So, while Nancy had been breaking her last ties with the Slade, Roger had been enjoying a minor South American revolution: 'Boat Race Night was Armageddon to this.' And while Nancy tried to make money selling Realsilk hosiery, Roger was merrily slaughtering alligators by the dozen and having more adventures than most people enjoy in a lifetime. As her confidence ebbed to zero, he was living out the adventure fantasy of his Edwardian heroes. While she was becoming involved with a young estate agent poet, almost by accident, he was—? She had no idea.

She heard that he had returned, but for a while she did not see him. No one did. And then one evening she looked across the room at a party and there he was, taller than everyone else, red-haired and hardened by adventure. Did he open his arms in greeting? Did they pick up where they had left off? Was it as if he had never been gone? Or did he break it to her that their strange sort-of romance was over?

No. None of the above. After all her romantic imaginings, Roger Pettiward quite simply ignored her. He was chatting with a group of men when she first spotted him, so she waited, expecting that at any moment he would turn around and slope up to her in the old familiar fashion, but he didn't. He just continued chatting in the group with his glass in his hand. And the next time she looked, he was gone.

She was shattered: she had become, in her phrase, 'a nonperson'.

After that she saw him several times at pubs and parties, but they never spoke. Taking her cue from him, she usually just pretended he didn't exist. Being blanked by him seems to have induced in her a kind of paralysis, both physical and emotional, neither flight nor fight, but freeze. Her response to his rejection highlights just how chronically inexperienced she was, without any of the resources necessary to deal with the complexities of a relationship. She had absolutely no idea how to react.

Apart from one occasion, when in desperation she made what she described as 'a rather pathetic' attempt to get his attention. Peter Proud, the friend who had introduced her to Realsilk, had invited a group of them to a party his mother was giving. Mrs Proud owned a small, exclusive couturier's business in Knightsbridge and the party was to launch the new season's fashions. A bright and enterprising woman, she was rumoured to be the mistress of the world speed record breaker and national hero, Sir Malcolm Campbell. Nancy knew that Roger was expected to attend the party, and she suggested to a group of her Slade friends that they should liven the 'stuffy' gathering by pretending to be drunk.

'I can still see,' she wrote, 'the smiles on the faces of the row of elderly men standing sipping small glasses of sherry at this unexpected turn as, with me leading, we rushed in at top speed, flung our arms round them and kissed them in turn, making some inane remark, giggling, and every now and then saying, "We're drunk!"' After they had pranced around for a while, they collapsed in a corner and did a little singing. Then they made a stumbling, kissing departure. Mrs Proud didn't seem to mind; perhaps she thought their performance improved the party.

Nancy must have confided the reason for the charade to her friend Carmen from the Slade. Later, when they were recovering in the Yorkshire Grey, Carmen passed on the information that 'Roger had been worried about her'. And that was it. End of story.

Almost.

A year later, by which time Nancy and Larry had left London and were living in Sussex, she made the trip up to town to visit the dentist and stayed the night with her old landlords and friends the Laings. Wandering down Tottenham Court Road, Nancy bumped into Roger Hilton, who took her along to a small evening gathering at the studio of a mutual acquaintance. Among the handful of guests there already was Roger Pettiward. He was sitting next to Diana, the fourth woman friend from Nancy's days in the sculpture basement at the Slade.

Hilton and Nancy sat on a couple of chairs near the door. Almost as soon as they were settled with their drinks, Roger got up and came over to her. He suggested that if she had nothing else arranged, they might leave together in a bit and go somewhere else. He then sauntered back to the chair next to Diana. A few minutes later Nancy was surprised to see Diana leaning towards him, smiling and cupping her hand as she whispered in his ear. He then crossed the room once more: he was sorry, but he had forgotten that he'd already promised to take Diana somewhere that evening. Nancy told him she was leaving London in the morning.

This meeting left everything unresolved, and not surprisingly it unsettled her. She concluded that Roger and Diana must be involved with each other, but she also felt that if Diana needed to stop him from spending an hour or two with her, then she must be afraid of her, afraid that Roger would be drawn to her again. But, 'it simply wasn't the way we had behaved to each other'.

Nancy never saw Roger again. He was killed, leading his men with great courage, in the commando raid on Dieppe in 1942.

In this final typed page of her own notes, she says, 'Looking back, I still think it's a pity we never had that explanation. What he did, whether he married or not, I don't know.' And in brackets she has written: ('More when I've thought it out'). But that 'more' never materialised.

Which is strange, because she could have found out very easily, even in 1982 when there was no internet to help the casual researcher. But Roger had sloped into Nancy's life at the time when she still wished to see her friends as existing – as she herself wished to exist – in a vacuum, without the encumbrance of family or antecedents. Roger, however, had plenty of both. He was born Roger Terry in 1906 at Onehouse Lodge, near Finborough Hall in Suffolk. When he was two his father took the name Pettiward by royal licence in order to inherit his cousin's estate and became lord of the manor. Thus Roger, his brother and two sisters grew up at Finborough Hall. After his Oxford degree he studied art in Munich and Vienna before joining the Slade. And in July 1935, at St Bartholemew the Great in Smithfield, he married Diana. She was the daughter of Frederick Berners-Wilson of The Hardwick, in Abergavenny, Monmouthshire. They had three children. Roger continued to paint, while enjoying a successful career as a cartoonist. In one of his *Punch* cartoons, a tall young man is leaning casually against a baronial mantel-piece, observed by a portrait of a supercilious eighteenth-century ancestor. His baffled father stands by the fire, uncomprehending as the young man drawls, 'Yes, Father, I know, but what virtue is there in gathering moss?'

Was Nancy, on this occasion, afraid of discovering the truth about this man who had made such an impact on her life? When she talked about him to me, she said her relationship with Roger was the only one that had its origins, on her part, with sexual attraction. Better that he should remain for ever a conundrum, perhaps, than accept the bitter truth that she never meant a quarter as much to him as he did to her. She hints at under-standing when she describes Diana as being 'very different in every way' from the other students, with the sort of 'diffident social confidence', the bored, drawling voice of the sophisticated upper classes.

The sorrow is not so much that Nancy fell in love with an enigmatic toff who blanked her on his return from terrific adventures, choosing instead a friend of hers who fitted easily into the world he knew. The agonies of first love and being jilted are a rite of passage rather than cause for lasting grief. For me the regret is that, briefly, Nancy had discovered within herself a spirit of joyous, extrovert anarchy, a vibrant enthusiasm for mayhem and fun, a huge well of energy and enjoyment, which she never really recovered. The roaring girl, glimpsed briefly when she and Roger disrupted the art-school dances with their whooping Lancers' gallop and crazy dancing, slipped from view, and after those few months in early 1932 never really flourished again.

'It is easy to imagine how we might have met,' Nancy said on the first page of her intended memoir. 'But what was it that made us team up together? And then, after living together for two years, get married? We were an odd couple – physically incompatible – Larry being short and thick-set and me at least three inches taller than him. And when we first met, in a pub probably, what were we like? How did we see each other, and what drew us together? What did each of us have that the other needed, or think they had?'

She never did get round to answering these questions directly. Still, it is possible to provide some answers.

Lawrence Durrell was born in Northern India in February 1912 and so was older than Nancy by just three months. He was the first child of parents whose families had lived exclusively in India for three generations, and although like everyone else they referred to England as 'home', none of them had never been to their almost mythical homeland. His father, Lawrence Samuel Durrell, was an engineer who worked for a while on the

Darjeeling Himalayan Railway. Later he set up his own con-struction firm, together with a couple of Indian partners, in Jamshedpur, which was then the centre of India's fledgling steel industry.

As a small child, Larry had had a Burmese ayah. The world Nancy had only glimpsed through the writings of Fielding Hall coloured his earliest memories – Kim's India, both sensuous and spiritual. In 1915 a second child was born, little Margery, but she died of diphtheria when still a baby. Not surprisingly, the next infant, Leslie, was given extra care and coddling by his recently bereaved mother Louisa, which exacerbated the inevitable rivalry between the brothers. Margaret, always known in the family as Margo, arrived when Larry was seven.

Like Nancy, Larry was sent away to boarding school at the age of nine, but the parallels end there. Rather than Lincoln High, its Gothic walls swept by the bleak winds off the North Sea, young Durrell's destination was the Jesuit college in Darjeeling, a place of breathtaking beauty in the foothills of the Himalayas where he was described in a school report as 'a sturdy young scamp'. He later claimed that he could see Mount Everest from his dormitory window, which is not strictly true but nonetheless evokes the wonder of the place.

There was no such wonder at the end of the next journey. In 1923 the pressure to provide his son with a 'proper' – i.e. English – education prompted Lawrence Samuel to take the entire family 'home' for the first time. Like Nancy, whose expec-tations of boarding school were coloured by the books of Angela Brazil, Larry had a head full of literary images to prepare him for his new life in England: he was looking forward to the vibrant and eccentric homeland of Dickens, Surtees and Thackeray. What he got was greyness, petty snobberies and a distinctly patchy education. Leaving behind 'the wild passes of Bhutan' he now had to endure 'mental sterility and cowardice and the thousand and one dreary shams of middle-class society'. Those scornful phrases come from his semi-autobiographical first novel, *Pied Piper of Lovers*, but they could just as well have been Nancy's description of Gainsborough. Although the English education was his father's idea, and his mother had argued hard to keep her family together in India, it was his mother he always blamed for the exile from the country of his birth, a country to which he never returned, but which remained a crucial part of his mental furniture for the rest of his life.

After six months spent with a succession of relatives, the family returned to India, leaving Larry behind at a school in Tunbridge Wells; his sister said he felt abandoned, and bore a grudge against this system all his life. It was two years before he saw his family again, by which time Larry had been transferred to Dulwich College. His mother visited England for a few months with her other children, including her last child, Gerald. The next time she went back to India, Leslie stayed in England with Larry.

School for Larry was a tedious necessity, made bearable by literature. In Dulwich he was near the world of the Elizabethan poets and dramatists he came to know and love and later, at St Edmund's School in Canterbury, he discovered Marlowe. Not a particularly distinguished scholar, or outstandingly popular, he survived by learning to box, which meant his piano-playing and book-reading tendencies were tolerated by his schoolmates.

In the summer of 1926 the entire family were once again together, and his father bought a large house in Dulwich; the eventual intention was to settle in England for good some time in the near future. When the family went back to India in the autumn Mrs Durrell insisted on taking Leslie with them. His school battles had resulted in much misery, and a permanently damaged eardrum. So once again, Larry was left behind when the family sailed away. He never saw his father again. Eighteen months later, in early 1928, Lawrence Samuel started to get headaches and his behaviour changed, becoming increasingly erratic; he died in April 1928 and three thousand miles away his eldest son received the shattering news in a cable. Within two months his mother had left India for the last time and sailed to England. From now on she devoted herself entirely to her four children, and was always known in the family as Mother Durrell. Financially well provided for, but without the support of her strong-minded husband, she found her brood increasingly diffi-cult to manage.

Larry left the school in Canterbury and went to a crammer where he seems to have spent a good deal of time failing to get into either Oxford or the army. Later he claimed he'd fluffed his exams repeatedly because he was – posthumously – thwarting his father's ambitions for him, but the failure rankled. He would have liked to go to Oxford and always felt as though he had missed out in some way. After a while the family solicitor, to whom she had turned for masculine advice, suggested to Mrs Durrell that a friend of his, an estate agent in the London suburb of Leyton-stone, might be able to employ her son.

Larry was still working there when he met Nancy, and though he had persuaded his mother to give him the use of her car, and though he was already writing poetry, he was almost as lost and unfocused as she was. 'We both started off,' said Nancy, 'rather using each other.' Looking back, she realised that outwardly she cut a very dashing and sophisticated figure, with an entrée into the literary and artistic circles that he had not yet achieved, while she was happy to find someone with the use of a car.

Superficially, they were an unlikely couple: her tall elegance must have made him seem even shorter and stockier than he was – a foot shorter than Roger Pettiward. But under the surface there was much to draw them together. Both harboured within them a sense of permanent exile, stronger than the common feeling of a lost childhood Eden that almost everyone carries into adult life. Nancy's was a memory of 'security, order, bliss, sun, nanny, back beyond the horrors' while Larry could have used the same words to describe the memory of his early years in North India. They both felt guilty that their parents had made financial sacrifices to educate them in order to satisfy social ambitions that they could not share, let alone achieve: the Durrells hoping their eldest son would become a fully fledged Englishman, the Myers aiming for a daughter who was a proper lady. Both had finished their formal education with a sense of failure, Nancy because lack of funds had forced her to drop out of the Slade and Larry because of all those abortive attempts to get into Oxford. By the time they met, they had both learned to navigate by different stars from those which guided their families: art and literature were all that mattered. But though they had turned their backs on conventional values, they were both conscious of having grown up in a social milieu which left them vulnerable to snobbery.

It was inevitable that anyone born in 1912 in either India or England was going to be acutely aware of the fine gradations of social hierarchy which carried an importance mercifully hard for a modern mind to unpick – not just upper, middle and lower class, but strict pigeon-holing according to employment prospects, as in 'servant class' or 'shop-keeper class'. The Durrells and the Dixies (his mother's family) had lived in India for three generations, but not as 'heaven-borns', those lords of creation who took their place at the apex of British colonial life for granted. Nor did they belong among the British-educated civil servants. The Durrells were India-educated engineers and technocrats, and it was Lawrence Samuel's social ambitions that meant his sons had to be educated in England. But when Louisa Durrell came back to England her accent marked her out. As one of her relatives cattily noted, 'No one with an accent is ever well-bred.' A proud and sensitive boy would inevitably suffer at these petty humiliations, even while seeing them for the idiocy they were.

Just as Nancy did. Her parents had concentrated on turning her into a young lady and had constantly emphasised that, in spite of their financial difficulties, they were superior people. Nancy despised their attitude, but like Larry she could not be totally immune to it. Like him, she had her own kind of snobbery, which reflected her devotion to bohemian values. After her death, I was intrigued to find, among her papers, a handwritten item headed 'Artistic Snob' which began, 'My daughter Joanna recently accused me of being an artistic and aesthetic snob' and she quotes me: '"as though other people don't really count" – At the time I was a bit offended, but now I think that it's true in a way, and was already an established part of my armoury at the time I left school. My experience both at home and at school had been one total lack of response or comprehension of any of the things I felt most strongly about. I found confirmation and inspiration only in books.' And, she adds defiantly, 'Thank heavens I did.'

Both had turned to books for a way to interpret the world. Both had found that what is now called the 'straight' world did not appreciate them. Both had forged a superficial way of engaging with people: Nancy because she was beautiful and unconventional, Larry because he could conjure up a bewitching charm at the drop of a hat. And both were ambitious, not for fame and fortune, though a bit of fortune wouldn't have gone amiss, but to carve a place for themselves in the only pantheon that really mattered, that of the arts. They wanted to create work in which they could take pride.

And along the way, this unlikely couple began to enjoy themselves.

In an attic room above a music publisher, two young poets were locked in literary battle. Even by the dismal standards of the time, this tiny flat was off the scale of discomfort, with ancient beams and crumbling walls and nothing whatsoever to sit on. The men had set the terms of the contest: they were going to do battle for Nancy with words. With tea and gin and immense good humour, John Gawsworth and Larry took up their swords of verbal dexterity and fenced and parried the night away, the Georgian poet against the modernist. As dawn light seeped into the scruffy attic, Gawsworth made an expansive gesture and declared, 'Well, the best man has won, Lawrence! May you take the fair lady!'

The fair lady had been present throughout. She was uncomfortable with their histrionics, and maybe she sensed something more, something that fixed this long night of wordplay in her memory even though she claimed to have been 'tired and uninterested'. Her Slade friends were ebbing away – apart from that single trip to the Falkeners' party in Reigate, Larry never met them – and in the world of writers which she was to inhabit from now on, she was becoming an elegant presence, not quite a trophy wife, but in danger of losing that fragile, and recently discovered, sense that she was 'someone'. Dismissive though she was of their self-important play-acting, the verbal duel was always one of the stories she told.

Competition out of the way – and John Gawsworth did not languish long: by October he was printing 'Sonnet for Miranda' – the friendship between him and Larry developed into an enduring source of pleasure for them both. Gawsworth was, Larry said, the first 'Real Writer' he had ever met, burning, as he himself wished to, with 'a hard, gem-like flame'. He was fascinated by Gawsworth's collection of memorabilia – a skull cap that had belonged to Dickens, Thackeray's pen – and relished the fact that he had actually met both Yeats and Hardy. Through John Gawsworth and Nancy's Wykehamist friends, Larry began to move in the circles where he was able to develop and shine.

And in return he gave her what she perhaps needed more than anything: a family.

Larry's family was as a revelation, even before Nancy had had a chance to meet them. With Larry, as she was discovering, every-thing was verbal, discussable, and that in itself was an education for her. Never in her life had Nancy come across anyone who talked about their family like this. He dramatised everything about them, just as later he was to dramatise his first lunch with her, and the episode as a flu-stricken chauffeur. To begin with Nancy found it thrilling. He warned her that his family had gone completely to pieces after his father died, his mother was an insane woman, practically certifiable, who had thrown her for-tune to the winds while the younger children were hopelessly spoiled and ran rings around her and everyone else. Nancy's deal-ings with her own tight little family triangle were too tortured for her to be able to joke about them. Indeed, she hardly ever talked about her parents at all, even to Larry. But Larry gloried in his family's faults and inflated them to such gigantic proportions that they became grotesque, ridiculous – and ultimately harmless.

When they drove down to Bournemouth for their first week-end visit together, Nancy's resistance to people's families had been eroded by this larger-than-life build-up. She was full of anticipation, because, as she said, he made them sound like the Sanger family, that unconventional brood in *The Constant Nymph*.

The reality was even better than she could have hoped. Louisa Durrell had moved to Bournemouth a couple of years earlier, and bought a large, ramshackle house which she named Dixie Lodge after her own family. Nancy loved it from the very first. She loved the craziness of it all, its air of improvisation, the fact that it looked like people playing at keeping house rather than really doing it. There were no fixed times for meals, everybody shouted at everyone else in a way that seemed to her uninhibited and honest, and, most important of all, everyone was free to be whatever it was they wanted to be. In this family, no one was forced into a mould.

She had already fallen under the spell of Larry's charm, his ability to turn the most mundane event into a colourful drama. And charm was what the whole family had in spades. Charm and humour. Over the years I met all of them except Leslie, and it was always their warmth and laughter that lingered in the memory. As a household of unruly teenagers, with an erratic and indulgent mother trying and failing to keep some kind of order, they must have been irresistible.

However, Nancy's first visit ended in disaster. On her very first morning at Dixie Lodge Larry came into her room and hopped into bed with her, swiftly followed by Gerry, who at seven was very much his mother's baby. When Mother Durrell found the three of them cuddled up cosily under the blankets she erupted in fury. Never in her whole life had she been so disgusted! 'Out you go!' she roared. 'Out you go this minute! Never darken my doors again!' Mrs Durrell accused them of corrupting her little boy and gave them five minutes to leave the house.

It was Nancy's first experience of Louisa Durrell's histrionics, and she was horrified. Larry was more sanguine. 'The silly woman,' he said. 'She'll soon be over it. Come on, we'll go now. In a day or two she'll be glad to have us back.' And he told his mother airily that she was a stupid woman. 'Don't be such a fool, Mother!' he said as Nancy slunk out of the house beside him. After all Nancy's fractured miseries with her own mother, one can sense the blissful release of hearing a mother being told she was a fool, and stupid, without the heavens crashing down and the known world coming to an end.

Just as he had predicted, a fortnight later they were welcomed back with open arms, and from then on his mother turned a blind eye to whatever corrupting activities they indulged in. To Nancy she was kindness itself, the doting and approving mother she had yearned for. Mrs Durrell decided that Nancy looked consumptive and set about trying to fatten her up with cream, butter and whatever else she could lay her hands on. As she was a marvellous cook this meant delicious meals. Delicious meals at unpredictable times with everyone talking at once and saying exactly what they wanted. A joyous combination.

From the first, Nancy loved being accepted as a part of this chaotic family, even if she did feel 'rather a goose among ducklings', being so long and thin when they were all so short and round. But a happy goose, nevertheless, and 'tremendously taken into the ducklings'.

In the autumn of 1932 the family of Durrell ducklings was, in theory, headed by Louisa. At forty-six, she had been a widow for four years and was struggling to cope with her remarkable offspring, as well as with the practicalities of surviving in a country she barely knew. Leslie was fifteen, and boarding at Dulwich College. Despite being taller than Larry, good-looking and not without charm, poor Leslie was never a match for his older brother. Larry could make him look like a fool any time he wanted – and he wanted to often. Whenever Leslie annoyed him Larry responded with a verbal flaying. Leslie had no defences against these attacks. As a small child he had held his breath and gone blue in the face when thwarted, a highly effective weapon, but now he had no means of retaliation. He developed a passion for guns.

Margo was twelve and a boarder at Cheltenham Ladies' College, so was only around in the holidays. To begin with she didn't make much of an impression on Nancy, though later they became close.

Gerry was a favourite from the first. Slender and delicate, with more than his fair share of the Durrell charm, he reminded Nancy of Christopher Robin, though with a rather more determined character than Pooh's friend. His mother took him to school every morning. Or rather, she tried to. He had a fierce resistance to school, what would now be called school phobia, and clung screaming to the railings as she tried to drag him along the street. Frequently, her efforts ended in failure and by the time they returned, exhausted, to Dixie Lodge he would be running a temperature and the doctor would have to be called. (As a school-hating child myself, I was in awe of his brilliance at school avoidance.)

At seven, Gerry still slept in his mother's bedroom as he was afraid of being left on his own, and he refused to go to bed without her. So early each evening she retired to her big bed, and anyone else who happened to be in the house came along too. She had an enormous silver teatray with silver teapots and milk jugs. Larry and Nancy would bring a bottle of gin with them and together they would sprawl on Mother Durrell's bed and chat and laugh while Gerry drifted off to sleep. Very cosy, as Nancy said.

When Margo and Leslie were home from school they played exuberant games of bicycle polo in the garden with Larry, and sometimes Nancy was persuaded to join in. With Mother Durrell's delicious meals, fun and shouting and laughter and games, trips to Dixie Lodge were always a delight. She said, 'I really fell in love with his family,' and described it as 'a great opening-up experience'.

For the next ten years, Mother Durrell and her younger children played a crucial role in her life with Larry, and it is no coincidence that when the final break came, the married couple had been separated from the rest of the Durrells for three years.

After years of trying to survive in London as a single person, Nancy was delighted to be part of a couple, no longer forced to steer a path between the twin horrors of being stereotyped as either a tart or a cock-tease but free to be herself. Together, she and Larry gave each other the courage they had lacked singly.

Nancy encouraged Larry to stop pretending to be an apprentice estate agent. Not that he needed much encouragement. By the time they got together he had pretty much given up the charade and his time in the Leytonstone office had become another source of good stories: the perils and adventures of the young rent collector, attacked by savage dogs and with doors slammed in his face. 'You're wasting your life doing this,' she told him. 'How ridiculous to do such a stupid thing.' And so he gave up the farce. Larry was twenty-one in February and around this time, with his usual bluntness, he persuaded his mother to give him his portion of the family money. 'You're chucking it all down the drain,' he told her. 'In another few years there won't be any left. I want my bit now.' And so she gave him the interest from his share of the family money, which amounted to three pounds a week.

When he was still at the crammer, Larry had made friends with Cecil Jeffries, a fellow student who had been equally determined not to get on in any conventional way, and they had kept in touch. It was Cecil who printed his first few poems. By early 1933 Cecil had decided to launch a nightclub. A beautiful young man, tall and lanky, with a pink and white complexion, baby lips and curly hair, Cecil was 'terribly unstable'. According to Nancy he was always either drunk or drugged and they regularly found him lying on the floor and frothing (at the mouth, presumably). In the intervals between lying on the floor and frothing, Cecil opened the Blue Peter in a basement in Soho. Its blue lighting made for a somewhat eerie atmosphere, and mostly people just went there to drink. Larry was taken on to play the piano. Though he had never been properly taught he could, according to Nancy, 'strum quite gaily', and this is what he did for two or three hours every night. When she had finished the evening performance of *Children in Uniform* at the Duchess Theatre, Nancy would join him there. He wrote a couple of songs, light-hearted celebrations of new love, like 'Out of the Blue':

> *Was tired of late nights*
> *Forbidden delights*
> *Was tired of the people I knew*
> *When all of a sudden*
> *The wind seemed to change*
> *And you came out of the blue*
>
> *Like a song without words*
> *Like a tree without birds*
> *Like a cottage without any view*
> *I was all on my own*
> *When the wind seemed to change*
> *And you came out of the blue.*

On several occasions Harold Nicolson, the diplomat husband of Vita Sackville-West, turned up with some of his boyfriends. Nancy was incensed whenever the eminent man went over to Larry, placed his hands on his shoulders and said, 'Do, darling, do play "Trees" again.' She had no experience of such matters: homosexuality was still illegal, and men were regularly sent to prison for indecency. For Nancy the main interest at the Blue Peter was the 'professional ladies'. Never having encountered prostitutes before, she was flattered when they took her for one of them. 'What have you got tonight, dear?' a hooker asked her when they were side by side, looking in the mirror in the ladies' room. Being taken for a whore, when she was safely in a relationship, was a delightful confirmation of how far she had migrated from her parents' hopes that she would become a lady.

Whores and homosexuals: the Blue Peter was an interesting, if brief, interlude. Not surprisingly it closed after only a few weeks, when the frothing proprietor ran out of money and the police raided the place. (Larry made good his escape through a window, as he had done when evading his mother in order to drive Nancy and her friends to Surrey, this time down a drainpipe.) By that time, Nancy had left the stage and taken up a new career as a photographer.

A fellow schoolgirl from the cast of *Children in Uniform* gave Nancy an introduction to a commercial photographer who operated from a basement off the Charing Cross Road. 'I seem to have spent my whole life in basements,' Nancy commented ruefully. She worked there for three or four weeks before telling Larry, 'This commercial photography is a piece of cake,' and they decided to set up their own studio. Looking back, she was horrified at their bumptiousness: to go into business after only three weeks as an assistant and no real training. She wasn't even sure that she had ever taken a professional photograph, and her experience of developing plates was minimal. But these considerations did not daunt them in the least; they had the confidence that comes from shared hopes and plans.

Now it was Larry's turn to instil her with courage. Having extracted as much money from his mother as he could, at least for the time being, he encouraged Nancy to write to her parents for funds. 'Why not ask your father?' he said. Amazingly, she did, telling him she was going into the project with a friend of hers who was very knowledgeable – 'that kind of rot', as she said. Even more amazingly, her father approved of the idea. Photography was something he understood, having taken it up during their happy years in Eastbourne. At last, he thought, Nancy was putting her artistic training to some profit. 'Certainly,' he wrote back, 'I think it's a very good thing to do,' and he enclosed a cheque for three hundred pounds.

Delighted, Nancy and Larry set about establishing themselves as commercial photographers. First they needed premises. Inevitably, they found themselves a basement, but a large basement this time, under a café in Lamb's Conduit Street run by a woman who was known simply as Cheffy. Cheffy was a well-known character, and her café was a favourite meeting place. She had a deep, croaking voice, and a cigarette permanently at the corner of her mouth. With rouged cheeks, black ringlets and a scarf over her head, she looked every inch the gypsy she claimed to be. She said she had been born in a hansom cab while crossing one of the London bridges (conceived seems a more likely story) and if she liked you, she gave you everything, but if she didn't, then out you went. Luckily she took a great liking to Larry and Nancy and they ate all their meals in her café.

There's a joyful air of play-acting about the whole photographic episode, and a friend who knew them at that time remembers it as an entirely harmonious partnership, with never a cross word between them (but then, she also remembers it as a summer when the sun shone every day). At this point, for the first time, it is possible to set Nancy's record besides those of her friends, and it is telling: whereas she emphasises her ineptness and naivety, others remember her apparent maturity. Whatever she might have felt like inside, she gave an impression of competence.

Larry was to be the manager, so a portion of the basement was separated off from the rest by a large velvet curtain, behind which was his large roll-top desk and an enormous imitation-leather armchair. At the other end of the room another section was curtained off for the darkroom. They put up shelves and bought a variety of lights and, of course, a camera. An assistant was hired, known simply as Pike. Unfortunately Pike knew hardly more about commercial photography than they did, and was none too bright, but he was at least cheap.

Then there was the problem of what the enterprise should be called. A great deal of time was devoted to thinking up a suitable name, which involved endless discussion and, when they thought they had found one, they'd say, 'Let's see what George thinks about it,' and off they trooped to George Wilkinson's flat and he would twiddle his ring with his long fingers and say, 'Well, I don't know that that's *exactly* right . . .', so they'd begin again. Eventually they settled on Witch Photos. Once they had a name, the writing paper had to be chosen and printed. (Confusingly, the address on the paper was Millman Street, while a contemporary directory places Durrell Commercial Photography in Red Lion Passage. Some of this confusion was probably deliberate, an attempt to prevent Nancy's parents from discovering she and Larry were cohabiting.)

Their first efforts at photography were not promising. The Wykehamist Peter Bull needed some photos to take to agents, so he sat for his portrait and the results just about passed muster. Their second subject was A. J. Symons, the writer George was working for. Chiefly remembered for his biography of Frederick Rolfe, *The Quest for Corvo*, Symons was then an impressive figure. Nancy remembered him as a dignified and rather frightening man who seemed middle-aged – over forty at least – though in fact he was only thirty-two. He arrived at the studio for his sitting and she solemnly took several shots of him, but when they were developed – disaster. All of the images were covered in large spots. It turned out that Pike had put all the plates into the camera the wrong way round. They had no option but to phone Symons and confess their mistake. He obligingly came back to be photographed again, this time with more satisfactory results, but not surprisingly the whole episode made Nancy feel 'very small'.

While Larry sat behind his velvet curtain, feet up on the roll-top desk, waiting for the phone to ring, Nancy and Pike made various attempts to produce a portfolio of images that would showcase their skills. The trouble was, as she was increasingly aware, the skills they wished to showcase were almost non-existent. All their demonstration shots, tasteful arrangements of china and silver and bits of furniture, emerged blighted with shadows and highlights in all the wrong places.

Nancy and Pike experimented with different poses and lighting, but the quality was still uncertain

Their only other customer was a man she described as 'very vulgar', who said he had a brilliant idea for advertising women's underwear. Pam Black was brought in to help with this money-making venture, and she and Nancy sat around in cami-knickers pretending to play strip poker while the vulgar man took the pictures. The results were not judged to be very marketable; as Nancy said, neither of them were cut out to be glamour models, she being much too skinny and Pam, at that time, rather butch-looking, with short hair and a beaky nose.

Some Witch Photos images of Nancy survive: they show her experimenting with different poses and lighting. Presumably Pike took them.

Along the way they had acquired a Fox Terrier puppy, and this led to problems with the outspoken Cheffy upstairs. Nancy was devoted to their new acquisition, even though it widdled every-where and knocked the lights over. After a while, however, Larry refused to take the puppy back home with them in the evenings, presumably objecting to its not being housetrained, and it was left on its own to howl miserably in the basement. Cheffy accused them of being cruel, and though Nancy agreed with her, Larry was adamant. Already Nancy was finding the gentle, cherubic young man had an immovably stubborn streak. The dog continued to howl in the basement; relations with Cheffy went downhill.

They were living in a couple of rooms not far from the studio, though Nancy had also taken a room in nearby Calthorpe Street in case her parents showed up, which they did on one occasion. For once her father was all enthusiasm. He visited Witch Photos and was thrilled with the whole venture. When Nancy saw him off at the station he told her that her photographic career had given him a new interest in life, which made her feel terrible because by then she and Larry knew quite well that the whole enterprise was going nowhere fast.

The next time Nancy's parents came down from Lincolnshire was for their daughter's twenty-first birthday. The news they brought changed everything.

In May, Thomas and Louise Myers travelled down to London and took a room in a hotel. They had brought Nancy a somewhat startling gift, a fox fur. Perhaps she had decided she needed a conventional outfit in which to convince bank managers and punters of the seriousness of Witch Photos, because Janet Laing, the daughter of her former landlord, had made her a sophisticated dress to a *Vogue* pattern in a soft plum-coloured wool. Now she could finish off the outfit by draping her fox fur round her neck, its tail held firmly between its little sharp teeth.

The surprises didn't end there. 'We've got something exciting to tell you,' her parents said, brimming with enthusiasm, as they dropped their bombshell. 'Your cousin Fielding Hall left you all his money when he died.'

Nancy's immediate reaction was one of tremendous pleasure. Fielding Hall, her father's cousin whose books had been such an inspiration to her when she was in her teens, had left her his entire capital when he died in 1917, and it was now worth over three thousand pounds. Almost as important as the cash was the knowledge that this man, to whom she had always felt a deep sense of connection, had marked her out for special attention.

Just why the old Burma hand left all his money to his cousin's only child, no one knew. After all, he had two young children of his own. Fifty years later, another of Nancy's paternal relatives died intestate and as the lawyers struggled to track down all his surviving relatives several unknown members of her family emerged from the shadows. One afternoon she received a phone call from an elderly lady, Fielding Hall's daughter, who straight away demanded, 'Why did my father leave you all his money?'

Nancy had no idea. She'd been five when he died and had no memory of ever meeting him. His motivation remains a mystery. It might simply have been because he was by then so estranged from his wife and children that he couldn't bear them to have anything of his. As his wife was independently wealthy, his own capital was not financially significant to them, though emotionally it is another matter, as his daughter's question after a lifetime of uncertainty makes clear. It may be significant that Fielding Hall made his final will in the summer of 1917, two months before he died, at exactly the moment Nancy's parents suffered whatever disaster caused them to leave Eastbourne and start again two hundred miles away in Gainsborough. Perhaps rumours of Thomas Myers's activities had reached him and he took pity on his daughter. Whatever the reason, his deathbed impulse had far-reaching consequences.

As the news sank in Nancy's excitement gave way to feelings of bewilderment.

'Why didn't you tell me?' she asked her parents.

Her mother looked coy. 'We wanted it to be a surprise,' she said with a smile.

It was. Nancy was frustrated and angry. If she had known about the money that would be hers on her maturity, she would have been able to plan. She would not have had to drop out of the Slade, but could have enjoyed the full three years without the constant anxiety about finances blighting every stage. Instead of drifting, she would have been able to work towards a goal. The futility and time-wasting of Realsilk Hosiery and *Children in Uniform* had been not just a bore, but completely unnecessary.

It was not the only surprise. A few months later her father wrote to her, a 'rather shame-faced letter' saying that it had somehow slipped his memory that Fielding Hall was not her only benefactor. His own father had left Nancy a substantial legacy when he died in 1928. Quite how Thomas had forgotten this after only seven years is a mystery, since he and his stepmother were joint trustees. Fielding Hall had sensibly put the public trustees in charge until Nancy reached maturity, but old Reverend Myers gave his widow and son discretion. However, with his usual money-repelling genius, Thomas had invested the money and lost a good deal of it, which perhaps accounts for the delay in telling Nancy about her inheritance. It was this money that had paid for Lincoln High, art school and even Witch Photos. So all those times when her parents had burdened her with the financial sacrifices they were making on her behalf were a fiction too: her grandfather's money, not theirs, had financed it all.

'I felt,' she said, 'enormously *done* and thwarted.' All those stomach-churning occasions when she had been consumed with guilt about asking her father for money, and he had grudgingly granted it and told her to keep some kind of account, it had actually been her own money he'd been dispensing. Even the three hundred pounds for Witch Photos had been hers all along. And now she and Larry were saddled with commercial photography, whereas if they had known what the situation was, they'd have chosen a different route.

From now on Nancy's somewhat unsatisfactory parents fade from view. Nancy saw as little of them as possible, though she never broke free of the emotional tangle in which they had enmeshed her. Phrases like 'the best woman in the world' and 'You can never make up to me for the pain I had bearing you', echoed in her psyche for the rest of her life. Her mother died in an asylum in Lincolnshire just before the end of the war, having suffered from some kind of dementia for several years. Nancy had not seen her for a long time. Thomas reappeared after the war, but Nancy was never close to him.

There is one final mystery, one final surprise, before Thomas and Louise Myers depart from the story. The details about Louise's family recounted earlier come from the information Nancy set down in her unfinished memoir, based on what her mother had told her. Much of it turned out to be fantasy.

Nancy writes that Louise's father was a tea importer. This could be a simple mistake, since he is described as a cotton broker on her parents' marriage certificate. She says that Louise had two sisters, Emmeline and May; true enough, but there were also three brothers, John, Harry and James, and at least one of them married and had a child.

The story that the three girls had been reared to be gentle-women, and that it was only their father's unexpected bankruptcy that forced them to work as ladies' companions, was also false, as the census records clearly show. Henry Shaw, Louise's father, had begun life at the bottom of the industrial heap. He was born in 1840 in the Lancashire town of Ashton-under-Lyne. Both his parents are described as roller-coverers, which meant they had a menial job in a cotton factory, working long hard hours for very little pay. In 1851 his two older sisters, aged twelve and thirteen, were also working at the mill, two of the children who had to keep the enormous looms running productively. Henry, however, is described as 'a scholar' so perhaps the family invested in their clever son, hoping that his achievements would lift them from the poverty and relentless grind of mill work.

Henry's ascent can be charted at ten-year intervals. By 1861 the family have moved to Oldham. The parents are both now listed as cotton spinners and twenty-one-year-old Henry is a bookkeeper. The 1871 census has Henry still living in Oldham, but now working as a cotton-waste dealer. He has married and little Louise, his third child, is two months old. Move forward another ten years and Henry has lifted his family out of obscurity and moved to the Wirral, a salubrious district across the Mersey from Liverpool, where he lives with his family and a servant. The good times have arrived and Henry is now a cotton broker. But their prosperity is short-lived. Ten years later they have moved to a smaller house and Henry is a salesman. After his death his widow and one of his sons return to Oldham. The family's brief moment of gentility is over.

But not for Louise. In 1901 she was thirty years old and had begun her journey south, working as a lady's companion in Leamington Spa. How better to learn correct manners and speech than as a lady's companion? Ten years later she has arrived in Eastbourne, where she impresses the jolly bachelor dentist with her melancholy, ladylike ways. Nancy never mentions meeting any of her mother's relatives, apart from the 'rather peculiar' Emmeline. My guess is that Louise took great care to break all contact with her family. For one thing, they would have had a distinct Lancashire accent, and the illusion of her genteel origins would have been shattered.

Poor Louise. Suddenly her obsession with appearances, the constant insistence that they were 'superior beings', makes perfect sense. Her daughter had to be an exemplary young lady because her own sense of her social position was so fragile. The burden of maintaining such an elaborate fiction must have been tremendous, especially when it turned out that her husband was unable to provide the lifestyle she needed to bolster her precarious self-image.

Nancy's origins, which caused her such soul-searching to the end of her days, were thus constructed on a base of lies, secrets and mysteries. It would have been fascinating to discuss this discovery, which goes such a long way to explain the tensions and contradictions in her early years, with her. How much Thomas knew about his wife's reinvention is a mystery. Nancy never guessed any of it. But when the young Nancy embraced modern art, wanting only to sweep away 'veils of sham and pretence', she had more reason than most to desire to do so, since veils of sham and pretence were precisely what she had been surrounded with all her life.

There was never going to be any common ground for Nancy and her parents, and from now on they play virtually no part in her story. The daughter on whom Thomas and Louise had lavished such energy was determined to follow a path as different from theirs as could be imagined. And after her twenty-first birthday she had the money and freedom to do exactly that.

5

PROVINCIAL LIFE

The Sussex village of Loxwood lies between the North and South
Downs, in that quintessentially English landscape known as the
Weald, an area of ancient oak woods, placid waterways and small
farms which seems, even now, much further from London than
a mere hour by train. It was here that Nancy and Larry, with their
new-found economic freedom, moved in the summer of 1933,
exchanging the smoky pubs and sociable evenings of Fitzrovia for
the English country idyll. Witch Photos was no more; their next
project would be Larry's novel.

It proved much quicker to dismantle their commercial
photography enterprise than it had been to set it up as the motivation was stronger. Even before the bombshell of her birthday
inheritance they had known that Witch Photos was going
nowhere fast, and they were both bored by the pretence. They
wound up the business with no regrets, though Nancy dreaded
telling her father. Larry strengthened her resolve: she must tell
Thomas that 'her friend Lawrence Durrell' deeply regretted it,
but had advised that to continue with commercial photography
would be to throw good money after bad; their only realistic
option was to cut their losses. Better to do it now rather than

later, and so on. So she did. After years of solitary struggle, Nancy was discovering the value of the authoritative male voice.

George Wilkinson was to live with them, and he too intended to write a novel. Like Larry he was in part inspired by the three-hundred-pound prize that Cassell the publisher was offering for a first novel. By this time he was as much Larry's friend as Nancy's, and on the whole their time together worked well. Pam Black, George's girlfriend, had taken Nancy's place in *Children in Uniform* and joined them when she could.

They found a picturesque cottage called Chestnut Mead on the edge of the village. It had been built around 1500 in the traditional Sussex method, with oak timber frames and a tiled roof, low ceilings and an open fire. Like most country cottages in the 1930s, it was primitive by modern standards: no electricity, no phone and no bathroom. The front door opened into a small hallway, with stairs that led straight up to the first floor. The ground floor comprised a small sitting room and a kitchen at the back, which they used for washing as well as for cooking. At the end of the back garden was a wooden privy. George insisted on taking the larger of the two upstairs rooms; he pointed out that as Larry and Nancy were a couple they would be sprawling all over the house, while he needed space of his own in which to work.

The cottage was unfurnished, so they equipped it in the bohemian minimalist style: a table in the sitting room served as both the dining table and a desk for Larry, and they got three chairs and a couple of beds. Their only extravagance was a Challen baby grand piano that Nancy bought for Larry and which must have taken up a great deal of space in the little sitting room. It was secondhand, cost sixty pounds and was in excellent condition.

Nancy bought Larry a Challen baby grand when they moved to Loxwood

The Weald was a good choice. E. V. Lucas, whose 1903 book *Highways and Byways in Sussex* had done much to popularise the region, lamented in his introduction to the 1935 edition the changes brought to his beloved county by 'motor cars, motor buses and motor charabancs'. This 'age of universal mechanical traffic' had led to 'the rise of petrol pumps and garages and the multiplication of the tea-cottage and the road-house ... All counties,' he added waspishly, 'seem to be given over to the tea industry, but none so much as Sussex.' Even though Loxwood had its very own tea gardens he liked the fact that it was 'on the edge of a little-known tract of country, untroubled by railways'. And so it remains to this day.

The majority of the village's 750 inhabitants derived their living from the land as they had done for hundreds of years: farmers, smallholders and labourers. Apart from the tea gardens, Loxwood also boasted a blacksmith, wheelwright, beer seller, boot repairer (boot, not shoe, testament to the working footwear of its clientele), dog breeder, district nurse and an artist – called, rather confusingly, Farmer. And the village was no stranger to eccentric outsiders.

In the middle of the nineteenth century a London cobbler called John Sirgood moved to the area and founded a non-conformist sect. As the sect gathered more and more followers in the area, they built several simple chapels. The charismatic Sirgood preached a message that was practical as well as spiritual, a gospel based on shared resources and communal living. He set up local shops to provide employment for the young women in the sect, thus freeing them from the tyranny of domestic service which did not allow sufficient free time for religious observance. Trade, when devoted to spiritual ends in this manner, acquired a higher value, as illustrated by the opening verse of one of their hymns:

Christ's combination stores for me
Where I can be so well supplied,
Where I can one with brethren be,
Where competition is defied.

By the early 1930s any local hostility to the group had evaporated and they had earned the nickname of Cokelers, said to be a reference to Sirgood's preference for cocoa over the usual beer, which must make them the only religious group ever to be named after a bedtime drink. They called themselves the Society of Dependents to emphasise their reliance on God for all things. They were sober, hard working and law-abiding. They were also on the decline. Though not insisting on celibacy, they did consider it a higher state, always a tactical error for a religious group with ambitions to expand. Still, in 1934 they were a familiar sight in and around Loxwood, the men all bearded and wearing dark clothes, the women in black dresses and poke bonnets, and their

Combination Store and Steam Bakery, purpose-built in the centre of the village, was thriving. Not only the usual groceries, haberdashery and paraffin, but clothes, china, even bicycles and gramophones, could be bought there. The new arrivals at Chestnut Mead, however, preferred to take the bus into Horsham to do the bulk of their shopping, Louisa Durrell having reclaimed her car.

Nancy loved being in real countryside at last, and enjoyed learning to keep house, or at least the culinary side of it. She had bought a couple of cookbooks and two large pots and experimented with cheap meals, many of them combinations of rice, beans, lentils and vegetables which she called Esau's potage. Their lifestyle was simple. They chopped wood for the fire. 'I did all the cooking and cleaning,' said Nancy firmly, before qualifying this with the statement that she never actually *did* do any cleaning – no one did. George washed up and from time to time complained about the mess made by her cooking. Larry's duties were confined to digging a pit at the end of the garden and emptying the chemical toilet into it, an unpleasant job, but one that only needed to be done once every two or three weeks.

After some initial teething problems – a letter from George survives, which seems to be attempting to smooth over a quarrel, though its cause is not given – they settled into a satisfying routine. In the mornings, Larry and George worked on their novels while Nancy, in her words, 'did things' downstairs. After lunch they went for long walks. The countryside around Loxwood is criss-crossed with old paths, drovers' routes and bridleways, giving them an endless choice of rambles: beside iris-fringed waterways, through the oak woods which in spring were a mass of bluebells, or along the tree-bordered green paths which had been tramped for hundreds, probably thousands of years. In the evenings they relaxed by the fire, enjoying what George later remembered as 'those never-to-be-forgotten evenings of fireside confidences'. And they made music. George had bought himself some drums and cymbals and he accompanied Larry, who played jazz piano and sang.

They made no attempt to join in with village life, and were looked at rather askance by the locals. They discovered they were known as 'the three sketches', which sounds like a comment on the extreme tallness and thinness of Nancy and George. They never entertained and the cottage was in any case too small for visitors. The only caller Nancy could remember was the Reverend Mainprice, who had completed nearly twenty years in the village; he dropped by only once, and did not stay for long.

But there were tensions. Freed from the charade of being an estate agent's apprentice, or even the manager of a photographic studio, Larry had got into his writerly stride and every morning he worked hard on the semi-autobiographical novel that was to become *Pied Piper of Lovers*. In his bedroom upstairs, George listened to the furious rat-a-tat of Larry's typewriter keys and what little inspiration he might have started with evaporated. Larry was on a roll; George suffered. Similarly, Nancy admitted that she had been very much at a loose end.

When Larry involved her in a creative enterprise, that too became a burden. He wanted to give Gerry a book of his poems for Christmas, each one to be written out in a beautiful script and accompanied by Nancy's illustrations. She hated doing it. 'I was chained to trying to make this wretched book,' she complained. In an effort to explain her difficulty, she said that with any creative enterprise 'you have to have some idea of why you are trying to do it' but she couldn't visualise it at all. Illustrating a home-made Christmas present for an eight-year-old doesn't sound like such a hideous burden for someone who has taken pride in their drawing since early childhood, but Nancy was suffering from the creative paralysis that had afflicted her before, and would do again.

Two years earlier, when she had worked alongside her friend Stephen Gilbert in the Robert Street studio, she had hoped that some of his 'moral fibre' might brush off on her. In fact, the opposite happened, and she became more inhibited about working than ever. Something similar was happening now, at Chestnut Mead. Throughout her life she was dogged with what always struck me as a distinctly unhelpful perfectionism. She was uneasy with the mess and mistakes of children's botched efforts at creativity, but no one suffered from her dislike of the second-rate more than she did herself. She was quite incapable of producing a 'good enough' set of illustrations for little Gerry's Christmas present, and suffered tortures of angst over the task.

From this point of view, her relationship with Larry was turning into a disaster, and through no fault of his. The sweet, unhappy youth who suffered from a weak heart and wanted mothering had, in less than a year, morphed into a purposeful and dynamic writer burning with that 'gem-like flame' he had so admired in John Gawsworth. If George found himself unmanned by Larry's creative ferment, how much worse was it for Nancy, whose artistic self-confidence was always so precarious?

So she pottered around and grumbled about the Christmas book, while upstairs George listened to the relentless pace of productivity in the living room and his own inspiration fizzled away to nothing. In the spring of 1934 George hit upon a drastic solution: he would leave the country altogether. He and Pam would marry and set off on a mammoth cycling trip through Europe which would lead them, eventually, to Greece, maybe settling in Corfu. Life was cheap there, so they had been told. Larry and Nancy followed their scheming with interest. If George and Pam sent good reports from Greece, they might follow the next year.

Once George's room was empty, there was a chance to have visitors to stay from London. If 'the three sketches' had caused a stir among their neighbours, then the guests who turned up at the door of Chestnut Mead in early June must have confounded them utterly.

The 1930s were the most intensely political decade of the twentieth century: in retrospect, the Great Depression, the Spanish Civil War and Hitler's rise in Germany dominate the landscape, to the extent that one sometimes gets the impression that people at that time thought of little else. Not so. Nancy and Larry, like most of their circle, were firmly anti-political and regarded the rumblings and threats of war on the world stage as inconvenient interruptions to the real business of life, which was to create art and literature that would outlive the muddles made by politicians. The only politics they had any time for were the fantasy kind, like the kingdom of Redonda and its dukedoms, courtesy of John Gawsworth and M. P. Shiel. Or, even more bizarrely, the Potocki brothers and their claim to the throne of Poland.

Geoffrey Potocki de Montalk and his younger brother Cedric had been born in New Zealand. Their father was descended from a Polish Count Potocki, and on this slender evidence the brothers were to stake their claim to the throne of Poland. Make-believe had sustained them through a horrific childhood. Their mother had died when they were still very young and their father's second wife was cruel in the worst tradition of wicked stepmothers: beatings, toil, hunger and being forced to go barefoot all year round made their childhood an unremitting misery. Remarkably, they emerged from this youthful ordeal with humour, intelligence and a zest for life, and after they moved to Europe, they became colourful figures in the pageant of London literary eccentrics. Nancy and Larry had got to know them when they were neighbours during the Witch Photos months.

Geoffrey, like Larry, was a passionate admirer of the work of Rabelais and Verlaine. His attempts to print a small edition of poems, including five translations, for private circulation brought down the full weight of the English legal system in an obscenity trial that was both comic and horrific in equal measure, and which illustrates the moral atmosphere in which Larry and other young writers were coming of age. Sir William Joynson-Hicks, while Home Secretary in the 1920s, had done his utmost to uphold decency without distinguishing between pornography and works of art, and this was a view that continued into the 1930s and beyond. Censorship was not just an irritant: it had real teeth. In 1915 the entire print run of D. H. Lawrence's *The Rainbow* had been destroyed; thirteen years later the publishers of *Lady Chatterley's Lover* did not even bother to attempt publication in England. And when the case was being heard for *The Well of Loneliness* in 1928, the magistrate refused to allow the testimony of experts, remarking, 'How can the opinion of a number of people be evidence?' Permission to publish was refused.

Even so, no one could have anticipated the reaction when Geoffrey tried to get his spicy poems privately published. The printer he chose agreed to do the work, and then promptly turned the poems over to the police. The court case was a travesty. Before it began, the Recorder of London, Sir Ernest Wild, invited the female jurors to withdraw from the trial as 'this was a very filthy case indeed'. A sample of the offensive verses shows what constituted extreme filth in 1932:

Here lies John Penis
Buried in the Mound of Venus.

It was Potocki's misfortune to come before a judge who had had poetic aspirations of his own; in his slim, privately published volume *The Lamp of Destiny and Other Poems*, subtitled *Being Some Indiscretions of the Long Vacation*, Wild had described himself without irony as 'the meanest bard that ever twanged on Lyre'.

And a very mean bard the Recorder proved to be, though Geoffrey hardly helped his own case by appearing in court dressed in his royal maroon robes – copied from medieval costumes in the British Museum – long hair flowing over his shoulders, and insisted on swearing not on the Bible but on the collected works of Shakespeare. When Wild asked him how he had become a poet Potocki replied airily that it was the choice of the gods. 'What gods?' the Recorder wanted to know. 'A man cannot call himself a poet if he is not a poet,' said Potocki perhaps tactlessly. In his summing-up, Wild told the jury: 'A man must not say he is a poet and yet publish filth. He has to obey the law the same as ordinary citizens and the sooner the highbrow school learn that the better for the morality of the country.' After which, farce turned ugly and the pretender to the throne of Poland was sentenced to six months' hard labour.

There was outrage. The *New Statesman* said that the law had been reduced to an absurdity, and W. B. Yeats wrote to Potocki that the sentence was 'criminal in its brutality', but even so, and in spite of the involvement of Leonard Woolf and others, the sentence was upheld on appeal. Potocki's sufferings in prison were horrific, and he emerged angry and embittered – but still witty and highly entertaining. His views, however, including his anti-Semitism, had become more extreme. A sign on the door of his room near Lamb's Conduit Street told 'Communists and racial enemies' to please abstain from calling.

The brothers were slightly built and very attractive, with

engaging smiles and a quick humour. The first time that Larry and Nancy visited Geoffrey they found him in a little upstairs room, which she described as 'even less furnished than other people's' – so no furniture of any description, presumably. Dressed in the robes they now wore at all times, Geoffrey's dark red, and Cedric's blue, the two brothers were kneeling over an enormous map of Poland spread out on the floor between them and squabbling over who would have which bit of their ancestral homeland after the coming war.

It was Cedric who startled the villagers of Loxwood when, some time in early June, he swept up to the front door of Chestnut Mead in his flowing robes, looking more eccentric than usual since acute toothache had prompted him to tie a white scarf around his head, with a knot on top. He was accompanied by his American mistress, who was the wife of an academic. She had been supporting him for some time, but as Cedric insisted she be addressed always as Madame, Nancy was unable to remember her name. She was big and Germanic-looking, rather in the style of Frieda Lawrence, with fair hair braided and coiled around her head. Her daughter Catherine was seven, with enormous dark eyes and long, straight hair; an enchanting child, she was understandably adrift in this unlikely ménage.

The visit did not begin well. In honour of their guests, Nancy had splashed out on what was to them a great luxury, a tin of chicken in aspic, only to be informed that the future ruler of Poland never touched anything out of a tin. She must find him something else to eat. Things improved, however, and Larry later regaled George and Pam, who were by now married and pedalling across Europe, with tales of their guest.

Cedric and his entourage had been prompted to quit London by the belief that the capital would be far too dangerous for him when the expected war broke out. They planned to live in Sussex for a short while, before setting off for the supposed safety of Scotland in a horse and cart.

A cottage was found for them at a minuscule rent. When the lease on Chestnut Mead came to an end, Larry went back to Bournemouth in a lorry with the piano, their books and few bits of furniture, while Nancy stayed on with Cedric, Madame and Catherine.

Midsummer, and the weather was glorious. Long, perfect June days of blue sky and sunshine. Nancy revelled in the whole experience. The cottage was tiny – she called it a woodman's cottage – like something out of a story book. Over a hill, about three-quarters of a mile from Chestnut Mead, Little Songhurst Cottage backed on to ancient oak woods. No other habitation or building of any kind was visible from its windows, and the only access was across two fields from Old Songhurst Farm; there was no road of any kind.

In the deep peace of the cottage, birdsong and insect hum and the timeless stillness of the woodland and pastures all around, Nancy felt inspired for the first time in months. Happily, she set to work painting the landscape around her, the cool blue shadows of the trees and the shifting greens of the fields. Though she did not make the connection herself, it seems likely that the absence of Larry and his all-consuming creative energy contributed to her sudden burst of activity, as much as the rusticity and the long days of sunshine.

Her second memory of the Little Songhurst interlude is more curious. They were having a picnic, and she had 'a first kind of memory of feeling myself *physically*. I was looking at her: Madame was then about thirty-five, bigly made, and she had blue veins all over her, which stood out. You could see the veins going down her thighs and across her chest. And I was looking at myself, and thinking I looked as though I was made of pale wood, because you couldn't see anything inside me.'

She gives no explanation, but it is obvious that the moment was significant to her and stuck in her memory long after other, apparently more important, events had been forgotten. As with the sudden inspiration to paint, Larry's absence played a part in this moment of corporeal self-awareness. After nearly two years of an intense sexual relationship, she was single again for a few days: a chance to see herself as separate, to reflect on her body as an entity on its own. Nancy was capable, all through her life, of regarding her physical self in a dispassionate, almost detached manner. Even so, to say it was the first memory of feeling herself physically is surprising, and it may well have meant something different to her altogether.

Life at Little Songhurst was even more primitive than at Chestnut Mead: they each had a wooden bowl and a spoon; nuts and rice predominated at meals; and when, after a few days, Nancy woke up covered in spots and running a high temperature, Madame gathered dock leaves and other wild plants to medicate her. Measles was a more serious illness then than now. Luckily, as well as providing herbal remedies, the Potockis raced across the fields to the nearest telephone to inform Larry of her illness and he came haring up from Bournemouth. In a crisis, he was effective. He brought in a proper doctor, banished the dock leaves and, as soon as she was well enough to travel, drove her back to Dixie Lodge.

The boomerang generation is not a modern phenomenon. Nancy and Larry had sufficient funds to live independently if they wished, but they chose instead to stay with his family for nearly a year. Though Larry was to complain bitterly about 'Pudding Island' and the 'English Death', Nancy recalled the months they spent in this most bourgeois of English seaside towns with pleasure.

Nancy in the window at Bournemouth

In 1934 Bournemouth was a town of over one hundred thousand inhabitants, but it had grown so rapidly that some elderly residents could remember a time when it had needed only a single postman. The residential areas had been built amid the pine woods that were one of its main attractions, since there was a widespread belief that the resinous perfume given off by fallen pine needles was beneficial for chest complaints. In the nineteenth century the budding Bournemouth tourist industry had specifically targeted invalids, claiming that 'the peculiar sedative influence of its climate' was due to the exhalation of plentiful pines 'giving off into the atmosphere a terebinthine oxygenating influence'. Perhaps because of this sedative effect, it had also been dubbed 'the ten o'clock town', as all the good people of Bournemouth retired to bed early and after that time there was no chance of getting a coffee or light refreshment of any kind. Indeed, in the hotels visitors could not even enjoy a hot bath, since the bathrooms (no en suite then) were all locked, not to be reopened until the chamber maids returned to draw the water the following morning.

Dixie Lodge was about ten minutes' walk from the centre of town, and typical of the comfortable, unpretentious houses that had been built during the town's rapid expansion over the previous fifty years. Set back from the road, its large lawn was sheltered by one or two of the ubiquitous pines. Inside, there were sofas and easy chairs, carpets and Larry's piano, what Nancy described as 'a rather *disarray* comfort'. Just the kind of haphazard, undemanding homeliness that she liked best.

Mother Durrell and her three youngest children had welcomed her into their unorthodox family. 'We all loved Nancy,' Margo was to say simply when she looked back. A postcard from Gerry to Little Songhurst Cottage, written when she was staying with Cedric, is addressed to 'Dear Auntie Nan', and as he was not a child known for doing or saying the dutiful thing, it seems genuine in its affection: 'Mummy says you've got measles. I am sorry sorry. I hope your better soon. Just eton a large bag of cherries lovely!! There is a nice river here. Were sitting by it resting. We want to see you again often soon. Thank you awfully for cake.' Nancy revelled in the novel sense of belonging. Larry had finished *Pied Piper of Lovers* and sent it off to Cassell's for their competition, so he was suspended in that limbo of waiting, when a book has ceased to belong to its creator and has yet to start an independent existence in the minds of others. He told his daughter Penelope that this in-between time was always an agony, even after he had become a huge success, and this first occasion must have been especially difficult. During this period, he was happy to initiate Nancy into the well-loved stories that bound the family together, most of which centred on his mother.

Louisa Durrell was fascinated by ghosts. One of Nancy's

favourite stories about her dated from her early married life in India. In one of their homes, a remote place that backed on to jungle, the locals had told her about a lonely spirit that cried in the night. Cue action from Louisa. After dark, with a little lantern and all the servants begging her not to be so foolhardy, she would trip out in search of the unhappy spirit, entreating it as though it were a bird or a timid wild animal: 'Come on, come on, come here!' she called into the darkness, but without success.

Another favourite story related to Gerry, who had been a babe in arms when his father died. One day, when he was three, he asked, 'Mummy, who is the man sitting in the breakfast room?'

'I don't know, Gerry,' she replied. 'I don't think there's anybody in there.'

'Come and look,' he said and, taking her by the hand, led her into the next room. She saw no one. 'Look,' he said, pointing to an apparently empty chair, 'the man there!'

'What does he look like?' she asked. Whereupon he proceeded to describe his father with complete accuracy, down to the last detail of his clothing. Perhaps she drew comfort from the belief that their father was still some kind of presence in her children's life. Though she was only forty-two when her husband died, there was never any suggestion that she might remarry: pretty, vivacious and warm-hearted, she settled into a lifetime of widowhood at the centre of her family.

Nancy was puzzled by Louisa's lack of interest in making new friends. She was gregarious, relied on the company of others and had masses of the Durrell charm, so that strangers were instinctively drawn to her; yet after her husband's death she made no new friends of her own. It may be that she was unsure how to slot into the social networks of Bournemouth, or there just weren't that many outlets for a single, middle-aged woman in 1934 – bridge? golf? the Church? – that would have suited her, or perhaps her children and their friends provided company enough for anyone. Or maybe the Durrell family's eccentric appearance, which so endeared them to Nancy, set them apart from other people. Whatever the reason, she remained a constant and underestimated presence at the heart of the family Nancy had come to love.

The final member of the household was the dog, Roger. Nancy and Larry's little terrier had succumbed to fits while they were still in Loxwood, and died, but Roger, large and black and eventually to have a starring role in *My Family and Other Animals*, was everyone's favourite. Nancy described him as 'staunch'. During that year in Bournemouth, Roger was hit by a car and his tail, in her words, 'went bad'. The vet was called and carried out surgery on the kitchen table, Nancy holding the tail while the vet cut it off. She was always pragmatic where suffering animals were concerned, and never allowed her devotion to them to make her squeamish.

In the makeshift comfort of Dixie Lodge, Larry and Nancy enjoyed the autumn and winter months. The town's sedative climate might have had its drawbacks, but there was no shortage of culture, and they went to events nearly every week. In 1929 the Victorian Winter Pavilion, which had been described as 'a concert hall in the style of a huge cucumber frame, especially adapted to the requirements of invalids and ferns', had been closed, and was replaced by a huge new Pavilion, with a theatre, three restaurants, a ballroom and two bars. The Municipal Orchestra had built a national reputation with its pioneering conductor, Sir Dan Godfrey ('an old boy who'd let it go to bits', in Nancy's view); it was now under the baton of Richard Austin, who persuaded world-class performers to visit. There they heard Kreisler and Cortot, Rubinstein and Horowitz. But the performance that affected them both most deeply was when the Russian-born pianist Benno Moiseiwitsch played Beethoven's Piano Concerto No. 4. From the very first notes there was a rapport between soloist, conductor and orchestra, and at the end the audience went wild, everybody grinning and hugging each other and cheering. Years later, when my mother employed me as a cheap (half commercial rates) and pretty much readily available artist's model, it was one of the records we listened to. 'Listen,' she would say as the needle began its scratchy progress, 'everyone expects the orchestra to begin. In a concerto, the orchestra always begin. But Beethoven changed everything with those opening chords on the piano.' Then she lapsed back into the silence of her work. Two years later, when Larry was writing *The Black Book*, he listened to their records of Beethoven's much-loved piano concerto constantly and told a friend that he knew the music more intimately than he knew his wife.

Fired by these experiences, they bought their first gramophone: one designed and manufactured by E. M. Ginn. The design, with its huge horn and a needle of sharpened thorn, looks antiquated to a modern eye, but the sound quality was excellent. Nancy and Larry slowly built up a collection of records: Beethoven's second piano concerto and, of course, the fourth, Ravel's *Daphnis et Chloé* and, like the rest of the British record-buying public at that time, Myra Hess playing her arrangement of Bach's *Jesu, Joy of Man's Desiring*.

They went to the theatre. In those days of repertory companies, provincial towns were better provided for than they are today, and Bournemouth, with its captive audience of the wealthy elderly, was no exception. They enjoyed plays, most memorably Noël Coward's *Hay Fever* and *The Circle* by Somerset Maugham, a witty examination of high-society adultery and family break-up.

And they bought books, lots of them. Larry at this time was getting into Rabelais, while Nancy was buying art books, including a beautiful volume on the work of Henri Gaudier-Brzeska. Their book-buying brought them into contact with Alan Thomas, who was working at the Cummins bookshop in Old Christchurch Road. Alan fell under Larry's spell almost at once, and became a frequent visitor to Dixie Lodge, joining in the family's games and arguments with gusto. Later, for reasons she never fully explained, he was to be one of the very few people Nancy actively disliked, but at this stage in their relationship she felt only a mild unease in his company.

She might have been buying books on art, but her own work was non-existent. Asked about her painting during this time, her reply was emphatic, 'No, no. I was completely unhinged,' adding that she would have to go into all that later. But she never did, so her statement – 'completely unhinged' – has to remain, a crude shorthand for what must have been a complex and painful inability to focus on her work.

All the while, the beguiling letters from George kept on coming. Progress by bicycle had brought him and Pam, by the middle of August, to Corfu. Why not come out for a while? George wanted to know. At the end of October he was tempting them with descriptions of sitting out in the warm sunshine, and at Christmas they received an enchanting pictorial map Pam had made of the island, complete with donkeys and memorable sites. Larry sent back lavish praise, adding that Nancy had been 'peculiarly impressed' by the little block, though her artistic pride would probably stop her from admitting the fact. A poem, written by George, accompanied the map and emphasised the seductive lure of the island:

> . . . *surely such fine December heat*
> *Must make the case for novelty complete?*

It did. The plan to head out to Corfu was taking shape. As soon as she realised their plans were getting serious, Mother Durrell declared that she and the rest of the family were coming too. They had lived in England for just six years, and in that time moved house frequently and had put down no real roots. Nancy quotes her as saying, 'Well, I'm not going to stay here if you're going to Corfu. What d'you expect me to do, with all these children? We're coming too!' Larry told George his mother had suggested 'with a certain charming timidity' that they should all continue to share a home once they had left England, but he, with 'an equally charming definiteness', insisted on separate domiciles. He intended to live alone with 'the lamp-post' – his current nickname for Nancy. He also scotched his mother's hopes that the whole family would journey out together. 'We're not going to travel with that lot,' Larry said firmly. 'You can't come till after we've got there. We'll scout out the lay of the land.'

Now that Britons flock to Corfu in their millions, it is hard to imagine what an adventure the journey must have been in early 1935. George's letters were full of advice. He warned them to steer clear of a shipping company called Schenkes, to whom he had entrusted his luggage, as they had apparently never heard of Corfu and had sent the luggage via the Cape of Good Hope. He said that the overland route to Brindisi might not be too expensive, and claimed there was an 80 per cent reduction on rail fares for honeymooners in Italy, adding cautiously, 'verify that'. Which, George thought, might be a good reason for them to get married.

Whether it was the prospect of reduced train fares or, as Larry claimed, as a Christmas gift for his mother, they did indeed get married at Bournemouth Register Office in January 1935. Nancy was unable to remember why they had decided to marry at that precise moment, but it seems an unlikely Christmas present for Louisa as she was not invited to the wedding and, indeed, did not even hear of it until a couple of weeks after the event. A decision not to involve family in their wedding probably had a good deal to do with Nancy's horror at the thought of having to invite her parents. Needless to say, Mother Durrell was delighted when they told her they had married: like the rest of the family, she was devoted to Nancy, and besides, she liked things to be regular – an increasingly forlorn battle as her unusual offspring matured.

The registrar also had a liking for regularity, and was predictably dismayed by Larry's flippant demeanour during the ceremony. Alan Thomas and one of his colleagues from the bookshop – 'some dim character' said Nancy dismissively, unable to remember his name – were witnesses. Larry wanted to swear on the works of Rabelais instead of the Bible, and the registrar was frightfully insulted. 'You're undertaking this deeply serious event very lightly,' he reprimanded stuffily.

A glorious myth has grown up around the marriage ceremony. Larry, who was nearly six inches shorter than his bride, was anxious lest the registrar assume the tall Alan Thomas was the groom and that the wrong couple would get married. He therefore came up with a plan to borrow a couple of midgets from the local circus to act as witnesses, but his efforts were thwarted when their employer was unable to spare them for the task. It's one of the many stories that ought to be true, but Nancy never mentioned it. One can imagine the three of them joking about it, saying what they needed was a couple of borrowed midgets, as they made their way to the Register Office, and from their laughter and irreverence the myth evolved. True in essence, if not in fact, like so much of the Durrell canon.

Nancy's inability to remember just why they got married at that time is significant. She was always puzzled by ceremonies and the conventional ways of marking life events, though she wasn't blind to the practical side. When she discovered that I had also married without telling anyone she made a half-hearted offer to pay for a repeat performance, but only so we could have wedding presents for our new home. (Twenty years later my daughter, who deplored the family avoidance of proper weddings, also found herself marrying in secret. 'The genes were too strong for me,' she commented ruefully when she phoned with the news.)

On 2 March 1935, the Clydebank-built SS *Oronsay* of the Orient line steamed out of the port of London, bound for Brisbane via Gibraltar, Port Said and Aden, a journey that would take six weeks in all. Among the passengers were the newly married couple, both in high spirits: at last the great adventure was beginning.

Nancy scribbled a postcard to Alan in Bournemouth, which was taken back to land by the tugboat that had escorted them into open waters: 'Just managed to catch bus, train, boat, breakfast, taxi and whatnot. Looks as though we're all going to be real pals and one big happy family on this boat.'

Soon, she and Larry were entertaining themselves by lampooning the rest of the on-board family in a series of merciless cartoons drawn by Nancy, with comments written by Larry. A

Nancy and Larry passed the journey lampooning their fellow passengers. For 'The Boss', Larry has written, 'He's been ordered out of the lavatory because the notice reads "Gentlemen"'

picture of a grim-faced elderly lady is described as 'An eminently devilish courtesan of the old school, 1812 vintage. Once a girl, always a girl.' And the distinguishing marks of a lugubrious look-ing gentleman in glasses are said to be 'Perpetual sickness'. At the end of the sequence, Larry has written incredulously, 'All the characters depicted here are entirely real. So help us.'

Ten days later they bade farewell to their fellow passengers, dis-embarked at Naples and took the train to Brindisi; from there it was a short hop by ferry to Corfu. At least, that was the theory. But they arrived at the port to find that no ferries were running. Their departure was delayed by a combination of politics and bad weather, as they kicked their heels and watched the rain come down, waiting for normality to return. 'This revolution,' as Nancy described it vaguely, 'Metaxas sort of taking over.' In fact, what kept Nancy and Larry holed up in Brindisi for nearly a week was an attempt by the followers of Eleftherios Venizelos to mount a coup in Athens.

The weather was atrocious. After all George's tantalising descriptions of balmy winter days, they were quite unprepared for the reality of late winter in the Mediterranean. '*Terribly* cold, *bitter* storms,' said Nancy. Marooned in their hotel, they made friends with an RAF officer who was similarly stranded and some-what lonely. Their precious Ginn gramophone was making its way to Corfu with the rest of their luggage, but the pilot had a portable gramophone with, for some reason, only one set of records: Rachmaninov's second piano concerto. As it was winter, the hotel was almost deserted, and the only public space was a big, draughty hall with a black and white tiled floor. There they sat every evening on their cane chairs, shivering and drinking and listening to the surging romance of Rachmaninov while the storm raged outside. Their time was not entirely wasted: Larry's second novel, *Panic Spring*, begins in a hotel in Brindisi, in the midst of winter, with a journey that has been held up by a revolution in Greece to an island not unlike Corfu. Every day Nancy and Larry, like the protagonist in *Panic Spring*, peered out into the blinding rain and wind until at last the weather improved, the attempted coup had been thwarted, the plotters sent into exile and they were free to resume their journey.

An overnight ferry journey brought them to the port in Corfu town, where Pam and George were waiting to meet them. Like all new arrivals in the 1930s, they spent a few days in the Pension Suisse, which no longer exists, but sounds wonderfully like something from an E. M. Forster novel. The Wilkinsons were already installed in a bungalow a few miles south of the town, and Nancy and Larry soon rented a little house nearby. It continued to be much colder than they had expected: April was chilly and unpromising. May started out not much better.

For Nancy, their first summer in Corfu was a revelation

And then, towards the end of May, the summer heat began. It was Nancy's first experience of Southern Europe, and they were both bowled over by the sheer intensity of their surroundings. Larry wrote that he could never do justice to the wonder of the place, and Nancy was intoxicated. During those first summer months, soaking up the beauty, the climate, the freedom, the sensuous pleasure of it all, Nancy fell in love with the island. She loved the sun, loved the warmth, loved the olive trees, loved everything about it. Her attachment to the island never wavered for a moment. Corfu was to keep a special place in her heart for the rest of her life.

When I was a child and she talked to me about her life before I was born, there was a special tone of voice, an echo of remembered contentment, whenever she talked about Corfu. There's a story that some of the islanders, who knew the family before the war, claimed that when Nancy left in August 1939 a part of her spirit remained behind. However one chooses to interpret that statement, in some essential way it rings true. In the spring of 1935, Nancy had arrived in the place that was to mean more to her than anywhere else, a place where she experienced a deep and abiding happiness.

6

PROSPERO'S ISLAND

You have had the best of your youth on the island.

Lawrence Durrell, *Prospero's Cell*

Early in 1994 my sister Penelope phoned me up. She was excited but also apprehensive. The White House in Kalami, the house her father made famous in *Prospero's Cell*, was available for rent. Should we go?

Like her, I was wary as well as curious. It was a bit like suddenly hearing that Shangri-La has been discovered by the mass-market tourist industry and a package holiday is on offer.

Needless to say, curiosity won. Though Larry had been back to Corfu from time to time after the war, Nancy never returned, and neither Penelope nor I had ever been there. But now that Larry had been dead for four years, and our mother for over ten, the opportunity to sniff the place out for ourselves was irresistible. We persuaded our husbands, booked up and went.

As it happened, the section which was let out to tourists was the top floor that Nancy and Larry, after living there for a while, had paid to have built. The lower part of the house was where the family lived – the same family that had lived there since the 1930s – as well as housing the bar and taverna. The White House in Kalami is a beacon for tour boats and so, every morning for a blissful week in early June, we took our coffee onto the balcony, looked out on the sparkling sea and watched the little boats as they puttered into the bay and paused below the balcony, loud-speaker systems belting out a glorious medley of misinformation: 'This is the famous White House where Lawrence Durrell wrote *My Family and Other Animals*.' 'This is the famous White House where Gerald Durrell lived with his father Lawrence.' 'This is where Justine Durrell wrote *The Alexandrian Quartet*.'

I can't think of any other place in the world which has been so closely identified with two brothers, which is all the more remarkable considering how young they were when they went, and how comparatively brief their stay was. In the spring of 1935 Larry was twenty-three and Gerald was just ten. By September 1939 the outbreak of war had brought their island idyll to an end. Yet during those four years Larry and his youngest brother absorbed images and experience that fed into both *Prospero's Cell* in 1945 and *My Family and Other Animals* ten years later, books that could not be more different except that both are as readable and brilliant today as they were when they first electrified a war-weary, colour-hungry British public with their description of a vanished paradise.

In *Prospero's Cell*, a lyrical evocation of the island, its people and its culture, Nancy is immortalised as N, a serene, painterly water nymph who dives for cherries, offers the occasional pithy comment, performs miracles of diagnosis when the peasants fall ill (armed only with a thermometer and a medical encyclopedia), speaks bad Greek, draws cartoons on the rocks, names their boat

and can sometimes be observed striking one of 'those fine unconscious attitudes'. All in all, N fulfils the role of the beautiful
consort whose presence completes the classic landscape. Her own
reaction to this image was typically enigmatic. Once, when the
diving for cherries episode was mentioned, she responded with an
all-embracing camel-like snort, a derisive dismissal of the masculine purple-prose memory – but whether the snort conveyed
the meaning 'what nonsense, it never happened', or 'really, that
was no big deal' or – my preferred interpretation – 'actually, I
can't remember but I'm not predisposed to approve', no one will
ever know.

Nancy and the Durrell family in Corfu

Nancy was more charitable towards *My Family and Other
Animals*, a book she loved. Given her passion for honesty this is
surprising, because in that book she has been painted out of the

picture with Stalinist efficiency, along with all the other wives. The Durrell family remains firmly nuclear. Mother Durrell, her four still-at-home children and Roger the dog hightail it out of England on a whim and set up house together. George Wilkinson appears as Gerry's tutor, but there is no Pam. Gerry's mentor, Theodore, is a childless bachelor and Larry never even has a girl-friend. Only Margo is allowed a romantic life, but that is because she is portrayed as a comically lovelorn teenager. *My Family and Other Animals* nonetheless escaped Nancy's usual dislike of mythologising because, she said, it was true in its essence: it described the island as she remembered it, and though the incidents were fictional and many individuals had been erased, Gerry captured the character and voice of those who remained with brilliant precision. She singled out one episode that nailed Larry's personality exactly.

Gun-obsessed Leslie has been boasting about his prowess at pulling off a 'left-and-a-right'. Larry, with maddening older-brother superiority, says he can't understand why Leslie's making such a fuss, since a left-and-a-right is obviously an extremely simple procedure, at least for someone (like him, of course) blessed with a 'mercurial' mind and the ability to keep a cool head. All right then, you try, says Leslie. The next morning the whole family set off early for the swamp to see Larry demonstrate his instinctive genius as a marksman, and he oblig-ingly puts a large feather in his tweed hat, giving him the appearance of a 'small, portly, and immensely dignified Robin Hood'.

As the snipe start to fly over the marshy ground, Larry takes aim and shoots, but the gun fails to go off. It's not loaded. Larry brushes aside his first error with ease: all Leslie's fault, of course, for not preparing the guns. The next time the birds appear he does indeed fire. Disaster.

The gun roared and kicked, the snipe flew away undamaged, and Larry with a yell of fright fell backwards into the irrigation ditch.

'Hold the gun above your head! ... Hold it above your head!' roared Leslie.

'Don't stand up or you'll sink,' screeched Margo. 'Sit still.'

But Larry, spreadeagled on his back, had only one idea, and that was to get out as quickly as possible. He sat up and then tried to get to his feet, using, to Leslie's anguish, the gun barrels as a support. He raised himself up, the liquid mud shuddered and boiled, the gun sank out of sight, and Larry disappeared up to his waist.

'Look what you've done to the gun,' yelled Leslie furiously; 'you've choked the bloody barrels.'

'What the hell do you expect me to do?' snarled Larry. 'Lie here and be sucked under? Give me a hand, for heaven's sake.'

'Get the gun out,' said Leslie angrily.

'I refuse to save the gun if you don't save me,' Larry yelled. 'Damn it, I'm not a seal ... *get me out!*'

'If you give me the end of the gun I can pull you out, you idiot,' shouted Leslie. 'I can't reach you otherwise.'

Larry groped wildly under the surface for the gun, and sank several inches before he retrieved it, clotted with black and evil-smelling mud.

'Dear God! Just *look* at it,' moaned Leslie, wiping the mud off it with his handkerchief, 'just look at it.'

'Will you stop carrying on over that beastly weapon and get me out of here?' asked Larry vitriolically. 'Or do you want me to sink beneath the mud like a sort of sportsman's Shelley?'

Leslie handed him the ends of the barrels, and we all heaved mightily. It seemed to make no impression whatsoever, except that when we stopped, exhausted, Larry sank a little deeper.

'The idea is to rescue me,' he pointed out, panting, 'not deliver the *coup de grace*.'

'Oh, stop yapping and try to heave yourself out,' said Leslie.

Eventually, he struggles out, and stomps off home. He gets a bottle of brandy and has the maid stoke up a roaring fire in his bedroom. By nightfall he is drunk as a skunk and merrily abusive: the family bank up the fire and leave him to drink himself into oblivion. In the small hours a log spills out of the grate and his bedroom floor catches fire. Pandemonium, with the whole family racing around, until Leslie finally drags the bedclothes off the still-sleeping Larry and puts the flames out. Larry wakes.

'What the hell is going on?' he demanded.

'The room's on fire, dear,' said Mother.

'Well, I don't see why I should freeze to death ... why tear all the bedclothes off? Really, the fuss you all make. It's quite simple to put out a fire.'

'Oh, shut up,' snapped Leslie, jumping up and down on the bedclothes.

'I've never known people for panicking like you all do,' said Larry; 'it's simply a matter of keeping your head. Les has the worst of it under control; now if Gerry fetches the hatchet, and you, Mother, and Margo fetch some water, we'll soon have it out.'

Eventually, while Larry lay in bed and directed operations, the rest of us managed to rip up the planks and put out the smouldering beam. It must have been smouldering throughout the night, for the beam, a twelve-inch-thick slab of olive wood, was charred half-way through. When, eventually, Lugaretzia appeared and started to clean up the mass of smouldering bedclothes, wood splinters, water, and brandy, Larry lay back on the bed with a sigh.

'There you are,' he pointed out; 'all done without fuss and panic. It's just a matter of keeping your head. I would like someone to bring me a cup of tea, please; I've got the most splitting headache.'

'I'm not surprised; you were as tiddled as an owl last night,' said Leslie.

'If you can't tell the difference between a high fever due to exposure and a drunken orgy it's hardly fair to besmirch my character,' Larry pointed out.

'Well, the fever's left you with a good hangover, anyway,' said Margo.

'It's not a hangover,' said Larry with dignity, 'it's just the strain of being woken up at the crack of dawn by an hysterical pack of people and having to take control of a crisis.'

'Fat lot of controlling you did, lying in bed,' snorted Leslie.

'It's not the action that counts, it's the brainwork behind it, the quickness of wit, the ability to keep your head when all about you are losing theirs. If it hadn't been for me you would probably all have been burnt in your beds.'

And that is where the chapter ends: last word to Larry.

According to Nancy, the image of Larry sitting in bed and telling everyone else what to do while he berates them for their ineptitude captured his personality exactly. And Gerry had an unerring ear for people's patterns of speech: Larry's – bombastic, witty and scathing – was wonderfully entertaining, unless you happened to be on the receiving end of his scorn. But what comes across most clearly in Gerry's portrait is the family's robust attitude to the genius in their midst. They never miss a chance to ridicule his posturing, and to his mother he is always just one of 'you children', to be remonstrated with from time to time. For much of the Corfu period, when Nancy and Larry rowed, it was all part of the ongoing squabbling of a noisy and basically affectionate family – and the family almost always took her side.

As Penelope and I discovered during our week at the White House, a touch of enchantment still clung to Corfu in 1994, in spite of the traffic and the buildings and the commercialisation. Though it was not exactly *terra incognita* in 1935. The most northerly of the Ionian islands, it had been marked by Byzantine, Italian, French and British rule, but was almost the only part of modern Greece never to have been under Ottoman rule. As a result of this chequered history of occupation, Corfu town had not one but two Venetian forts, the smart cafés on the Liston were shaded by a replica of the rue de Rivoli in Paris, there was a Greek royal palace called Mon Repos, a Swiss pension and a substantial Jewish quarter, and, the legacy of Britain's nineteenth-century protectorate, cricket had been adopted as the sport of the island, and had developed its own highly eccentric terminology.

Their first joyous response to Corfu makes clear how powerful the impact of the island was on both Larry and Nancy. For Nancy, who had only ever hopped across the Channel, it was her first experience of the Mediterranean. But the memory of those four years was inevitably coloured by what followed. Whether in the brothers' books or Nancy's memories, it always seems as though pre-war Corfu is glimpsed at the far end of a long black tunnel, its colours more vibrant, its pleasures more intense, the sunshine brighter and the sea bluer because of the long horrors that followed. They never had a chance to run out of steam, get disillusioned or bored. They wrote and spoke of a vanished world. The lack of financial worries was an important factor: despite Larry's occasional frets about poverty, the Fielding Hall money was always there as a cushion and 'Nancy is writing to the bank' was a frequent refrain.

While they were there, and even more so in retrospect, Corfu functioned as a dream come true for each member of the family: for Mother Durrell it was an escape from the alien mores of England and a chance to recapture some aspects of the colonial life she had been accustomed to in India; its rich fauna fuelled Gerry's growing passion for wildlife; Margo plunged into the world of the locals; and Leslie discovered a rustic world full of all manner of creatures just waiting to be shot. Larry was to develop his unique authorial voice, while for Nancy the island was, quite simply, a place to experience the joy of being. She said that whereas Larry always wanted to learn about a place, to discover its history and culture, she was content simply to let the atmosphere wash over her, to breathe it in, absorb it by osmosis.

Corfu was a visual feast. Nancy was entranced by the colourful clothes worn in the south of the island. The women were decked out in wonderful combinations: a yellow print skirt combined with a pink flower-pattern bodice with perhaps a plain bolero over that and yet another floral design on the shawls with which they covered their heads and shoulders. Like the wild flowers that covered the landscape in spring and autumn, whose colours should have clashed, but didn't, these combinations displayed an effortless artistry that delighted her.

Nancy and Larry had formed the advance guard; the rest of the family arrived soon afterwards, and brought with them the news that though *Pied Piper of Lovers* had not won the prize for first novel, Cassell wanted to publish it and were offering a fifty-pound advance. For Larry, that first vindication of his ambitions to be a writer was a landmark, a terrific confidence boost at the beginning of their new life on the island that contributed to his turbo-charged creativity over the next two years. Nancy produced a design for the jacket: a harlequin figure split down the centre, dark and light, the ambivalence at the heart of so much of Larry's writing – and of their relationship.

Nancy's cover for Larry's first novel

Larry and Nancy had found a little villa close to the Wilkinsons' bungalow. It was on the hillside just south of Corfu town, overlooking the sea and Pontikonisi – Mouse Island – with its little monastery. Their first home, which Larry dubbed Villa Bumtrinket, was primitive, 'a little hut, really', said Nancy: just a sitting room and a bedroom, with a kitchen at the back. A headlong plunge through the olive groves brought them to a shingle beach, mundane by the standards of their later swimming places, but in those first weeks of discovery it seemed miraculous to be able to scamper down to their own private stretch of sea. Soon Larry's mother and the rest of the family were installed at the nearby Villa Agazini, the strawberry-pink villa of *My Family and Other Animals*, so that during their first summer they were all within walking distance: Pam and George became honorary Durrells – George was roped in to give Gerry lessons, never an enviable task, since his school phobia extended to any kind of education – and the three households enjoyed a relaxed and easy social round. George and Pam already had a boat, though they were novice sailors, but they all learned the basics fairly quickly. The two couples read together in the evenings, rather grandly calling themselves the Shakespeare Reading Society.

Sailing, swimming, soaking up the sun, reading, talking, exploring ... that first summer was everything they had hoped for and more. One day Nancy, Larry and the Wilkinsons packed up a picnic and set off to walk the seven miles across the island, having heard that the beaches were better on the west coast. Nancy was bowled over by the beauty of their route along ancient paths and tracks. As they arrived in one remote village, all the men rushed out with chairs, bowing and gesturing to them to sit down while the women crowded round to examine these exotics who had appeared in their midst. Nancy was wearing only a little halter-neck top in checked cotton, which she had made herself, plus matching shorts, a straw hat and sandals; the women couldn't make her out at all. 'You a boy or a girl?' they asked, pinching her as if to see if her skin offered any clues. Having ascertained her sex, they made them welcome with figs and cheese and drink; it was her first experience of the warmth and curiosity of the locals and for her the whole experience seemed fabulous. Then, when they arrived at the other side of the island, the beach was amazing. It was their first sight of the rugged and dramatic west coast that was to become so important to them over the next few years.

During that first summer the Durrell family met the two men who were to dominate and infinitely enrich their years in Corfu. The first was Spiro the taxi driver, who adopted the whole Durrell family. He was a big, growly-voiced man with a peaked cap, who used the enchanting pidgin English Gerry captured in *My Family and Other Animals*. Soon he was Mother Durrell's major expense; she used him to take her everywhere. He either accompanied her on shopping expeditions or would do the shopping for her. He was passionately pro-British. Nancy remembered him saying once, 'Honest to gods, Mrs Durrrell, you cut me opes, you find the Union Jack inside!' Sometimes, if the weather was particularly fine, he would drive his battered old American car up to the house and suggest an impromptu expedition.

Their second new friend was Theodore Stephanides, a complex and fascinating man. Tall, with bright blue eyes, fair hair and a little beard, he spoke perfect English. He was quite a bit older than them – forty – and at first sight he seemed rather stuffy and old-fashioned; that impression soon evaporated. As soon as he got to know them, his sense of fun erupted. He was a terrific giggler, and joined the family in their games of hide-and-seek behind the house; when the male members of the family had mock battles round an improvised fort he galloped around, waving branches and hurling pine cones and clods of earth with the best of them. He was steeped in the folklore of the island, folklore which was still alive in the 1930s: certain trees were believed to have special powers and stories were told of shipwrecks that were avoided because the sailors had the wit to call on the still-living Alexander the Great.

Theodore's passion for wildlife was a godsend for Gerry, though among the locals he had earned a reputation as something of a witch doctor who concocted potions from pondlife, an accusation rooted in fact. He got the idea that microscopic organisms were a rich source of protein. To demonstrate this he occasionally dredged a whole lot up, drained them and made them into sandwiches. Nice, he declared, munching appreciatively, but no one else was tempted.

He was soon absorbed into the Durrell clan, but his wife Mary remained somewhat apart and gave the impression she disapproved of their unconventional ways. Nancy described her as 'prim and proper', but their daughter Alexia was enchanting, 'a little fairy'. However, Alexia was often unwell; whether because of this, or for other reasons, Mary and Alexia did not usually accompany Theodore on his visits.

A radiologist by profession, Theodore was an erudite man who wore his learning lightly. On one occasion he invited Larry and Nancy, together with Pam and George, to look round his laboratory. He showed them a series of joke slides he had concocted for the occasion, what appeared to be strange creepy crawlies.

Theodore and Nancy on a caique

He then moved on to tell them about some of his interesting cases and showed them his collection of curiosities, such as a Siamese-twin fetus. A particularly interesting stomach proved too much for Pam, who keeled over in a faint. At once, Theodore was all concern and efficiency. 'Oh yes, pick her up,' he said. 'Put her head between her knees.' As soon as she was vertical again, he resumed where he had left off. 'As I was saying, the interesting aspect of this stomach is—' George interrupted him, 'Theodore, I don't think Pam can stand any more of that.' Theodore was surprised. It had never occurred to him that his beloved specimens might upset anybody.

In his reminiscences of the Durrell family, Theodore's courtesy and humour are combined with his scientist's powers of observation. On his first visit to the Villa Agazini he was immediately struck by Larry's overwhelming confidence and bubbling energy. The younger man gave the impression of being everywhere at once, dominating the company and showering everyone with advice and suggestions – whether wanted or not. Larry assumed control of any activity, irrespective of whether he knew anything about it. Years later, during the war, their paths crossed again in Cairo and Larry undertook to teach Theodore billiards. 'Incidentally,' wrote Theodore in his immaculate, sloping handwriting in his journal of reminiscences, 'I never learned if Larry actually *knew* how to play billiards, but this was no obstacle to *teaching* someone how to play.'

Though various tutors were employed to educate Gerry while they lived in Corfu – George did not survive the course for long – it was Theodore who transformed his boyish delight in the natural world into a focused and lifelong passion. Right from the start, Gerry's patience was phenomenal. Nancy remembered how he made tiny lassos out of grass and stayed for hours crouched in front of a little hole where he knew a lizard was resting. The moment it came out he lassoed it and pulled the noose tight – another creature for his growing collection of wildlife. Gerry's unconventional schooling – or lack of it – paid dividends: his three elder siblings had all been to some extent damaged by the 'proper education' which had been the reason for quitting India. Not so Gerald: Theodore and the island itself seem to have taught him everything he needed to know.

To begin with at least, the novelty of Corfu life was combined with a rather old-fashioned Englishness: Nancy and Pam baked cakes; they enjoyed traditional afternoon teas; they made jams and chutneys. When not occupied swimming, sunning and walking, the women were often to be found in the kitchen while Gerry hunted insects, Leslie shouldered his gun and tramped the countryside, and Larry worked at a feverish pace.

It was another characteristic noted by the observant Theodore: Larry's ability to cram more into the day than anyone else. Like the rest of the party he might give the impression of day-long lotus-eating, but in fact his output during his first eighteen months on the island was prodigious. He was gratified that *Pied Piper of Lovers* was being published, but he had already outgrown his first book and had embarked on the novel that was to be published as *Panic Spring*. He was still keen to find a winning formula, maybe even to write a best seller and make lots of money from his love affair with words. Within months, however, his horizons had altered for ever.

A new landscape called for a new literary geography, and this is exactly what Larry found when his American friend Barclay Hudson lent him a copy of a book by a little-known fellow American called Henry Miller. Reading *Tropic of Cancer* changed everything for Larry: a literary *coup de foudre*. Later he admitted that although he'd been aware at once that the book was important, he had at first found it hard to come to terms with its brutality. But as he absorbed its radical message, he discovered much to admire and was soon trumpeting Miller's praise to all around him. Alan Thomas, back in Bournemouth, was bombarded with letters telling him to read it, read it, *read it!* It was several months before Thomas summoned the courage to admit to Larry that he had read it and it was not to his taste. Nancy shared her husband's enthusiasm: she appreciated the book's raw energy – it has been characterised as a book that swallows life whole – and she was unperturbed by the indigestible lumps of misogyny which create such obstacles for a post-feminist readership. *Tropic of Cancer* is above all an unflinchingly honest book, and for this alone Nancy would have loved it. Against a background where D. H. Lawrence's *The Rainbow* had been destroyed by order of the courts and Potocki's harmless little rhymes had earned him six months in prison, Miller's book was a clarion call for freedom of expression and a literature in which everything could be said, everything discussed, everything described. Now that the battle has been won, at least as far as 'obscenity' is concerned, it is easy to underestimate Miller's achievement, but in the summer of 1935 reading his book was almost equivalent to a religious conversion. And indeed, a fair bit of his language is religious in its tone. Art, he says, consists in going the full length. Do anything, but let it produce joy. 'Do anything, but let it yield ecstasy.' Amen to that, from Larry and Nancy both. Larry composed a robust fan letter; Henry replied, and the two men struck up a literary friendship that was to endure for nearly half a century.

At the end of the first summer, with storms battering the island, their tiny cottage by the sea south of Perama no longer seemed quite so idyllic. Mother Durrell had moved with the rest of the family to the Villa Anemoyanni near Corfu town, and Nancy and Larry shut up the Villa Bumtrinket and went to join them for the winter months. All through the Corfu years this pattern was repeated: long periods of comparative isolation interspersed with a few days or weeks – in this case, months – back with the family. As Larry told Theodore, you can have too much of paradise: sometimes you need a bit of family hell to make you appreciate it. The Villa Anemoyanni was a large, comfortable house about four miles north of Corfu town and Nancy and Larry shared a bright room, which was soon awash with books and papers, which Mother Durrell, like any mother of an untidy stay-at-home son, battled endlessly to get tidied up.

As in Bournemouth, Nancy slotted easily into the life of a family so unlike her own, a household where she was accepted for herself. Nancy enjoyed herself in the kitchen with Mother Durrell, where they improvised jams and lime chutney. Surprisingly little fruit grew on the island, so their jams were mainly variations on a marrow or tomato theme, which according to Nancy tasted better than it sounds. On one memorable wet afternoon Theodore visited with some records of Greek folk music and taught them traditional Cretan and Corfiot dances, clumping round and round in the large downstairs room.

Larry and Nancy were full of schemes. They would travel; they'd make money writing a detective story in which the culprit would hide the murder weapon in his anus. On winter evenings, while an aromatic fire of olive wood and pine cones burned in the grate, they played those paper games which almost entirely died out with the advent of television. Their take on consequences, enhanced by liberal quantities of cheap wine, led to such libellous things being written about friends and neighbours that Mother Durrell carefully burned every scrap as soon as the game had ended.

On a fine April morning in 1936 Spiro drove Nancy, Larry and Theodore to visit Madame Gennatas, an acquaintance of

Theodore's who lived in the north-east of the island. The road was bumpy, but the landscape was stunning: Mount Pantokrator rising up on their left; the sparkling Ionian Sea below them on the right; olive trees, cypresses and flowers vibrant in the spring sunshine. Nancy described Madame Gennatas as 'a stony-faced, chunky old woman' who lived alone in a beautiful old house which had once been a Venetian look-out. She spoke excellent English, though the origin of her Liverpudlian accent was a mystery; her guests were served an old-fashioned tea with seed cake and goats' milk (no cows in the rocky north of the island). She lived in Kouloura, an exquisite little bay with a row of eucalyptus trees lining the inlet. Naturally sheltered – *kouloura* means 'ring' in Greek – it was the place where the caiques that plied back and forth to Corfu town were harboured in bad weather.

Larry and Nancy were smitten with the area. In *Prospero's Cell* N is reported as saying 'the quietness alone makes it another country'. Spiro was charged with finding them a couple of rooms to rent for the summer. Nancy had been feeling for some time that their existence near Corfu town was 'too tame', and was keen to be in the wildest place she could find, while Larry wanted peace and quiet away from the 'pack of brats' – his siblings – so he could work without interruption. The rest of the family were dismayed at their defection, but as soon as Spiro found suitable lodgings for them in Kalami, just south of Kouloura, Nancy and Larry headed north. In 1936 Kalami barely merited being called a village – just a few little white-washed houses on a gentle bay, the steep hills behind rising up towards Mount Pantokrator. They weren't completely cut off from the expats of the island: their American friends Barclay and Jane Hudson had rented a villa just ten minutes' walk away, among some trees near the point. There was no road to the Barclays' house, just a rocky path that

involved a certain amount of scrambling, but in the summer of
1936 they spent a lot of time in each other's company.

Nancy and Larry took two rooms in a house built on a flat rock
on the southernmost curve of the bay. It belonged to a carpenter
called Athenaios and his wife Eleni. Athenaios, whom Nancy
always called Totsa, was dark, good-looking and quiet, as was
his wife; Eleni, following the custom in the north of Corfu,
always wore dark blue or black: dark blue or black full skirts, a
full-sleeved white blouse with a dark jerkin over it and a white
scarf covering her head. Nancy was as intrigued by the clothing
of her neighbours as the peasants were by hers. Even in the
height of the summer the peasants wore thick woollen vests
with long sleeves, believing that to leave them off would mean
certain pneumonia. They were horrified to see Nancy and Larry

The White House in Kalami before the top storey was added

wandering around in shorts and swimming costumes – or worse still, nothing at all. They made an effort to find skinny-dipping spots that were out of sight of the locals, but in their passion for taking their clothes off they probably didn't always succeed.

In some ways, Nancy and Larry plunged into local life, but while they were enjoying what Nancy later called 'the life of Riley', daily existence was tough for their hosts. Because the terrain in the north was so steep and craggy, the local Corfiots couldn't walk barefoot, or carry things on their heads as they did in the south. Anything to be transported had to be roped onto their backs. And as there was no fresh water at sea level, the women had to virtually crawl all the way up to the road where the spring was in order to fill their jars with the day's water – hard work, whatever the weather.

Having rented out two of their house's rooms, Totsa and his family slept in the third. The two families shared the kitchen and dining room. Close contact with their hosts meant that Larry and Nancy soon picked up enough patois to understand and be understood. Larry became fluent, but in *Prospero's Cell* he refers to N's 'bad Greek', so though she could always get by it is unlikely that she bothered much with grammar or speaking correctly, as he did.

Nancy liked and respected their new neighbours, but she never had any illusions about the hard choices imposed by their environment. When people talked nostalgically about the 'good old days' when families took care of their elderly, she said that, on the contrary, when food was in short supply it went to those who worked. Of necessity, the elderly were often allowed to go hungry, even starved.

Totsa and Eleni had two daughters: Frosso was about seven years old and pretty, with big brown eyes. But the younger daughter, Tihouli, was 'a pathetic little thing' of about five, whose front teeth were so rotten she was unable even to chew her food. Her devoted parents lavished cuddles and attention on their puny child, but when Nancy suggested taking her to a dentist they looked at her in astonishment. 'But she's only a girl,' they said.

Later that year, Eleni had a new baby and that too failed to thrive. One day, when it was particularly cold, Eleni came to Nancy and said, 'The baby's ill, kyria, will you come and have a look at it?' Nancy found the infant thinly clad and wheezing in its wooden cradle. 'I think it's in a draught, and it's cold,' she said. 'Wrap it up a bit more.' When she reported on this to Larry he advised her not to get involved. 'Leave it alone,' he told her. 'Have nothing to do with it at all. If anything happens to it they'll only blame you. Absolutely no good.' She ignored him and did as much as she could whenever they asked her for help. In time the baby did indeed die, but she was not held at all responsible.

Eleni's next baby was a boy, to the great delight of the family, a happy, bouncing, healthy child. Giorgios was a wonderful baby who responded to colours from an early age. When he was three months old Nancy showed him coloured pictures from the magazines she'd brought back from Athens; his eyes popped wide, his hand shot out to grab them and he panted with delight. Larry was made godfather to this thriving boy.

The journey to Corfu town by road, as they had discovered on that first springtime visit, was long, arduous and expensive. Their main contact, at least until they got their own boat, was by the twice-weekly caique that called in at Agni, a cluster of houses on a little bay a mile or so to the south. The walk to Agni along the path through the trees beside the rocky shore was magical, and took them past a spot that became one of their favourites for swimming, just below the shrine to St Arsenius. A short walk in the other direction brought them to Kouloura with its little shop selling matches, paraffin, hard cheese and salted cod, but not much else. For the most part they ate the same food as the villagers. Apart from greyish-brown bread and macaroni, the staple diet was some kind of fish stew made from small fish cooked with carrots, potatoes, onions and garlic. In the evenings, Totsa and his family and the other villagers often joined them for talk and singing, and Eleni handed round little cups of Turkish coffee and glasses of ouzo while Nancy offered biscuits or sweets from a tin.

They bought a boat. They became boat-mad and before long had three of them. The first was an elegant sailing boat, painted black all over, which gave it a sinister appearance, in Theodore's opinion. He suggested adding a white stripe just below the gunwale. Larry countered by proposing a broken white line, which would give an impression of gunports: his boat was going to look like a twelve-gun sloop of war. Of course, said Theodore, 'Larry was just pulling my leg. But sometimes he would get so carried away by pulling other people's legs that he would end up by tweaking his own.' The sailing boat remained unadorned and they named it *Van Norden*, after the character in *Tropic of Cancer* who is driven half mad by his need to have sex with a different woman each day. Their next boat, a little cockleshell of a rowing boat almost as broad as it was long, was named the *Bumtrinket*, like their first villa, after the flatulent maid in a play by Thomas Dekker. The name of the third, a flat-bottomed boat with an outboard motor that could achieve impressive speeds in comparison to the other two, is not recorded.

The boats, as boats do, demanded a lot of their time. They were turned upside down on the flat rocks below their house, scraped, painted, cleaned. Larry and Nancy were enthusiastic rather than expert sailors, but the *Van Norden* did give them the freedom to explore the bays and coves around the island. Squalls blow up out of nowhere in the Ionian, and they were frequently caught out. On one occasion they had taken Captain Severn, an elderly gambler from Corfu town who was devoted to Mother Durrell, and who liked to join them on their sloop. An enormous black cloud loomed overhead, and Nancy wanted to head back to shore. Larry disagreed. A row developed, with Nancy, who knew their limitations as sailors, insisting they return to land and Larry equally determined to stay at sea. To her dismay, Captain Severn took Larry's side, not because he thought he was right, necessarily, but because 'a captain must rule absolutely'. This was a novel idea to Nancy, who had never for a moment looked on Larry as the captain and had no intention of doing so in the future. However, on this occasion 'the captain' got his way, the storm erupted and they were duly scared and soaking wet by the time they reached land. Some variation of this scenario, with or without Captain Severn, was a frequent occurrence, especially when sailing back and forth to Corfu town, a journey of an hour or more.

Larry had finished *Panic Spring* the previous December, and all that summer he was working furiously on what was to become *The Black Book*. Inspired by the example of Henry Miller, he was attempting something that was, for him, entirely new. After a morning of intense work, the boats provided relaxation. Nancy would say, 'Let's take a picnic and go to that bay three bays away,' or 'Let's go as far as we can.' Sometimes they'd simply row across the bay, sometimes they'd go exploring in the *Van Norden*. As their confidence increased they sailed round the top of the island and discovered a deserted beach. No road led down to it, and from the beach it was a steep scramble up the cliffs to get to the road at the top. They stayed there for a fortnight, sleeping under the stars, doing nothing very much apart from swimming and sailing and lounging about. As it was impossible to take enough provisions for a whole fortnight – even their drinking water had to be brought by road – they arranged for Spiro to come with supplies in the middle of their stay. For Nancy that fortnight was pure delight, combining her great love of simplicity and wildness, and they returned every summer. When she was in her sixties, surrounded by books, furniture, paintings, she sometimes seemed baffled by this accumulation of worldly goods and commented in a puzzled way that she had always imagined ending her days in a cave, owning nothing but a tin mug, plate and spoon: she was remembering those timeless summer days of solitude and freedom on the wild western beaches of Corfu.

Reading the published extracts of Larry's letters to his bookseller friend Alan Thomas in Bournemouth, one gets the impression that his mind was entirely taken up with literary matters. He raves about *Tropic of Cancer*, curses Cassell for their spineless attitude to censorship in *Pied Piper of Lovers* and talks about the books he is reading and his progress with his own writing. In actual fact, a fair chunk of their correspondence dealt with altogether more mundane matters: 'Life is very beautiful and drunken ... Nancy's period is 37 days overdue. Pattering feet? Curse this tropical air. It makes one as fertile as the stoats ... PS *Are* stoats fertile?' And later he reports that a hell of a scare last month had left them running round Corfu town trying to buy 'ergetol' and finding a doctor who would 'abort the wretched thing if it didn't turn up'. Then, 'Another panic this month over Nancy's period. That girl is a pest.' Somehow, in the move up to Kalami, what Larry called Nancy's 'beautiful anti-aircraft device' had gone missing and they were now paying a heavy price. He lamented, with perhaps unconscious imagery, 'Now we also are at a loose end.' Not only was birth control unavailable on Corfu, but contraceptives were not allowed through customs and the officials had taken to opening their parcels. The poor Hudsons had had what he describes as 'gunch' and a ring-pessary languishing on the quay for months.

Get an occlusive cap, he begged Alan, and wrap it in newspapers, or *Time and Tide*, to evade detection. Poor Alan, that inhibited Quaker bibliophile, must have been slow to make the purchase, because in desperation the couple were reduced to the locals' reliance on chopped-up bits of sea-sponge soaked in olive oil as a home-made deterrent. And, as Larry added as an afterthought, '69 is a bore too.'

Inevitably, Nancy became pregnant and they were both terri-fied; neither had any desire for a child at this stage and 'bombing it out', as Larry put it, was neither pleasant nor safe. In despera-tion they turned to Theodore. He put them in touch with a gynaecologist whom Nancy described vaguely as 'very nice', though he was at first disapproving and not inclined to be help-ful. Find a medical reason, they begged the doctor, so he obligingly declared Nancy to be anaemic, which was plausible enough, given how thin she was. She was booked into a nursing home in Corfu. Larry was frantic with anxiety, and when the pro-cedure had been successfully performed his relief exploded in a storm of panicked rage. The next day, he reported to Alan that 'the slut' was sitting up in bed, and that the staff of the nursing home had wanted him to examine the fetus, but he was so furi-ous and worried he told them to stuff it up their arse. He could have kicked it 'for all the jitters it gave me'.

There was reason to be frightened, as abortion was not without serious risks, but Nancy had a fairly robust attitude to the psycho-logical side of it. Some time in the 1970s, when a friend and I were discussing the pros and cons of abortion, she chipped in with the information – new to me – that she had had two and they had both been absolutely fine. She then added that the second had been difficult because of the circumstances, but not because of any scruples she had about it. I was too surprised to ask for details, more's the pity, and so have no idea when the second occurred, though I imagine it must have been after she and Larry had parted. Anyway, 'praise be' as Larry said at the time: the first abortion had no ill effects. As soon as she was well enough, Nancy left the nursing home and went to recuperate for a few days at the Villa Anemoyanni. Mother Durrell had not been told the reason for her stay in hospital, and was predictably furious, and extremely upset, when she found out. She thought it was wrong and told them so.

Nancy made a full recovery and life went on as before, but the pregnancy scares, and the abortion, had a far-reaching impact on their relationship, though neither realised this at the time. They were both young and naive enough to think that being happy with the person you loved was a simple business. Three years later, in 'A Small Scripture', a poem dedicated to Nancy, he wrote:

A bleeding egg was the pain of testament,
Murder of self within murder to reach the Self . . .

For Larry the image of the egg had parallels with the cosmos, but even so this couplet surely resonates with the experience of the abortion; it suggests that Larry's response to this episode was far more sensitive than he let on. As so often, his correspondence told only half the story.

During those first two years on the island, though they had an eclectic and interesting circle of friends, Larry was aware of being cut off from his literary peers; in fact solitude is one of the recurrent themes of *The Black Book*: he talks of 'the fantastic loneliness which tells me that I exist', and describes as 'primordial in its loneliness, the mood in which I set out to meet you'. Even then, their marriage was perhaps less harmonious than it appeared, but one area that remained rock solid between them was Nancy's passionate commitment to his development as a writer. In some ways she took this even more seriously than he did. Larry was sometimes tempted to produce something with a commercial appeal, while Nancy was only interested in the creation of work of lasting value, and never mind if that meant it was doomed only to be appreciated by a handful of discerning readers. They had sufficient money to live on, and that was enough. The impossibly high standards she set for herself were useful to Larry, who had the energy and self-confidence she so obviously lacked. During their first years together Larry relied heavily on her opinion, at least with regard to prose. When it came to poetry she had no language in which to express her views, though she had an instinctive response and was able to feel if a poem worked or not – which is never very satisfying feedback for an author. Ever since they gave up Witch Photos and moved to Loxwood, she had believed in his potential and had encouraged him, but she was lukewarm about his first two novels. *The Pied Piper of Lovers* she described, always the mistress of the throw-away rebuff, as 'a bit dull'. *Panic Spring* had not impressed her much either, though she came up with its title: why not call it *Panic Spring in Limbo*, she had suggested. Larry cut off the last two words.

The Black Book was another matter entirely. It came, she said, 'bursting out' at great speed and she thought it was terrific, marvellous, wonderful. The 'great speed' must have been a retrospective gloss, because although Larry worked with maniacal intensity its creation was traumatic, a quite different experience from either of his first two books, and the effort of digging so deep inside himself brought him to the verge of breakdown. In a letter to Henry he described the state of his soul as 'shaky', adding that he had become prey to 'rages and fears and psychological tics'. In another letter written just after he had finished *The Black Book* his grasp of syntax collapsed under the strain and he said, 'It ruins one living to become writing'. He admitted that he had taken out most of his frustration and nervous exhaustion on Nancy. She probably did not remember that, and if she did, she would have thought his behaviour was more than justified by the finished result.

The Black Book centres on a collection of characters based on people Larry had known in his London years, with two voices, Lawrence Lucifer and Death Gregory, being two aspects of himself. In it he attacked what he called 'the cultural swaddling clothes' which collectively he named the English Death and he began to explore themes and techniques – different narrative voices, the need for rebirth, the supreme importance of 'loving well' – which were to culminate in *The Alexandria Quartet*. T. S. Eliot was to call it the first work by a new English author to give him hope for the future of prose fiction. By any account it is a bravura performance, a sheer avalanche of words and images that instantly proclaimed him a talent to be reckoned with.

Larry himself, once the manuscript was finished, was generous in apportioning credit. If *The Black Book* had any merit, he told Miller, it was 'all due to TROPIC, I think. And my wife, who is divinely mad.' He quoted Nancy's opinion that he was at last writing with a new, authentic voice. And when Miller confirmed her view, declaring it to be stupendous and saluting Larry as a master, she was delighted. Larry told Henry that 'Nancy is as proud as punch, it being her book.' He inscribed the manuscript with the words, 'To Nancy from Larry. In memoriam: stars, Ion, butter, Κολόυρα, [unreadable – quarrels?] dung, insults, tears, love and <u>Laughter</u> – and a promise of bigger books as yet!!' The dedication to the first edition, published in Paris the following year (it was dropped after they separated), was *To Nancy, onlie begetter, etc* – an echo of the title-page dedication of Shakespeare's Sonnets. *The Black Book* remained her favourite of his prose works. When Henry Miller praised his surrealist 'A Christmas

Carol' – later published as 'Asylum in the Snow' – Larry cheerfully responded with Nancy's opinion that it was not a patch on *The Black Book*, 'NOT A BLOODY PATCH'.

The final section of *The Black Book* was first published separately under the title *Coda for Nancy* and addresses the 'you' with whom the book had opened, who shares the room over the Ionian. He touches on the strain of creation, the terror of writing, before declaring that he becomes too afraid to continue. But the remedy lies close by. 'It is then that I get up in a panic and go to where you are sitting, working, and knitting, and put my hands on your hands. Then in a moment or two my courage is restored and I return to the pages, turning them over, reading them slowly, wondering.'

All the tenderness of their early years in Corfu lies in those words, the loving partnership that fed into his bold experiment with prose.

His creative progress during those first Corfu years is easy to chart; hers, almost impossible. As almost her entire output from the 1930s was destroyed or vanished in the war, one has to turn archaeologist to get any impression of what Nancy was doing. *Prospero's Cell* describes the high-ceilinged room in the White House 'where N's lazy pleasant paintings stare down from the walls'. The end results might have looked lazy; their creator was anything but. Later in the same book he describes how N, at an open-air dance, begins to make her 'slow painful notes' for paintings. Painful and slow was at least an improvement on 'completely unhinged', which was how she described her attitude to her work during their Bournemouth year, but she remained bogged down in the swamp of her self-doubt and inhibition. The behaviour of Francis, the beautiful young woman artist who has fetched up on a Greek island in *Panic Spring*, owes a lot to Nancy. Walsh, the narrator, describes how she 'would stand for hours on the hillside in a torn straw hat, trying to build up the form of a landscape by an interrelation of the colours'. Furiously Francis associates and reassociates her groups of colours – an approach reminiscent of Nancy's first teacher at Westminster Art School and his insistence on 'transposing the colours'. Francis sets herself impossibly high standards and screws up her face with 'self-immolating dissatisfaction' – an image which sounds exactly like Nancy. The contrast with Larry is stark. He breezily refers to an entire novel as 'a small turd' or 'a leprous distilment' (two of his own verdicts on his second novel, *Panic Spring*) and moves on with buoyant optimism to the next task. Not so Nancy. One longs for Francis/Nancy to let go, play, allow herself to take risks and make mistakes, but no. Instead, she ratchets up the pressure by propping reproductions of landscapes by El Greco or Cézanne – both artists Nancy revered – against an olive trunk, and while 'slowly crunching a dwarf pear between her teeth, or peeling an orange' she would stare and stare at the image as though she could draw out its secrets. Often, Francis ends by kicking her own canvas down the hill in disgust.

Walsh, who happens to be in love with Francis, cannot understand such brutal perfectionism. She tries to explain: 'When Cézanne couldn't get what he wanted,' she tells him, 'he left a blank on the canvas.' In her opinion, 'That was real conscience. If mine were half as strong I should produce nothing, but a series of blank canvases.' Her statement is pure Nancy: better a blank than run the risk of producing a dud; better silence than saying something inauthentic. The phrase 'the best is the enemy of the good' might have been coined just to torment her.

It is a wonder Nancy ever silenced her inner critic long enough to produce anything at all, but she did. Theodore has written that the Swiss artist René Berlincourt especially admired her watercolours, and singled out for high praise a painting of a large white

Persian cat that used to lounge near the milk shop in Corfu town. But praise from others, even that of a fellow artist like Berlin-court, had to do battle with her own unforgiving internal voice, which was forever telling her she wasn't good enough.

When she did achieve a measure of success, it came from an unexpected quarter. *Night and Day*, a literary magazine that had just been set up as a kind of London-based *New Yorker*, bought a couple of her cartoons. The first shows a Roman soldier who has just dragged a group of cavewomen out of the forest. 'The woods are full of them,' he declares smugly – a popular catchphrase of the time. Larry, writing to Anaïs Nin in July 1937, said that 'Nancy has just lifted five quid for a comic drawing and is quite unbearably aloof today.' Without pausing for breath he immediately goes on, 'And I have found a goddess in the flesh. Nausicaa,' who turns out to be a seventeen-year-old who 'looks at men with the impersonal mindless way that cattle look at trees', for which he adores her. It may be wrong to read too much into that swift

'The woods are full of them!'

Nancy was delighted when her cartoon was bought by *Night and Day* transition from Nancy's achievement to his raptures over a bovine adolescent, but it conveys the unmistakable impression that, though he was proud to have a beautiful artist as a wife, he was, to say the least, ambivalent about the possibility of her success. Luckily for him, her own 'self-immolating dissatisfaction' was more than enough to inhibit her development as an artist.

Her confidence cannot have been increased when Larry began painting as well, perhaps inspired more by Miller's example than by any desire to compete with her. As with music, he had a natural facility and his paintings, some of which survive, had an engaging charm. He never took his artistic endeavours very seriously – he told Henry cheerfully that they made Nancy vomit – they were never the products of anguish, as Nancy's were.

A month later *Night and Day* took the second of her cartoons, though a less successful one, and she also drew some chirpy illustrations for 'Obituary', a short story by Charles Norden – the name under which *Panic Spring* was to appear – featuring the comic demise of a big-game-shooting country squire in which his old school tie looms large.

Another frequent contributor to *Night and Day* was Roger Pettiward who, since the days when he and Nancy had decorated the Slade with their caricatures, had developed into a quirky and original cartoonist. He wanted to be known for his serious paintings, so his cartoons appeared with the name Paul Crum or a simple spiral as the signature. As Nancy's were signed Nancy Norden it is impossible to know if either was aware that they were once again sharing a platform.

Just as *Night and Day* was shaping up to be a fine home for the Nordens' lighter offerings, it suddenly and dramatically went out of business. In October Graham Greene, the magazine's film critic, wrote a blistering critique of the nine-year-old Shirley Temple's appearance in the film *Wee Willie Winkie*. He said that in her case infancy was a disguise and that many of her admirers – 'middle-aged men and clergymen' – were devoted to her films for all the wrong reasons. Two years earlier, in the film *Captain January*, she had already been 'a fancy little piece' but in this film she was 'a complete totsy' with 'a well-shaped and desirable little body'. The film studio sued, the judge found in their favour, *Night and Day* folded and Nancy's career as a cartoonist came to an abrupt end.

As far as I know, she had no further cartoons published. Her sense of fun bubbled up from time to time in a love of simple jokes, the simpler the better. 'What do you do if you meet a lion when you're out for a walk?' – Larry relayed Nancy's question in a letter to Alan Thomas – 'Don't know? Push your umbrella down its throat, and then open it.' Could this be developed into a dirty joke, Larry wondered.

In May 1937 Alan Thomas came out for a long-awaited visit. Larry and Nancy had been looking forward to seeing him, and in a detailed letter (rare, she was never much of a letter writer) she advised him on what to bring – 'old clothes, shorts if you have them' – and waxed lyrical about the joys of early summer on the island: 'It's still quite English summer weather here in May – cherries and strawberries and the first figs.' They greeted him with enthusiasm, and shared all their favourite places and activities with him over the three weeks of his visit.

Superficially, it was all a great success, and Alan returned to Bournemouth full of memories of happy times and conversations, but both Larry and Nancy were, in their different ways, disappointed by it. Perhaps it was a measure of how much their two years on the island, and the correspondence with Miller and Nin, had changed them, but the old familiar conviviality was strained. Larry complained to Henry that Alan had not understood a word they said, while Nancy often mentioned her fury at his refusal to record what was actually happening. One morning, after she and Larry had engaged in a particularly blistering row, yelling furiously at each other all through breakfast, she happened to look at Alan's journal, in which the faithful Boswell was noting the day's events. To her amazement she read, 'Sitting having breakfast in this magical place with the wonderful sunshine streaming in and the delightful conversation of the Durrells.' She was outraged by this mendacity. As far as she was concerned, Alan was living in a dream-land. He had decided in advance that the Corfu trip was to be a kind of A *Dream in the Luxembourg* experience, romantic and wonderful, and so wrote the fantasy, not the reality. Unforgivable, in Nancy's opinion. Ever since that moment in the new house in Gainsborough, when her mother had told her she was wicked to say their 'beautiful' garden was horrid, she had an abhorrence of anything that smacked of falsehood. Of course, she could tell white lies when it suited her, like anyone else, but she was unable to be dishonest in any fundamental way. It is a cruel irony that she had joined forces with a man for whom actual truth was less important than poetic truth, and Larry had no problems with Alan's contribution to the Durrell mythology.

After Alan left they moved for a couple of months to the west of the island, to the two bays at Paleokastritsa. They rented a tiny cottage from a Greek called Kostas. Mary and Alexia Stephanides were next door and Theodore joined them at weekends. Alexia, who was then about seven, remembers Nancy and Larry living in complete harmony, never a cross word between them. They were both painting busily, but whereas Larry never minded the little girl watching him as he worked Nancy, who set up her easel in a quiet spot, tended to shoo her away after a little while. It was Alexia, an acute observer like her father even then, who remembered Nancy as 'innocent'.

*

On his way south, and at Larry's instigation, Alan had stopped off in Paris and visited Henry Miller at the Villa Seurat. Since Larry's first fan letter in the summer of 1935, the correspondence had matured into a vibrant exchange of views which combined lavish praise – 'It's so damned perfect it makes me green with jealousy ... a masterpiece, the most perfect thing of its kind that I have ever read' (Henry on 'Carol') and 'You are such a very great man I'm continually surprised at you' (Larry to Henry) – with real insights and criticism. Larry declared that *Tropic of Cancer* and *Black Spring* were 'the most religious books written since the authorized bible'. (It is easy to mock this exaggerated mutual admiration, but both men were battling against the established literary scene – the kind of attitude expressed in George Bernard Shaw's extraordinary letter to Larry later that same year, telling him not to become 'a commercial traveller in obscene literature' and ending 'you are young and foolish. So you had better do what I tell you' – and generous affirmation was vital.) Their exchange had widened to involve Anaïs and Nancy: Henry sent the manuscript of Anaïs's *House of Incest*, which was read with huge enthusiasm in Kalami. Henry asked for a photograph of Nancy, which Larry dispatched, saying, 'The photograph? Nancy says, "But dear, make it clear to him will you? I AM A PERSON!"' Perhaps she was afraid of being an adornment only, but Henry responded with enthusiasm, saying firmly, 'I was tremendously impressed by the photo of Nancy. She looks like "a person".' Larry also sent off one or two of Nancy's paintings, and often quoted her opinions in his letters to Miller. From time to time Larry tried to persuade Henry to visit them in Corfu, but Henry was not much inclined to travel and, anyway, he was always broke. When they did meet, it was Nancy and Larry who travelled to Paris, arriving at the beginning of August 1937.

After such a build-up, that first meeting could so easily have been an anti-climax, but no. It was a milestone for them all. Nancy adored Henry right from the start and she was fascinated by Anaïs. 'At first,' she said, 'we were both wild with excitement at entering right into the very heart of this dazzling, intriguing, fascinating world of bright lights and shadowy corners.' Henry was bowled over by Larry's charm and conversation and Anaïs felt as though she had known him for ever. The party lasted all day and into the night. In retrospect, it sometimes seemed as though the party had continued, off and on, all through that late summer and winter: laughter, conversation, shared enthusiasms and a real meeting of minds. It was everything they had all hoped for and more. The steaks Nancy cooked that first day were so delicious they found their way into at least two of the memoirs of the event. Outwardly, it could not have been more successful.

But within only ten days Nancy and Larry were troubled: homesick for Corfu and thinking of leaving. They visited Anaïs and confided their anxiety to her as they sat on cushions on the floor of her apartment by its enormous window and drank coffee in the dark. Anaïs believed she understood. 'They recoil from what I recoil from,' she noted approvingly in her diary, believing they disliked 'the slippery, greasy, putrid world of Fred ... Brassaï, et al'. She was glad that she was able to share their revulsion, and to reassure them and persuade them to remain. But in actual fact, though she might think they had spoken intimately, Larry and Nancy were never able to discuss their real fears with anyone. That initial instinct of flight had had a deeper cause: they feared that what Nin termed 'the Villa Seurat and the Dôme circus' would harm them as individuals and as a couple, and they were right to be afraid. From the point of view of Larry and Nancy's relationship, the Paris months were a total disaster.

7

SAFE FROM EVERYTHING
BUT OURSELVES

Safe from everything but ourselves

Lawrence Durrell, 'At Epidaurus'

In Paris, Larry had morphed again. During their first months together in London, the poorly 'child man' Nancy had first noticed behind the wheel of his mother's car, the uncertain estate agent whose weak heart and baby talk had triggered her maternal instincts, had evolved into a dynamic and single-minded young writer. In Corfu he had begun to evolve his unique authorial voice and he now knew that he was capable of much more than a mere facility with words. Nancy wrote that, having established himself as a writer, he was now determined to establish himself as a *person* (that word again). Larry regarded this as an essential component in his literary development: the previous year he had written to Miller that to have art it was necessary first to have 'a big personality', which one should 'pass through the social mincer, get it ready for misery'. At the Villa Seurat he hung out with a group who were on his wavelength and with whom he could explore ideas and projects without restraint. Here, he was the long-awaited crown prince in the court of King Henry. And Nancy, who had expected to enjoy this new phase of their life together alongside her mate, just as they had shared every experience in the past, found herself assigned a very different role. In Paris Larry was determined to keep her on the sidelines. He wanted her to admire silently, but on no account to be part of the action. She must be decorative but insignificant – a 'lady-in-waiting', as she put it.

Nancy adored Henry from the beginning

It was the Paris period that gave rise to most of the misconceptions about Nancy. Several people commented on her silences and reserve, and Betty Ryan, the young American artist whose flat they first stayed in, even went so far as to say she lacked 'spark' and kept herself aloof. Most people assumed that this was due to shyness and a naturally quiet personality, and this impression has found its way into chronicles of the period, in which she is characterised as placid, gentle, shy and entirely dominated by her brilliant husband. Deirdre Bair's judicious biography of Anaïs Nin is fairly typical: '[Anaïs], Henry and Larry engaged in night-long talkathons, with Nancy (whose money paid for her husband's peripatetic life) sitting shyly outside the triangle or playing the role ... of handmaiden to literary men and provider of their food and drink'. The reality is far more complex, and unpicking it goes to the very heart of their marriage.

From the moment of their arrival, Larry set out to conquer this new literary landscape. He unleashed the Durrell charm to devastating effect; he was funny and profound, sensitive, erudite and endlessly entertaining. His laughter reverberated round the room and on that first day at the Villa Seurat Henry was so overwhelmed by the charisma of his protégé that he was moved to tears of affection and admiration. But all the time that Larry was enchanting his new friends with his pyrotechnic displays of lyricism and wit, he was fighting an equally determined rearguard action against Nancy. As a boy he had honed his skills on his younger brother Leslie, and now they were deployed for the first time against Nancy.

Which is not to say his charm and sympathy weren't genuine. Because a person's mask does not give the whole picture, it is tempting to imagine that the hidden part of them is somehow more real, but this is not necessarily true. The Larry who captivated Henry and his entourage was as much the real him as the person who was expending such savage energy to keep Nancy out of the frame. He was someone in whom the extremes are more extreme than most, and it was these extremes that he had first mined in *The Black Book*: the lyrical tenderness and the devastating cruelty existed side by side, and sometimes brought him to the brink of madness. When, much later, he said that he began each novel as an alternative to committing suicide, it was not rhetoric but a kind of truth.

Larry had been ambivalent about Nancy's place in this new order right from the start. He first wrote to Henry Miller in August 1935, two years before they arrived in Paris, but it wasn't until his third letter, more than six months later, that he mentioned 'my wife'. He was describing how much fun they'd had, sitting on the floor as a December storm crashed round outside, imagining the responses of all the great critics, like F. R. Leavis and T. S. Eliot, on reading *Tropic of Cancer*. In his next letter Henry sends his regards to 'your wife' and asks, 'how do you call her, par example?' But it is another six months, and ten more letters, before Larry provides the information, and then only after Henry has again insisted that he ought at least give him his wife's name. The time it took for 'my wife' to become 'Nancy' was significant, and maybe Nancy herself had a premonition that the changes ahead would not all be positive. There was her insistence on being 'a person', and in one of the letters Henry wrote before their August meeting he seems to be emphasising his goodwill towards her.

It was always going to be impossible, but Larry wanted to be simultaneously married and single as he embarked on his conquest of the Villa Seurat. The resulting tensions triggered shock waves from which their marriage never recovered. And all this against a background of laughter, fun and creative mayhem, a period which, for all its pain, Nancy looked back on with real affection.

*

The Villa Seurat is actually a street, a quiet group of houses and flats off the rue de la Tombe-Issoire in the 14th arrondissement, just south of Montparnasse. Number 18 is a simple art deco structure divided into five small flats, and Henry had been in residence there, off and on, for over three years. His rent was paid by Anaïs, with whom he'd been having an affair for several years. Betty Ryan, with whom Henry was also rumoured to be having an affair (she always denied it), had the flat below his. As Betty was away, Henry had arranged for Larry and Nancy to stay there until they found a place of their own.

Nancy fell in love with Henry from the beginning, fell in love with his huge grin and his big, warm-hearted welcome. He was the second of those larger-than-life, anarchic men – the first being Roger Pettiward – for whom she had nothing but admiration. When they met he was forty-five, twenty years older than she and Larry, and he seemed to her an old man. She described him: bald with delicate white skin, he had a long clown's face and faded blue eyes behind thick-lensed spectacles. Two great lines ran down from his nose to his large, generous mouth. Even now he is a man who provokes strong and contradictory reactions: part hobo, part seer, part sex-obsessed predator and part mystic visionary, he is impossible to categorise, though that hasn't stopped huge numbers of people from trying. What has vanished, what no one who didn't meet him can capture, is the impact of his personality, his zest for living, infectious passion and sheer exuberance. Anaïs described him as a man who made life drunk. Nancy used to say that he probably wasn't very good to his girlfriends, but he was always a good friend to her. Most important of all, time spent with him was never dull.

After their simple rooms with Totsa and his family in Kalami, Betty's studio apartment seemed to Nancy 'like something out of a film'. All pink and white, a staircase led up to a little bedroom in what Nancy called the 'surtout' above. She was entranced by the glamour of the arrangement. Two weeks later Betty came back and they moved across the road to stay for a little while with Henry's friend Alfred Perlès – who was always known as Fred. In the early days of their relationship, when Henry was down and out, homeless and hungry in Paris, Fred had taken him under his wing, but by 1937 the relationship had evolved and now it was Fred who was Henry's sidekick or, as Nancy describes it, Sancho Panza to his Don Quixote. As such, neither she nor Larry ever took him very seriously. They probably underestimated him, since his monograph *My Friend Lawrence Durrell*, which was written as a companion piece to a much longer book about Henry, is remarkably perceptive.

Fred was Austrian, and to Nancy he was always 'a funny little character, like a sort of mouse'. He was small, with very thin, mouse-like hands, a reddish face and big black, rather damp eyes. He was constantly excusing himself and giggling, and he gave Nancy the impression of being completely unreliable and, even more than that, 'utterly corrupt'. But in the short time they spent in his flat, during those first happy Paris days, Fred was primarily a source of huge amusement. Nancy and Larry used to lie in bed and watch his morning routine, which involved talking to his reflection in the mirror while he shaved. 'Hello, Joe,' the little man remarked to the soapy face looking back at him. 'How are you this morning, Joe? You all right, Joe?' He was playing to the gallery, and his audience found it hilarious.

Joe was the name that he and Henry had adopted for each other in their impromptu clowning – 'taking the lead', they called it, a simple way of letting off steam or keeping boredom at bay. 'Take the lead, Joe?' one of them would say (and when taking the lead, everyone became Joe). 'Yeah, take the lead, Joe!' the other responded, which was the signal for Fred and Henry to leap to their feet and cavort around the room. One finger in an ear, the other in a nostril, they'd dance about on crooked knees like monkeys, laughing and emitting war cries to the astonishment of the other people in the bar or café or wherever they'd been sitting. Of course everyone else was free to join them. 'Taking the lead' appealed to Nancy's love of mayhem, the zaniness that she'd enjoyed with Roger when they'd disrupted the art-school dances with their wild dancing, and even quite late in life she performed an excellent and affectionate impression of Henry's whooping, simian extravaganza.

His life-enhancing energy was carefully nurtured. Nancy noted how well Henry looked after himself, for all his disregard for bourgeois comforts. 'He always had a finger on his pulse, so to speak,' she said, adding, 'there was never much danger of him overtaxing himself' in spite of his sexual marathons. As soon as he felt a draught he immediately put on hat and muffler, which she and Larry found very funny, and whenever he felt the slightest bit tired he had a nap. His instinct for self-preservation meant that if he was feeling depressed, or guilty, he would, in his phrase, 'hibernate it away'. One morning Nancy and Larry took steaks to the Villa Seurat to cook for lunch, but they arrived to find Henry in a state, having received a letter from his parents in Brooklyn. Stricken with guilt over what a bad son he was, he immediately went next door to the bedroom to sleep it off while the rest of them – Fred, Larry, Anaïs and Nancy – enjoyed their steaks. When he woke up some time later the guilt had been successfully hibernated away, he was lively as a cricket and once more ready to 'take the lead'.

Alfred Perlès was responsible for the timing of the Durrells' Paris visit. Given their intense correspondence, it's likely that Larry and Henry would have met up before long, but in August 1937 they had a particular project in view: masterminding one of the most unlikely literary magazines of all time.

Since coming to Paris Perlès had taken various jobs; that summer he had been acting as a tout for the American Country Club that operated on a new golf course at Ozoir-la-Ferrière, about ten miles south-east of Paris. His job was to find new members and to collect their initiation fees. In a moment of generosity he must have quickly regretted, the club's director offered Perlès the editorship of the club magazine, *The Booster*. Perhaps he thought it would raise the profile of what was really the equivalent of a 1930s in-flight magazine – which it did, but in ways he never dreamed of. *The Booster* offered some financial stability for the impoverished Perlès and Miller as it carried a good deal of advertising, directed at the wealthy golfers and their families whose exploits were detailed in the back pages with Pooterish

Nancy's cover for their first issue of *The Booster*

precision. Nancy described a typical report as 'Mr and Mrs J. B. Finkelmeyer arrived on the *Aquitania*, and their beautiful daughter ... that sort of thing.' An actual notice reads, 'Mr and Mrs Léon Iché and their son Jean have spent 10 days at the club. In spite of many rainy days the Iché family played golf every day.'

For Fred and Henry, the challenge was irresistible.

The story of the American Country Club magazine and its swift demise was in many ways my favourite myth when I was young. The way Nancy told it, Henry, who had no money at all, was offered a golden goose that would have given him a regular income without any real bother. But the American Country Club, its clientele and the banal chronicle of their arrivals and departures, teas and lunches and rounds of golf, represented everything that he most despised and making a sensible go of it was never an option. Larry was made literary editor and Nancy became art editor, but 'Let's see how quickly we can run this thing into the ground!' was Henry's brief to his team. They decided to target the advertising. One, vividly illustrated by Nancy, carried the strapline: 'If you must walk in shit, wear Lotus shoes!' The advertisers duly left en masse and the magazine folded after two issues.

Alas, not true.

While researching this book, I hunted eagerly through every issue of *The Booster* (and there were more than two) for this memorable advertisement, but without success. Apart from some rather facetious advice to 'Keep Your Feet Fit for Golf' by visiting Mrs Baratta Alexander, graduate of Illinois College of Chiropody, the ads remain untampered with. Nancy must have been remembering the riotous sessions of what would now be called brainstorming as the editorial team planned their epoch-making magazine. No doubt she relished drawing an elegantly shod lady plunging her foot in a pile of steaming muck, but the picture never made it into the final version – more's the pity.

The only one of her drawings that does survive is the cover of the September issue, a face turning two ways, mouths open in shock, or delight, or exclamation. It might be intended to convey the outrage their little magazine was going to cause; but as an illustration it was hardly scandalous.

Still, Henry's cavalier attitude to a magazine that might have provided him with some cash, as well as offering a showcase for their work, was genuine. I think his lack of respect for money is the reason he is still regarded as beyond the pale. The sexual revolution of the 1960s meant that a new generation finally caught up with his views on sexuality, but his total contempt for 'getting and spending' was a harder freedom to accept. He has frequently been characterised as a scrounger, but that is to miss the point. If he had cash he gave it away; if he didn't, then someone else could provide. His courage in consistently biting (off) whichever hand was feeding him was one of the things that Nancy cherished about him – though when she and Larry lent him money, he was always touched and grateful.

The magazine lasted for four issues before the director of the country club severed the connection. The fifth issue, renamed *Delta*, carried a characteristic disclaimer on its front page: 'Beginning with this issue *The Booster* becomes *Delta*. It should be remembered that circumstances imposed on us a title which we did our best to live down to.' The third issue of *Delta* came out in the spring of 1939 and was entirely devoted to poetry. By then Larry and Henry had gathered a distinguished list of contributors, though their determined hilarity in the face of the disastrous international situation came in for a good deal of criticism. Their response was that when politicians are tipping the world into insanity it is the job of the artist to stay true to their calling, a view Nancy, who never involved herself in political debate, wholeheartedly endorsed.

But after the first issue of *The Booster* in September, her name was removed from the editorial team: all part of Larry's campaign to exclude her from the gang.

Another name that didn't make the editorial list after the first issue was Anaïs Nin's, who had been down as society editor. She was dropped because of her impatience with what she saw as Henry's infantile and vulgar side. 'What made Henry hysterical with amusement,' Anaïs wrote tartly, 'did not touch me.' She had no patience with the horseplay that Nancy enjoyed and it's hard to imagine her ever joining in when Fred and Henry 'took the lead'. In fact, she seems to have had almost no sense of humour at all. What she did have was beauty, an acquiescent banker husband, courage and intelligence, an apparently limitless fascination with her own sexuality and emotional life, and, most important of all, her diary. Her life story reads like two parallel lives, her own and the virtual one she created in her diary. Nancy, like many others, was in awe of this diary. 'Everybody talked about it,' she said. 'Anaïs talked about it, Henry talked about it.' And she was renowned for being able to 'canalise' (her own word) experience into art. As Nancy said, 'She had an appalling abortion in the morning and by the afternoon she'd written about it and transformed it into a work of art. It was a kind of terrific monster lurking in the background, and everyone was a bit scared of what Anaïs was going to write about them in the diary.'

Anaïs was nine years older than Nancy and Larry, and as reigning queen in the court of King Henry happily assumed the role of den mother to the young couple; she herself said that, in a symbolic way, Larry could have been Henry's and her 'writer child'. Of mixed Cuban, Spanish, French and Danish extraction, she had been brought up in Brussels, Paris, Cuba, Barcelona and

New York. Her dashing young composer and pianist father had abandoned his family when Anaïs was nine, a devastating blow from which she never fully recovered. Like Nancy, she emerged from an ugly duckling childhood to be a great beauty, though in contrast to the tall, blonde Nancy, she was small and dark, with huge eyes in a perfect oval face.

Anaïs was famous for her diary, which already filled many volumes

Since Anaïs's death in 1977, and more importantly that of her husband Hugo (Hugh Parker Guiler), more explicit extracts from her journal have been published and much more detail has emerged about her life. Nancy had read and enjoyed her dream-like *House of Incest*, but it is unlikely that she was aware that Anaïs had a passionate affair with her own father when they were reunited after an interval of twenty years. In fact, Nancy never got to know Anaïs that well. She subscribed to the accepted view that she supported Henry out of the generous dress allowance that Hugo gave her, whereas in fact Anaïs was involved in labyrinthine financial manoeuvres. She had elevated lies to the status of fine art and had coined the phrase '*mensonge vital*' – necessary lie – to justify her increasingly convoluted strategies for compartmentalising the different areas of her life. Nancy was also under the impression that the affair between Henry and Anaïs was more or less over by the summer of 1937, whereas in fact not only was it continuing, but during this time of what her biographer calls 'relative sexual stability' Anaïs was limiting her sexual activity to Hugo, Henry and Gonzalo Moré, a Peruvian of Scottish, Spanish and Indian descent. Nancy referred wistfully to the fun she might have had if she'd been able to join Anaïs with 'the Spanish refugees' she was support-ing, unaware that 'helping the Spanish refugees' was code for Nin's affair with Gonzalo.

In time, Nancy herself became caught up in the subterfuge. Anaïs writes in her journal that Nancy found a little house for her, without realising she wanted somewhere that she and Gonzalo could meet in secret. Anaïs was enchanted by the place and took it at once, but told Nancy it was too small and had in any case already been rented out. 'And thus the secret was estab-lished,' she wrote with satisfaction. Nancy would have enjoyed nothing more than being in on her friend's secrets, but Anaïs's need to compartmentalise her life, combined with Larry's deter-mination that Nancy forge no bonds with anyone apart from through him, meant their friendship never had a chance to grow. Thirty years later, after they had met up again in California, Anaïs wrote to Nancy that it had been pleasant to see her again, before adding the significant qualification, 'or rather, to really see you for the first time as I did not really know you in Paris – Henry and Larry were in the limelight'.

Thus their relationship was mediated through their menfolk. In the 1930s, even a woman as groundbreaking as Anaïs was torn between her belief that a woman artist should be the equal of a man, and a residual sense that a woman's primary role was as a handmaiden to a great man (in her case, Henry). It is hard to imagine now just how difficult it was in the 1930s for women artists to break through in a male-dominated environment, not just in a practical way, but in the far more complex matter of self-belief.

Larry had instantly impressed her, but that did not stop Anaïs from noting his increasingly public bullying of Nancy. She describes an evening the four of them spent together, which seemed to her like a long voyage, because their conversation ranged so widely, a 'beautiful flow'. She goes on to describe how Nancy's 'stutterings and stumblings', and the way she seemed to look to Anaïs to speak for her, reinforced her determination to forge a genuinely female voice, to write 'as a *woman*, in a different way from Henry and Larry'. And a little later she writes, 'Poor woman, how difficult it is to make her instinctive knowledge clear!' Anaïs understood the woman's sense of being handicapped; her own sensitivity derived from the feeling that she too was sometimes a stutterer.

'"Shut up," says Larry to Nancy,' Anaïs writes in her diary. 'She looks at me strangely, as if expecting me to defend her, explain her.' Nancy's inarticulateness inspires Anaïs to speak for all women. 'Nancy, I won't shut up,' she insists. 'I have a great deal to say, for June [Miller's estranged wife], for you, for other women.' But in the end she couldn't speak for Nancy, because they didn't know each other. Nancy didn't help the situation either, as her faith in honesty was not appreciated. Anaïs writes that when she asked Nancy her opinion of the diary, Nancy replied that she thought it was marred by 'a straining for effect'. After which, Anaïs cooled rapidly. Larry was more tactful, at least to begin with, and Anaïs had been bewitched from the start, feeling an instant connection with him, as though they had known each other for a thousand years. Like Henry, she might be dismayed by what she saw of Larry's public rudeness towards Nancy, but he was the star, the main attraction, the one whose creative ferment and brilliance was the whole reason for their friendship. In a showdown between Larry and Nancy, his new circle of friends would inevitably take his side.

But why was Nancy unable to speak up? She was not lacking in guts: she'd had the courage to break away from her stifling family and forge an independent life in London. In England and Corfu she had defended herself vigorously from Larry's bullying and in rows she was always able to give as good as she got. She was neither shy nor inarticulate, but in Paris she was in a kind of psychic purdah.

For all his *épater la bourgeoisie* bravado, Larry retained a core of conservatism and conventionality that was totally at odds with Henry's buccaneering free spirit. In Paris this tension was magnified almost unbearably. People observed the demands this conflict made on him. Fred Perlès, who had been assigned the role of court jester and had Feste's ability to observe from behind his clown's mask, noted that although Larry's conversation was brilliant, and he never stammered or groped for a word, even the most sympathetic observer was left in the dark as to his emotions. Under the Rabelaisian laughter and gusto, Larry was forever watching his audience and calculating the effect. And the person he was principally watching was Nancy.

'He could be carrying on a conversation,' Nancy explained, 'and his eyes would be darting about all the time. He'd be seeing what I was doing and then he would interrogate me afterwards.' He was jealous, fearing that Nancy would become a part of his exotic new world. He insisted that she keep her distance from everyone, even Henry and Anaïs, the two people they'd come to Paris to be with. 'We are not going to have anything to do with these people,' he'd tell her. 'We are quite different. We have quite different standards.' And if, when they were hanging out together at their favourite meeting place, the Dôme, a stranger came up and sat beside her and chatted, the repercussions were monumental. As soon as they were alone again, the interrogation was unsparing and quickly escalated. 'What were you saying to him?' Larry wanted to know. 'Why did you look at him like that? I saw you smile. Did he touch your hand? What are you becoming? You're becoming a whore!'

Nothing had prepared her for this obsessive jealousy. In Corfu they'd had rows in plenty, but there was no one there for him to be jealous of, and their arguments had been simple battles of will around how to do things, such as whether to return to shore when a storm was brewing, and in these arguments she had felt herself to be 'more or less an equal'. If his family was near by, they usually took her side. She didn't feel that she was out on a limb the way she did in Paris, where there was no one to back her up. Instead of an unimpressed Margo or Mother Durrell telling Larry to stop being a pompous ass, he now had Henry or Anaïs telling him he was a genius and a creator of miracles. Nancy was isolated, and Larry made sure things stayed that way.

To some extent it was straightforward sexual jealousy. Though he might write about sexual freedom and a freewheeling style of living, Larry had no intention of letting his beautiful young wife join the party. Double standards, sure, but he was largely faithful during the ten years they spent together, and infidelity was never one of Nancy's complaints about him. Also, now that more of Anaïs's journals have been published, it is clear that Larry had good reason to be anxious about the possible consequences if their friendship took off. A couple of years earlier, before the present period when Anaïs was limiting her sexual activity to the men she referred to as her three husbands, she had described her 'recipe for happiness' was to 'mix well the sperm of four men in one day'. Not an influence any husband would want for his beautiful wife.

One of the things Nancy always said about their Paris period was that Larry would never allow her to be alone in a room with anyone taller than him. Small-man syndrome at its most extreme. As he was five feet, four inches, this prohibition excluded pretty well all of their friends, Anaïs included. His shortness was a significant factor in the story of their marriage: years later Nancy told a friend of mine never to choose a wife taller than himself. She was not the only person to regard Larry's lack of height as significant. Perlès twice uses the word 'homunculus' in his description of Larry's appearance: 'He baffled me from the start,' he reports, and writes that he was 'a phenomenon which even slightly disturbed me ... as if I were placed face to face with a *homunculus* produced by some magician.' So not just a short man, but one whose physique was in some way abnormal. Fred said he thought Larry's lack of height was a cause of 'secret sorrow' to him, but it wasn't so secret. There had been the lighthearted suggestion that they should borrow a couple of dwarfs to be witnesses at their wedding, in case the registrar married her to Alan Thomas by mistake. A joke, yes, but a joke fuelled by insecurity. In *The Black Book*, his alter ego Lawrence Lucifer declares, 'My disease is the disease of the dwarf', and then explains that: 'To make myself plausible I am forced into a sort of self-magnification of action, of thought. I am forced to make myself transcend reality'. It must have taken huge courage to write those words, to confront his own deepest fear that he was in some way a physical freak. It must have taken even more courage to leave it in the published version. And his relationship with Nancy had been a factor, as the final section of *The Black Book* described.

He needed Nancy to remain the calm presence knitting quietly in the same room while he explored the further reaches of the wonderful and challenging new Parisian world he had set himself to conquer. The fact that she was resolutely determined to explore the world alongside him triggered all his most fundamental fears of abandonment. If the conflict between them was unequal it was partly because the stakes were different: Nancy wanted to have a good time and enjoy herself with her new circle of friends. For Larry, making sure this never happened was at some level a question of survival.

Whenever Larry fixed a goal, he was relentless. It was part of the secret of his great success, whether in writing or forging a name for himself or just simply surviving. In Kalami Theodore had noted the way he bullied Totsa over the question of windows in the top floor that was being added to the White House while they were in Paris. Totsa, knowing how winter storms pounded the house, was planning to put in small windows, but Larry 'buzzed around' and insisted 'I want two *big* windows that will take up the whole of the wall facing the sea. I *insist* on two *big* windows. I *must* have two *big* windows so that I can look out at the sea and feel as if I were actually riding the waves. Two *big* windows, mind you, each one must extend from here to here. See, I am making it so that there should be no mistakes. Two *big* windows. If I don't have two *big* windows, I shall just get up and leave and you'll never see me again!' His determination over the matter of the windows was insignificant compared to his determination that Nancy remain separate from the Miller entourage, but it gives an idea of his inexhaustible drive. As Nancy said wearily when she was asked how it was possible for one person to prevent another from making friends, 'Larry had energy enough for anything'.

*

Larry's second daughter, Sappho, was born in 1951, the only child of his second wife, Eve Cohen. She was a beautiful and apparently placid child; I remember Eve telling me, when Sappho was in her teens, that she'd 'never had a moment's trouble with her', and ever since I have been wary of children who are too docile. By her late twenties it was obvious she was seriously unhappy, and the main focus of her unhappiness centred on her relationship with her father. Through Penelope, Nancy had come to know and like Sappho, and by this time was concerned about her. Because she thought Penelope was the best person to help her sister, Nancy sat down and wrote her a long letter, by far the longest of her letters to have survived. In it she tried to explain Sappho's apparently chaotic behaviour – which her Durrell relatives put down to the fact that she was 'spoilt' – through the prism of her own experience. It is a letter full of the wisdom and honesty that was the mature Nancy at her best, wisdom that had been hard won, and to which she had no access in 1937. In fact reading it now, one gets the feeling that she is trying to give Sappho the wise counsel she herself had so desperately needed when her relationship with Larry first started to sour.

'I've been thinking about Saph,' she wrote, 'and being drawn back into my own past and the more I think the more I feel that I can understand what's been happening to Saph, perhaps better than anyone, because a lot of it happened to me.' The first thing Nancy does in her letter is to demolish the 'spoiled daughter' theory, which has been latched on to, she thinks, because it shows Larry in 'a good light as the indulgent father, and obviously Saph in a poor one. But,' asks Nancy, 'who bothers to wonder how Saph manifests any of the accepted characteristics of a "spoilt" person?' On the contrary, Saph's behaviour – 'tortured, self-hating, deprecating' – is the very opposite of spoiled. Although, she writes, 'Saph has obviously never opened her

heart to Larry, he can hardly believe her to be a happy, rollick-
ing soul.'

Larry's accusation that his problems with his daughter were all
because she was 'spoilt' was so unjust that Nancy went on to
examine exactly where the accusation had originated: who had
been spoiled in their twenties? Not Sappho, certainly, but Larry
himself. In Corfu and in Paris they had lived the life of Riley.
'During the burgeoning years,' she remembered, 'he had *no*
responsibilities of any sort. Money was unimportant. The interest on his inheritance came to three pounds a week – two could
eat on that in those days and pay a small rent. But all the travelling, books, boats, furniture etc was eked out of my capital.
What all this adds up to is that Larry was really completely
spoiled during those pre-war years and has ever since been dis-
playing the qualities typical of a spoiled personality – viz.,
insisting on having your own way in everything, insensitivity to
the feelings of others, unreasonable and violent reactions when
thwarted. Add to this a great deal of charm and Irish blarney
which can be turned on and off in a flash, and you have a picture
of someone as unlike Saph as it is possible to imagine.'

Nancy's concern for Sappho had reopened old wounds. 'When
Larry uses the adjective "spoilt" to explain Saph's behaviour, I
feel he's not just making a wrong analysis but is actually betray-
ing Saph in a way that was immediately recognisable to me and
brought back vividly the means he used to do the same to me.'
Betrayal might seem an odd word to use in this context, so she
goes on to explain by giving an example from her own experience. One incident in particular came back to her 'suddenly,
vividly, like a kick in the stomach'. It happened a few weeks after
their arrival in Paris. In Corfu, as she explains in the letter to
Penelope, they'd had a small circle of friends, but in Paris they
were part of 'a very complex, sophisticated world of people' who

were quite a bit older than themselves – 'artists and writers and bohemian café society'.

To begin with all was well. They'd had a 'tremendous welcome', but after the first few weeks Larry began to have doubts about the wisdom of letting her loose in this atmosphere of 'opening up ideas and relationships, where everyone was an individual as well as a member of the group'. It was now, Nancy wrote, that Larry began to stop her from becoming intimate with anyone in the group, or to share the experiences he was having. 'It may seem unbelievable, but he even forbade me to go and have tea with Anaïs on her barge on the Seine.' In this he was 'quite categorical. "I'm not going to have you have anything to do with them."'

Behind the scenes their rows intensified, but 'outwardly, we put up a wonderful show of being an absolutely devoted couple'. He was still proud of her 'as a possession' because she was beautiful, accomplished and apparently easygoing. But, she said, 'and this is vitally important to the understanding of this story and its meaning to me', to their new circle of friends she remained an enigma because 'I was never seen or spoken to alone; I didn't take much part in discussions.' This was all the harder as 'I loved it all and longed to join in, but I knew that, all the time when he was being his apparently most extroverted and gay self he was always conscious of what I was doing and that afterwards I would be grilled unmercifully: "What had I been saying? Why had I smiled? Did I want everyone to think I was a tart?".' As usual, it was Larry's energy that won the day. 'He had the stamina,' she said, 'to go on hour after hour.' Given all that was happening in private, it's not surprising that she was 'a bit inhibited' in public, but she knew, to her dismay, that this reserve was taken to be her natural character.

And then, it seemed, she had her chance. The Obelisk Press

was to publish the first three books (in the end, the only three books) in the Villa Seurat series: one each by Henry, Anaïs and Larry – and Nancy was going to put up the money. She was delighted, and though she'd forgotten where the idea came from she thought perhaps it had been hers. At last she'd found a way to be part of the group. The joint enterprise made her feel 'very happy and important' and gave her a feeling of 'belonging and being an active partner'.

By this time they had moved out of Fred's place in the Villa Seurat and had taken a flat overlooking the Parc Montsouris. Nancy had been so enchanted by Betty Ryan's apartment with its big windows and the bedroom and bathroom on a higher level that she had found another as similar as could be. Number 21 rue Gazan fitted the bill perfectly: a large airy studio room in a modern block, it overlooked the park and had huge, double-height windows and stairs leading up to the bedroom and bathroom on the upper level. One evening, when they were alone there together and they'd been quarrelling – again – Larry announced at about eight o'clock that he was fed up and was going out. Nancy said that, in that case, she would go out too. No, he said, he forbade her to – 'or else'. He left the unfinished threat hanging in the air as he banged out of the apartment. A little later Nancy did go out, though with no real friends in Paris she had nowhere in particular to go, so 'just wandered miserably down to Raspail and on down to the Seine' before returning home, most probably by bus. She was 'a bit apprehensive that Larry might have returned before I did', but when she got back there were no lights on. She switched on the main light by the entrance and set off up the stairs to bed. 'As I got to the top, Larry charged out of the dark bedroom and knocked me straight back down to the bottom of the stairs again.' He was 'remorseful and alarmed at the damage because it was obvious it couldn't be covered up'. As Nancy said, 'you don't get a black eye from trip-ping over'.

The next morning they had a visit from Henry. Nancy couldn't remember what story she and Larry had cooked up to explain her black eye, because in the event 'it wasn't needed'. Henry put two and two together, made an obvious five and immediately supplied the answer. Directing his apology at Larry, he said he was sorry if they had been quarrelling over using Nancy's money for the Villa Seurat books. Nancy tried to put him straight. 'Oh no, Henry—' she began, but as Henry's attention was still fixed on Larry, she turned to him, expecting him to endorse her denial. He said nothing, 'just looked sad and slightly embarrassed, as though he would deny it if he could but, in all honesty, well . . . '

Game, set and match to Larry. Not only did Nancy have 'a black eye and a limp' but she was discredited and alienated into the bargain. 'Larry, the supreme opportunist, had turned the situation to his own advantage and furthered his aim of dividing me off from the group – all with no effort at all.' The point of this story, and her reason for telling it now in her efforts to help Sappho, was that it was this sort of betrayal, 'so difficult always to put your finger on, or fight, that is so damaging and hurtful'. The black eye soon returned to normal, but the emotional hurt was harder to recover from. To Nancy it was 'not the bashes' that were important, but 'the being done down, sold up the river' and all this 'under the pretence of a united front'. The betrayal, in fact. Falling in love is a process of falling into trust, of daring to be vulnerable in the belief that the person loved will protect that trust. The betrayal comes when the person who claims to love you, whether partner or parent, uses the weapons of intimacy to score points and inflict pain.

Again the question arises: why didn't she speak up? Defend herself? Set the record straight? They'd had rows before, so why stay quiet now, when so much was at stake? For one thing she was bewildered: this was a new development and she 'didn't see the pattern'. Also, she was under his thumb, perhaps more so than she realised at the time, and not yet ready for a major confrontation. Like most people when a relationship starts to go off the rails, she thought and hoped it was a phase that would pass in time. But more importantly, as she wrote to Penelope, 'one must understand the priorities' of what she called 'Henry's world', the world of which they were both now so happy to be a part. Here, rows about money were commonplace – Henry and Anaïs had such arguments all the time – so that 'it would seem quite reasonable to them that I might say to Larry that I didn't see why I should spend my good money publishing other people's books'. The reality, the fact that Larry had left her in the flat alone and forbidden her to go out, would be quite incomprehensible to their friends, the apostles of freedom. To blow the lid off the fantasy they had created would have undermined the whole basis of their life in Paris, and this Nancy was not yet ready to do, even if she had seen clearly what was going on. For the time being Larry, the 'supreme egoist', was calling the shots.

Sexual jealousy was only one factor in Larry's almost pathological need to keep his wife apart from the Miller crowd. In fact, Nancy did not believe he really feared she would be unfaithful, because 'he knew I was utterly loyal'. In spite of the rows, they were still a couple welded together by common purpose, experience and love. He needed her, and she was far from ready to abandon him. If anything, his dependence on her was intensified during this period of dramatic change, and he was afraid that if she had allies his power over her would be weakened. But above all he was afraid that if she was ever free to talk intimately with another person, male or female, then their shameful secret might be disclosed. That must be prevented, no matter what the cost. 'They must know nothing about us,' he told her. 'Our private lives are sacred.'

In Miller's writings and in *The Black Book* sex is far more than pleasure and procreation: it is elevated to religious heights, the single most effective means of transcending the suffocating null-ity of the 'English Death'. Time and again Larry uses religious imagery to describe the sexual act: 'It is a new nativity when I enter her, the enormous city couched between her legs' and 'I lean down over you, and in a breath I fill every artery in your body with psalms.' Sex is self-discovery and revelation, the ulti-mate fulfilment and a rallying call to freedom. The primacy of loving well is an article of faith. Larry had long admired Rabelais's robust celebration of the physical and had no time for the genteel restrictions placed by bourgeois society. As apostles of this new credo, it went without saying that Larry and Nancy, like Henry and Anaïs, enjoyed a sex life of Rabelaisian proportions and intensity. Even if he was sometimes savage, cruel even, his relations with Nancy were in the spirit of their new-found religion of guilt-free, no-holds-barred sexual enjoyment. More, they were the greatest lovers since Antony and Cleopatra, Abelard and Héloïse, Romeo and Juliet ... In this they were simply adopting the kind of extravagant superlatives common in their circle. Hugo, in his diary, said of Anaïs that that she was Cleopatra, Sappho, Helen of Troy and even Christ and the fourth dimension in the flesh. (No one could ever accuse the Villa Seurat crowd of understatement.) If Larry and Nancy were part of a new race of literary titans, then their lovemaking had to be titanic as well.

But it wasn't. Among my mother's papers are a couple of hand-written pages which she jotted down as an addendum to the spoken tapes, so they must date from a few months before her death. They touch on issues it was easier to write down than to speak, but which she felt were important enough to record, almost the last words she ever wrote. For most of their married life, she says, their sexual relations had been far from easy, and on many occasions Larry had reproached her for her sexual 'passivism and apathy'. She then quotes his words directly: 'I don't want a bloody fucking block,' he used to say to her when things weren't going well. ('Fucking block' should be read as a compound noun, like 'chopping board', rather than simply a term of abuse.) The accusation had stuck in her memory, and even after forty years she quoted him verbatim.

Having read her handwritten note, it was a shock when I came across the following passage in *The Black Book* in which Lawrence Lucifer addresses his lover:

> I am weary. Do not speak to me, because you can only utter imbecilities. Shut up and function, you stale fucking block. Would you be happy if I went for your carotid with a razor, and showed you the nest of tubes and bladders which live disgustingly in your white throat?

I am always wary when biographers plunder an author's novels for details of their private life: 'Imagination!' I want to shout. 'Novelists draw on their imagination!' But Lawrence Lucifer's savage words echo Nancy's memory so precisely that it is reasonable to assume the bewildered lover's response is hers also. The passage goes on, '"Your poetry," she says in the letter, "is wild and unformed. Concentrate on style. And I don't understand *how you can both love and hate the same woman at the same time*."'

But simultaneously loving and hating his woman was precisely what Larry did. In 'Asylum in the Snow', written while they were still in Corfu, he said, 'I was the magic man. I would breathe quickly and murder my wife with language and heavy instruments ... In this way you can lie quiet beside your wife in bed and have no fear.' In Paris the ambivalence was intensified. He knew he was being unfair and cruel: he told Anaïs that after spending wonderful hours with her he went home and hacked away at Nancy with a little hatchet. Anaïs also reports the occasion when Nancy challenged him directly:

Nancy says courageously to Larry: 'Perhaps you are dissatisfied with me.'

Larry answers: 'I am, but that does not mean I want to change, or that I want anyone else.'

Although Anaïs's diaries were written and rewritten many times, and cannot by any stretch of the imagination be regarded as verbatim reports, this exchange has a definite ring of truth. Larry was tormented by a killer combination of frustration with Nancy and his profound need of her: the frustration and the conflict had poured out in *The Black Book* and in Paris it haunted him with the fear that their shameful secret, which would in his opinion have undermined his credentials as an apostle of the sexual life-force, would be revealed.

The reasons for Nancy's sexual inhibitions are not hard to uncover. Quite apart from an unfortunate choice of words – as a term of endearment, 'stale fucking block' is hardly seductive, and would be well calculated to kill all chance of spontaneous passion – there was the ever-present fear of pregnancy. In the pre-pill years it was impossible to separate sex from the risk of procreation, and late periods and pregnancy scares had dominated their first months in Corfu. Even in Paris, baby barriers at the ready, prevention could not be guaranteed. Nancy had already undergone one abortion and was not eager for another, nor, at that time, did she want a child. (Ten years later, a woman friend of Larry's told him fear of conception was a woman's greatest fear, a 'constant and besetting dread'.) Nancy was unable to relax and fully relish their lovemaking until she wanted a child.

Another element of their sexual mismatch was her complete inability to give an impression of any emotion that wasn't genuine. Faking pleasure, let alone orgasm, would have been impossible for her. It wasn't so much that she believed in being honest, more that she didn't know how to be anything else. I think this may also have contributed to her pariah status at Lincoln High. Most schoolchildren learn how they are supposed to behave in the group, to act a role in order to blend in with their peers. Nancy hadn't known how to act the part of provincial schoolgirl then, and she didn't know how to act the part of sexual partner now, unless she was genuinely aroused. Larry became more frustrated and more unreasonable, which only sapped her desire still further. It was a vicious circle in which both suffered horribly.

And so the myth of Nancy the Silent was born. After their first sojourn in Paris Anaïs wrote to Larry, saying how much she and Henry missed them both, and adding, 'I think often of Nancy's most eloquent silences, Nancy talking with her eyes, her fingers, her hair, her cheeks, a wonderful gift. Music again.' Her silence became a part of the group's mythology, turning her into a romantic child of nature, in her own words 'straight from the woods or the trees'. Anaïs would say to them, 'You're like creatures from another world. You have a secret language. Nancy is like a puma.' But Nancy was nothing like a wordless member of the big cat family, and being reduced to trying to communicate with her hair and her cheeks, far from being a wonderful gift, was a burden. She was trapped in a charade that gave her no joy and she became increasingly fed up. She had a clear memory of sitting on the edge of the group and thinking, *I might as well be part of the wallpaper. What am I? I'm wallpaper.* But she had no idea how to break free of this impossible situation.

One of the things that strikes me most about this period when Nancy was getting a far from deserved reputation for being shy and wordless, is how it echoes her childhood experience. How do you stop someone from making friends? With great difficulty, is the usual answer. But this wasn't the first time it had happened to Nancy. On family holidays her father had done his best to stop her from having friends because he needed her to keep Louise company while he played golf. She didn't make the connection herself, but the repetition of childhood patterns created a further snarl in the tangle in which she was now trapped. Larry and Thomas Myers, so unalike in most ways, were united in their desire to keep Nancy in social isolation, and her father had made Larry's job much easier. There is another uncanny echo: Larry's insistence that they had different standards and must keep apart from their bohemian friends is not so very different from her parents' belief that they were superior people and should not become intimate with their lower-class neighbours.

By December Nancy was desperate to break free, and when the opportunity arose she seized it with both hands.

Frank Capra's film *Lost Horizon*, based on the novel by James Hilton, had come out that year, and it made a huge impact on Henry and his circle; they all went to see it again and again. It tells the story of a group of survivors of a plane crash who are taken to Shangri-La, a hidden valley in the Himalayas. This mythical land, where old age and illness are unknown, is ruled with benign wisdom by a mysterious High Lama (played by Sam Jaffe). Henry was especially taken with the Jaffe role, and rather fancied ending up as a benign oriental sage. At the end of the film the outsiders leave the valley along a narrow mountain pass. George, the hero's headstrong younger brother, takes Maria, the beautiful young woman he is in love with, along too, not believing it possible she could be over a hundred years old. As they leave the magical air of Shangri-La Maria's skin wrinkles and sags on her face, she ages before their eyes and dies. In December 1937, Nancy thought she had discovered her very own Shangri-La, but the joy of it was short-lived and the consequences almost as disastrous.

Larry announced that he was going to spend three or four weeks in London over Christmas. Without her. Nancy didn't know the reasons for this decision: 'I can't remember what he wanted to do or what he said he wanted to do, or whether that was really what he wanted to do,' and nor did she care much, so long as she too was free to do her own thing. Most probably she was careful not to enquire too closely, since someone as possessive as Larry would only have been able to countenance her freedom if he had another woman in view. In Paris he had been unfaithful to her for the first time, a short affair with Teresa Epstein, though she didn't find out about this until much later. The companion he had chosen for the London trip was, unbeknownst to Nancy, a young painter called Buffie Johnson, whom she described dismissively as 'just a cheery, rather rotund girl'. Buffie and Larry had the same birthday, and she regarded Larry as a kind of twin spirit; certainly they were the same height and build. Larry told Buffie his marriage was as good as over: Nancy had gone to get a divorce and when that came through he wanted to marry his new-found twin. Together they set off for London.

Divorce was not uppermost in Nancy's mind, but she was looking forward to some uncomplicated fun and decided, for the first time, to go skiing. She told people she wanted to get away from

the city and have some fresh air and, having kitted herself out
with dark blue ski pants and jacket, and a bright yellow bobbly
sweater she'd knitted herself, she set out. Henry saw her off at the
station. He was troubled by the obvious rift between his friends,
and expressed to Larry his dismay at seeing them heading off in
different directions. He hoped Larry would soon return and nestle
down in their Paris flat, adding gently, 'I rather think you'd be
better off.'

As Switzerland was the conventional place to go, she thought
she'd have more fun in Austria and besides it was less trouble. At
the Hotel Goldener Adler in Innsbruck, where she stayed for a
night or two, she was told that Mutters was a good place, and
not far away. But Mutters, high in the Tyrol, turned out to be a
disappointment, though she did get invited to a dance in a nearby
village by a local youth, whom she described as 'a rather dull
chap'. The dance turned out to be not much better. She and the
dull chap took a taxi to the next village but, 'My memory of this
is that it was an extremely *dim* dance, only a glass of beer and
people stamping and wearing Lederhosen, very dreary.' At any
rate, not what she had travelled across Europe to find. She wrote
Larry a postcard telling him Mutters wasn't much fun and so she
was moving on.

Someone told her of a place that sounded suitably remote,
being inaccessible by road during the winter. She took a bus part
of the way, then proceeded through the snow on foot up the
valley to the single hotel at its end, and her bag was conveyed on
a sledge. She fell in love with the place at once: a small hotel
standing all alone against a backdrop of small hills and mountain
slopes. 'It was absolutely marvellous,' she said. 'Just what I was
longing for.' The sun was shining, adding to the effect which
made it, she added significantly, 'tremendously like Shangri-La'.
Not just the situation, but the company were what she needed

after those difficult Paris months. There were maybe a dozen
young people in the isolated little hotel, most of them novice
skiers like herself and none of them very expert. Even better, there
was a handsome young ski instructor who straight away paid particular attention to the beautiful, solitary girl in her bobbly yellow
sweater who had tramped through the snow to join them.

The first morning was 'absolutely lovely'. They set off for the
nursery slopes and skidded around in the snow, falling down and
laughing and generally having a wonderful time before coming in
and having lunch. In the afternoon they returned to the exhil-
aration of the slopes and in the evening after supper they played
games, including 'a sort of bar billiards', said Nancy vaguely – she
was never one of life's games players – adding that it was 'that
thing where the billiard ball goes into the holes, or knocks things
over. Or something.' The precise details of the game were unimportant, compared to the sheer fun of it. And they sang songs.
The next day the same blissful formula was repeated: sunshine
and hilarity on the ski slopes, good humour and easy company
over meals and in the evening. The ski instructor was showing
definite signs of interest, which Nancy enjoyed, but most important of all she was relaxed and happy, revelling in uncomplicated
pleasures almost for the first time in her life. It was 'a wonderful
release after Paris. Absolute bliss.'

On the third night, soon after she had gone to sleep, she was
woken by a noise at the door. The light came on, and there in
the doorway stood Larry. He was in a foul temper, claiming
he'd had to walk from Paris – a slight exaggeration – but he had
made the last part of the journey on foot, stumbling up the
valley through the snow while someone walked beside him with
a lamp. 'I don't think,' said Nancy, 'my heart has ever sunk quite
as much as it did at the sight of a cross, cold, damp Larry arriving just as I thought I was going to have a most wonderful time

in this place.' His luggage was weighed down with a couple of very heavy art books he'd brought her as Christmas presents. 'I know,' said Nancy, 'because he practically hit me on the head with them.'

Then came the inevitable interrogation. What had she been doing? She tried to fend him off with vague statements: 'This is an awfully nice place.' But he was having none of it. 'Why did you tell me you were *not* having a good time?' he wanted to know. 'You've been lying to me again!' The cross-examination lasted most of the night, and when they went down to breakfast the following morning he refused to say good morning to her new-found 'jolly friends'.

'As soon as you've finished breakfast we're off,' he told her. They ate their breakfast and, while everyone else went off to enjoy themselves in the sunshine on the ski slopes, she and Larry trudged miserably back to Mutters, where they checked in to a 'most dreary hotel' though at that moment it is probable that any hotel would have seemed dreary to her. It got worse, because they had no money to get back to Paris, and had to wait in the Goldener Adler while Nancy telegraphed the bank for cash. In the meantime, they made a pretence of having a skiing holiday; she bought Larry skis and a skiing outfit, and they slid around for an hour or two most mornings, but Larry wasn't really interested and refused to mix with any of the other holidaymakers. Most of that week was spent cooped up together in the hotel bedroom. The details were vague in Nancy's memory. 'He wanted me to do a drawing of some sort, a woodcut of two animals. He wanted it for a card or something.'

Their new-year card survives: an image of a lion and a unicorn, nursery-rhyme creatures famous for their fighting. 'The lion beat the unicorn / All around the town'. And Nancy's unicorn looks most subdued. All Nancy remembered clearly was that it was a

'The lion beat the unicorn / All around the town', goes the nursery rhyme

'*nightmare* week'. The interrogations were unremitting, to a degree which she found almost incredible when she looked back. 'This doesn't sound believable,' she commented when talking about this period, but when Larry learned that she had been in a taxi with someone (the chap who had taken her to the dance) he reacted with horror. 'He said his faith in me had entirely gone. He'd never trust me again. How could I have done it? I was nothing but a whore, and so on and so on . . .'

Writing to Henry, Larry put a mock-heroic gloss on the whole dismal business, describing it as his 'crazy catapult jump across Europe to join Nancy', and invoking the spirit of the film that was so much a part of their mythology at the time. 'I tell you Conway made no more violent attempts to reach Shangrila than I did to deliver my little Christmas present.' He congratulated himself on the clever detective work which had made it possible for him to run her to earth at four o'clock on Christmas morning, though he did let slip that now they were tearing each other's hair out. But he ends by addressing Henry as 'my dear Conway' and saying blithely, 'Shangrila for ever!' As so often, the conventions of their correspondence meant private misery was portrayed as farce.

This striving for jollity masked deep hurt and pain. A notebook entry, dated 2 January in the Goldener Adler, seems to hark back to the tranquillity of Loxwood: 'Let /A sedative evening bring steaming cattle, contagion of sleep, / Deeper, purer, surer even than Eden.' There is nothing worse than a reunion where both parties remain resolutely, wretchedly alone, and that week trapped together in a dreary hotel room was hell for them both. Just why Larry had abandoned his London trip is not known, though Buffie, in spite of his mention of marriage and her devotion, had insisted on separate rooms. It was the decision of a moment. 'Have fled' he scrawled in a note dated 23 December. But the speed and fury of his dash across Europe was the product of real panic and the fear of losing the wife who was still central to his life.

Miserably, no longer enjoying being together but by no means ready to separate, they returned to Paris. If things had been bad before, Nancy's Austrian adventure made everything ten times worse. From then on their marriage in its down periods forced each of them to live out their worst nightmares. Larry, advocate of lovemaking as a religious imperative, was harnessed to a wife whom he still loved and didn't want to part from, but who was sometimes as unresponsive as a 'fucking block'. Nancy, for whom honesty and authenticity were all important, not just as ideals but as a way of surviving, was obliged to live a lie, to pretend, cover up and create an illusion that all was well when it wasn't.

It was a grim contrast to their joyous arrival in Paris less than five months earlier. The year 1938 had got off to the worst of all possible starts.

8

TIME TASTED

In early April 1938 Nancy and Larry boarded the train in Paris and headed south once more. Nancy was excited at the prospect of returning to Corfu and seeing the family again. The beginning of the year had been hard for both of them: 'sad and difficult days', in Larry's words, and after eight months of city life, they were more than ready to let the island work its summer magic. In spite of the fractures in their relationship, both were making strides with their work. Larry had continued to consolidate links with writers whose opinion he valued, such as T. S. Eliot and Dylan Thomas, *The Black Book* was about to be published by Jack Kahane's Obelisk Press, and two more issues of *The Booster* had appeared, with another due in April. Nancy meanwhile had finally broken through and achieved a degree of recognition as an artist in her own right within the Villa Seurat group. 'A PERSON' at last.

It was Henry who first singled out her painting. He took a keen interest in the visual arts and had begun to create his highly original paintings a few years before. Though painting was for him always a secondary activity, he brought his trademark passionate intensity to the work. While in Paris, Nancy mostly did water-colours – probably because they were more portable than oils.

Nancy was delighted to return to Corfu

She was painting 'made-up things' at this time and, she said, 'they were very distinctly not like anyone else's'. A poem they had been reading and which had a particular meaning for Henry inspired one of her few oils: a forest fire in vibrant reds and purples, with abstract animals racing through the flames. Henry's response was electric. 'Gee,' he told her, and Nancy felt his whole attitude towards her change in an instant, 'I never thought you could do anything like this! The things of yours I'd seen before I didn't think much of them' (praise with a distinct sting in the tail, but Nancy seems not to have minded), 'but gee, this is marvellous!' Overwhelmed by his enthusiasm, she promptly gave him the painting, which he hung over his desk and showed off to everybody who came by. His praise gave Nancy what she had longed for all along: the feeling that she really belonged to the group on her own terms. Now she was in the club, 'because

Henry kept wagging his head in his very sweet way and saying, "Gee, that is marvellous!"' – her rendition of Henry's New York accent consisted of simply sticking 'Gee' before every phrase. For once, Larry didn't mind her getting the attention because it was acceptable for her to be an artist. And so, in those first months of 1938, she started to believe in herself again.

A painter whose approval carried even more weight was Hans Reichel, a dramatic character who was revered by Henry. According to Nancy, Reichel had an almost sacred place in the Villa Seurat circle; his dedication to his work and his utter disregard for money meant Henry saw him as 'inviolate and pure'. Nancy regarded him as ancient (he was in his mid forties) and, far from appearing 'inviolate and pure', he reminded her of the child murderer played by Peter Lorre in the film M. He was a shambling, fat, rather drunken figure, 'squat and toad-like and speaking quaint English with a heavy German accent'. He gave an impression of being tragic, pathetic and tremendously over-emotional. But this penniless and physically unappealing man created small paintings of astonishing vividness and colour, which she deemed '*exquisite*', rather in the manner of some Paul Klees – not so surprising, as Reichel had shared a studio with Klee before coming to Paris in 1929. These beautiful watery jewels showed eyes and fishes and flower shapes, all filled with mystery and translucent colours. One phrase of his stuck in her mind as being particularly beautiful and capturing something of what he was trying to achieve: 'Two flowers looking mutual in each other's eyes.'

According to Nancy, Reichel loathed having to sell any of his paintings, and only did so when driven by absolute desperation. What he liked best was to sit in his tiny room surrounded by his work, only occasionally consenting to be winkled out for a meal: whenever he got the chance he would drink as much as he could.

Nancy was amazed and delighted when this strange man singled out one of her unfinished paintings for scrutiny. The piece was more abstract than anything she had attempted before, a peasant woman in a Henry Moore-ish shell-like coil, done in greys and blacks. Reichel regarded it for a long time before pronouncing his verdict. 'It is good,' he told her in his heavily accented English. 'You see, there is a way in *here*, and there is a way out *there* also.' She never forgot what she called the 'savour of generous appreciation' of her paintings as an interesting small world in embryo. And then, as 'a salute from one artist to another', he gave her one of his paintings. An early work, it was intensely dark with a moon and a fragment of house. She was delighted, as much by the recognition as by the painting itself, and she took it back to the studio flat overlooking the Parc Montsouris. Larry's reaction came as a shock: he was 'absolutely livid' and insisted she return it at once. 'I don't know why,' she commented, because 'he couldn't possibly have been jealous of Reichel. But he didn't like me having anything he didn't have.' In fairness to Larry it's also possible that he didn't think a painter as hard up as Reichel should ever give his work away. Anyway, the painting was duly returned, to Nancy's lasting regret.

But the boost to her self-confidence remained and was reinforced by Henry's continuing encouragement. Soon after their return to Corfu, Henry added a message for her to his letter to Larry: 'But a word to Nancy, the old gal, who I suppose is "you" always in the Black Book. Who is this "you"? Nancy, how are you? . . . Will I be seeing you soon? I wonder. But I am happy that we got to know each other finally. You were sprouting like a cauliflower – the last few days in Paris.' And he concludes with some advice: 'Don't let Larry browbeat you! Give him tit for tat! Incidentally, everybody finds your pictures interesting, original etc.' After that, Henry's letters often contained a message for

Nancy. And although he complained that 'the old girl never writes me', he added that 'I think of her always, and wonder how to make her more of a success than she already is.' At one time Henry toyed with the idea of a joint exhibition of their work in London. Also, during those first months after their return to Corfu, Larry wrote enthusiastically that Nancy had begun to paint the most astonishing stuff – 'So assured and herself that it is wonderful' – though as the summer wore on and visitors arrived she had less and less time for painting. One gets the impression that he was trying to repair the damage of the winter by praising her work, at one time telling Henry that only being with him and his swollen egotism held her back. Yet none of this work remains. All was lost or destroyed in the panic and dislocation of war.

Or so I had thought. But in the Henry Miller archive at the University of California Los Angeles, among a pile of letters from Larry to Henry, I found a folded piece of cartridge paper with an unfinished sketch in bold colours of a peasant woman standing in front of two cows. Across the bottom he has written, 'All these I found among her throw-outs – a hopeless ass (unofficial) about destroying her own stuff!' Is it any good? I find it impossible to judge, but considering it was an unfinished and rejected sketch it offers a tantalising glimpse of what her 'good' paintings might have been like. Poor Nancy, how mortified she would have been to think that the only example of her painting to have survived from the 1930s was something she had thrown away.

Looking back on those years before the outbreak of war, Larry gave the impression they had existed in a self-made bubble of almost pre-lapsarian innocence, entirely untouched by the worsening political situation, but their letters tell a different story. From their very first months in Corfu, Italian expansion was a genuine threat: twelve years earlier the Italians had occupied the island for almost a month, and during that summer of 1935 they seemed to be about to do so again. Mussolini's troops had over-run Abyssinia and, as Larry wrote at the time, if there was any place the Italian leader wanted more than Abyssinia, it was Corfu. Italian bomber planes flew over the town to reconnoitre, and Larry and Nancy, like the rest of the population, were 'scared shitless'. The League of Nations remained passive in the face of Italian aggression, just as it had when the Japanese invaded Manchuria in 1931. The 'peace' between the two great wars was anything but peaceful. For most of the Durrells' Corfu years, Spain was being torn apart by civil war, as savage as such fratri-cidal conflicts always are. Most English writers took a stand and some, like George Orwell, even joined the fighting.

In 1936 Hitler had moved troops into the Rhineland and by 1938 he was calling for the Sudetenland to be annexed as well. On 12 March 1938, just a few weeks before Nancy and Larry left Paris, Austria was absorbed into the Third Reich, yet another contravention of the 1919 Treaty of Versailles. By the summer the German military machine seemed unstoppable, and the proper response was by no means as obvious as it seems in retro-spect. In France and England, those in favour of appeasing aggression were in the ascendant. 'No more Passchendaeles!' was a popular sentiment. Later that same year, as German pressure on the Sudetenland increased, President Roosevelt made it clear that America would remain neutral in the event of a new European war.

Against this backdrop, Larry's position was clear. On their first trip to Athens in 1936 he had mocked the Germans who were infesting the Acropolis and filling everything with their 'fum-phen sthinekel language, just like a lot of men imitating trains'. But he was neither an appeaser nor a hawk. He deliberately retreated into his 'Heraldic Universe', which he described as the proper place for that 'queer fish' the artist to inhabit. It was his belief that writers who felt driven to engage politically had confused the inner struggle with the outer one. He said that politics was 'an art that dealt in averages', whereas the artist was driven by 'his self isolation and the dislocation of the societal instinct'. Nancy sympathised with this position; she never expressed anything but the vaguest political opinions, since she was not one to pontificate on anything unless she felt well-informed. Larry's instincts were essentially conservative, and to some extent this is true of Nancy also, but her elitist love of excellence was tempered by an instinctive sympathy for the underdog, so simple political loyalties were alien to her.

They might try to distance themselves from events on the world stage, but they were anything but oblivious to what Larry termed 'the impending cataclysm'. It was impossible to ignore the fact that something terrible was going to happen at some stage in the future – but what or when was anyone's guess. People as diverse as George Orwell and Henry Miller were clear that the world they knew was about to be swept away, and no one had any notion of what might take its place. They were staring into a dark tunnel, with no certainty of light at the other end. France and Britain might be convulsed by bloody revolution, as Russia had been twenty years before; or torn to pieces by civil war like Spain; or, perhaps most likely, the German Empire could come to dominate Europe entirely. With the future so uncertain and so dark, it is perhaps not surprising that people turned to fortune-tellers and seers, like the astrologer Conrad Moricand, who had such an influence on Henry and who provided detailed horoscopes for both Larry and Nancy. All that could be predicted with confidence was that their Mediterranean idyll could not last.

And so they made the most of it. As Larry said at the time, the continuing threat of war sharpened the minute 'so that each tick of time going through is time tasted; unbearably sweet even if trivial things and idiots intervene'. But until those trivial things and idiots destroyed their fragile equilibrium, they intended to devote themselves to what they believed in: creating lasting works of art and having a roaring good time.

Back on the island again, Nancy was delighted to be reunited with the family. While they had been in Paris, Mother Durrell had shifted her younger children to the third of their Corfu villas, Villa Cressida, the snow-white villa of *My Family and Other Animals*. Idyllic in retrospect, the Corfu period was, in Nancy's opinion, a mixed blessing for Larry's siblings. Gerry had no proper education – though Theodore's mentoring probably more than made up for this – and as Nancy was so keenly aware of the failings of her own schooling she didn't like to see others missing out. Margo had received no education of any kind since 1935, when she was sixteen. Worse, she had begun to suffer from some kind of glandular complaint that caused massive weight gain – putting on 'a pound a day' according to Larry. She had been packed off to England, where they tried to figure out what was wrong with her, but she remained plump, with the result that the usual self-consciousness of the teenage girl was magnified tenfold, and for a while she was so embarrassed by her ballooning figure that she refused even to join the family for meals.

But it was Leslie who fared worst. He had always been the butt of Larry's mocking humour and vitriol, and a damaged eardrum, legacy of fights at school in Dulwich, prevented him from swimming with the others. Instead he hung out with the local field police, whom Nancy described with hauteur as 'a very low category of person': young men who tramped about the countryside with rifles over their shoulders but no very clear idea of what they were looking for. As she said, 'it wasn't much of an existence' for a twenty-year-old, though at the time Leslie would probably have disagreed. His consuming passion was weapons, and he had three or four different guns which he was always polishing and cleaning. When he got angry with Larry – a frequent occurrence, as Larry would needle him mercilessly, telling him what an idiot he was and how he'd wrecked his life – Leslie often turned his gun on him. Having suffered himself, he hated to see Nancy on the receiving end of Larry's verbal battering and took on the role of her champion. Sometimes when they were quarrelling Leslie rushed into the room with his gun aimed at Larry and roared that he'd shoot him if he didn't stop.

'And,' added Nancy thoughtfully, 'sometimes I really thought he would.'

When I started on this memoir Nancy had been dead for more than a quarter of a century and Larry for nearly twenty years. Theodore, Henry, Anaïs, Larry's siblings – all were dead. I assumed that every link with pre-war Corfu had been severed, but I was wrong. Nancy always referred to summer 1938 as 'the summer of the dancers' and one of those dancers is still very much alive. In March 2010 I took the train to the north-western tip of Devon to meet her, and over a thoroughly enjoyable visit gained a fresh perspective on a period I had previously only seen through the lens of Nancy's memory.

During the winter of 1937–8 Larry had met a young woman called Veronica Tester at the Players' Club in London. He was taken with her at once – hardly surprising, since as well as being an accomplished dancer and acrobat, Veronica was highly intelligent and widely read. On a later trip to London he met her friend Dorothy Stevenson, the daughter of an Australian bishop and an excellent classical dancer who was later offered a coveted place with the Ballets Russes. Enchanted by their mix of showbiz glamour and intellectual curiosity, he invited the two women to visit Corfu in the summer. When she received fifty pounds for a twenty-first birthday present, that is what Veronica did. Dorothy followed soon after.

Veronica remembered her summer months in Corfu as an enchanted time. She was impressed by Nancy, who welcomed them warmly even though she had never met them before, and took care of all the practical arrangements. The days in Kalami followed a simple pattern: they all rose early, at about six o'clock, and went for a swim. After breakfast they worked through the morning – Larry writing, Nancy painting and the girls doing their dance exercises. A simple lunch was followed by a siesta and then a late-afternoon swim. They ate supper on the flat rock beside the house while the light faded and the Albanian coastline was swallowed by the darkness, talking, listening to music, enjoying the precious moment – magical, never-to-be forgotten evenings.

As the summer progressed they made the trek over to the deserted beach on the west coast of the island. Veronica went with Larry in the boat, while Nancy and Dorothy took a donkey with the supplies. Here they slept on the beach and lived a life of almost mythic simplicity: they were woken in the mornings by the shepherd and shepherdess who wound their way down the hillside with their flocks; they danced naked on the edge of the sea, drew patterns in the sand and sat round a fire in the evenings, while Larry brought the Greek myths to life and sketched out the germ of his idea for the multi-layered novel he was planning to write. His conversation was intoxicating and seductive, but in spite of the rumours that grew up around their presence on the island Veronica was adamant that there had been not a hint of sexual engagement between them. And through all this Nancy seemed kindly and practical, but reserved and always a little remote.

Veronica and I talked on. What had that summer been like for my mother, she wanted to know. 'Well,' I said, 'she had felt excluded, a little left out. It was an uncomfortable time for her.'

'Yes,' Veronica replied, recognising the truth of this at once. 'I always wondered.' They had admired the way she coped; they thought she and Larry complemented each other and were well suited, but then she added, apparently contradicting herself, she had felt the presence of the two women that summer had acted as a safety valve. Still, she said, they had never felt they knew her at all.

What about the trip that she and Nancy made to Athens in October, after Dorothy had returned to London, I asked. In one of his letters to Henry, Larry describes being alone in Kalami while 'Nancy and V are somewhere in Athens bless them, probably celebrating their escape from the tyrant.' In Athens, surely she and Nancy got to know each other a little more, but Veronica was perplexed. She remembered Larry being with them, even when in Athens. I have puzzled over this anomaly, and two possibilities occur to me: either they made two trips to Athens, one with Larry and one without, or else the memory of his personality was so indelibly printed on that whole summer that it had become impossible to imagine him not being there. The inconsistency is salutary, I think, though at first I was keen to iron it out. Nancy never mentioned the trip to Athens, but somewhere between the written evidence and the vivid personal memories the events of that summer fracture and shimmer, for ever out of reach. So many versions, so many stories, flow from those simple summer days.

Nancy's memory of those months was less rosy. She bore no ill will towards the two dancers. In fact, she and Veronica met up again after the war and might have become friends except that Veronica was moving to Northern Ireland and they lost touch.

Nancy's verdict was typically understated: '1938 wasn't a good summer for me. Larry was being very pesky. He loved having a flock of young girls. It was wonderful for him to dance about pretending to be Pan, dancing naked on the beach. And Veronica did the most wonderful acrobatics.' When they slept under the stars on the western beach he placed himself between the two girls, with Nancy kept at a distance. In the circumstances, pesky seems quite mild.

As we talked on, Veronica indicated that she had in fact been aware that all was not well between husband and wife. She asked me if Nancy's childhood had been unhappy, saying she had got the impression that she'd had negative experiences in the east of England. Yes, I told her. Her family was not happy. I thought so, said Veronica, and repeated what she remembered of Larry's opinion: 'Just the kind of depressed Englishness I can't stand' had been his take on the emotional baggage Nancy was still carrying from her childhood.

When Veronica saw them again, in London the following winter, she noted how Nancy was relegated to the role of skivvy, preparing meals and clearing up while the literary men and the unattached young women enjoyed the talk and the laughter. Being a canny young woman, Veronica decided the life of a literary wife was not for her – a chilling echo of Nancy's reaction to the faded and depressed artists' wives she had encountered during her time as an object of desire at art school. Now, although her financial independence made some difference, she was in danger of sliding into that dismal situation herself.

Then, in the autumn of 1938, as Europe hovered on the brink of catastrophe with the Munich Crisis and her relations with Larry had still not recovered from the dramas of the previous months, Nancy made one of the strangest decisions of her life: she wanted a child. Larry, not surprisingly, was baffled, as indicated in a letter to Henry: 'Bored to death by uncertainty: now of course, Nancy wants to have a child the slut ... What sort of animal vegetable mineral is a woman's mind?'

Looking back, Nancy struggled to find the answer. 'We've got to the summer in Corfu after Larry's and my first winter in Paris,' she wrote, 'when the unhappiness of our marriage has obviously shown – had become really restrictive to me. I had made an attempt to get a temporary respite which made everything worse afterwards.' As she herself wrote at this time, 'there seemed to be no trust, no love' and in brackets she has added 'what is love? – no loving kindness between us'. And yet, not only did she remain with him, but they were still inseparable. 'What kept us together?' she asks. 'For if it takes two to quarrel it equally takes two to stay inseparable, as we were supposed to be – and were in fact.' She was coming to regard Larry as 'disloyal and traitrous, dissembling, domineering and in many other ways impossible to combine with satisfactorily', and so wondered 'why then did I deliberately decide I wanted a child with him?'

Good question. In retrospect it seemed as if her marriage had already turned into a battle ground, the second European war was imminent and their money was running out. The timing could not have been worse. Nonetheless the reasons for her overwhelming urge to have a child are perhaps not so hard to find. Knowing Larry as well as she did, it is unlikely that she saw a baby as a way to fix a failing relationship. Probably their relationship did not at the time seem as hopeless as it did in retrospect. Once they were back in Corfu there was so much they both loved: his family and the island forged bonds that must have felt unbreakable. But, more than anything else, I think she was simply lonely, and wanted something – someone – to love. Her first impulse towards Larry had been a maternal one: his baby talk during their first weeks together elicited her instinctive love of nurturing the helpless. Now the needy child had become 'the tyrant' and her mothering instincts were thwarted. She wanted a baby.

The immediate effect was on her attitude to sex, and this became for her the most relaxed and enjoyable period sexually of their married life. 'I couldn't have enough of it,' she said, which reinforces the idea that her memory of 'all love gone' did not apply to this period after all, since she would never have felt voracious desire for a man she no longer loved. As a result of her new enthusiasm, Larry stopped being importunate; in fact, as far as she could remember he failed to take full advantage of her active enthusiasm. She was slightly disappointed after all his reproaches at her passivity. Passive no longer, she was happy to relax and enjoy herself.

Like much else about her parenting, my mother's take on sex education was quite unlike that dished out by the mothers of my friends. When I was sixteen, a time when my friends were being told (this was the mid 1960s) to save themselves for Mr Right and never to be 'cheap'. ('Men won't respect you if you go all the way' was the usual threat.) Nancy took a different view. One afternoon, in the furnishing fabric department of Heals, our conversation drifted from the relative merits of William Morris or modern Swedish design to the 'how far should you go?' debate. She said firmly and clearly that *not* to make love when you were *in* love was selfish and wrong, which drew the attention of our fellow shoppers. 'Let's continue this at home,' she said with a smile. But as so often with Nancy, what might have been a straightforward green light came with a subtle caveat. Being in love was critical, and making love was not to be confused with just having sex. Once back at the flat she said with equal clarity, 'Making love when you're in love, and just having sex with some-one is like the difference between Rubinstein playing Chopin on a concert grand and an amateur playing chopsticks on a broken-down old upright.' As an image, it was an effective prophylactic. For some time, whenever things started to get steamy her words echoed in my mind, and as I drew breath and contemplated the current youth I was with, 'chopsticks on a broken-down old upright' seemed the most likely scenario.

But now, reading what she wrote about that last year before war broke out, I wonder if she was being entirely accurate. It is impossible to know how much in love she was with Larry at this time. Perhaps for her the truth was even simpler: making love when you're not frightened of becoming pregnant, making love when you want to create a new life to love – that, for Nancy, was the secret of sexual happiness.

And so we come to the end of her spoken memoir. Her voice captured on the tape recorder, with my father prompting her as best he could, Nancy said thoughtfully, 'It's funny that at the moment I can't think about what really happened [in the summer of 1938] except for Veronica and Dorothy, who stayed with us. I can't think of what else we did that summer particularly. Perhaps there wasn't anything very particular about it. We just went on our boats and lived our lives.'

With those words the final tape ends. Though Edward suggested from time to time that they carry on, in the last few months she couldn't summon the energy, or was simply too focused on her battle to beat her illness, to continue with her reminiscences. Which is a loss, of course, but as an epitaph to the Corfu days it is singularly fitting, all the simple ease and contentment of their summer idylls caught in those last few words: 'we just went on our boats and lived our lives'.

Most of the last winter before the war was spent in London. They borrowed a flat in Campden Park Road, near Notting Hill Gate, from Anaïs's husband Hugo. Paris was still important to them, but London was the centre of the literary action and Larry was trying to get T. S. Eliot to publish his poems on the Faber list. Eliot regarded him as, to his dismay, primarily a prose writer. (Nancy's view, all her life, was the opposite. She thought that poetry was the core of Larry's creation, and she took a somewhat dim view of most of his prose after *The Black Book*, including *The Alexandria Quartet*.) They enjoyed hooking up with the friends they had made the previous winter, but now Nancy was, if not resigned, then at least getting used to her subordinate role in their social life. She made the practical arrangements and provided the meals. 'My mum made an omelette for T. S. Eliot' was a happy teenage boast in certain situations. If ever she felt aggrieved by her lot, she only had to look at the fate of most other literary wives to know she was well off by comparison: Caitlin Thomas, stuck in a primitive cottage in Wales with no money, was having a wretched time, and Nancy was keenly aware of the difference her financial independence made. She might be virtually silenced but she was not, thank God, impoverished.

The exception to this pattern of exclusion was Henry Miller. In the last months of 1938 the Durrells' relations with him underwent a subtle transformation, and here again Nancy's money played a role. In September 1938 the Munich Crisis made all-out war seem inevitable and Henry fled Paris, first to Bordeaux and then Marseilles; from there he could, if need be, get a boat to the United States and safety. A pacifist through and through, Henry was as honest about his lack of courage as he was about his other shortcomings. Anaïs poured contempt on him for running away, but his abject panic was all of a piece with the rest of him. If real courage is acting bravely even when terrified, it would clearly have been alien to a man who believed only in acting how he really felt, and in that month he was definitely afraid. Marooned in Marseilles, he fell into a depression, which was made worse because he couldn't afford to leave. Nancy arranged for funds to be sent to him from London, and though in the event he didn't need to use them he was enormously touched by her prompt response, and in his next letter to Larry asked him to thank Nancy 'personally' for all her trouble.

Three months later they offered financial rescue again. Henry's birthday fell on 26 December, but since childhood he had always loathed and dreaded Christmas; and this year it looked as if he would be broke and alone as usual. With Larry, Nancy and Fred all in London, Anaïs with Hugo, and no money at all, he was contemplating a lonely and meagre few days. Once again Nancy arranged funds to be sent, he travelled to London and they had a thoroughly enjoyable time together. As always, Nancy loved Henry's ebullience and straight talk and he continued to champion her paintings and give Larry sensible advice, telling him he should stick with Nancy because she would give him the whole technique of life. On another occasion he told Larry to prepare for Nancy making a big hit with her paintings, and added, 'Don't squelch her! Give her plenty of time and space!' But time was what none of them was going to have for long.

While they were in London, the peace that had been brokered in Munich was unravelling. 'England facing war', declared the newspapers in January. The catastrophe was only a matter of time and return to Corfu, so vulnerable to Italian aggression, seemed an unlikely prospect. Where were they to go? Cornwall and America were two possibilities, but as spring advanced the heart of England, the most English bit of the despised 'Pudding Island', produced an unexpected surprise. Nancy and Larry visited Stratford-upon-Avon, and Larry was bowled over. He wrote ecstatically to his new friend, the poet Anne Ridler who worked with Eliot at Faber, about the Warwickshire countryside: 'As you drop over the border by Long Compton there is an air of another territory; the country arches and curves, and ... you feel you have reached ... a kind of green limbo ... From this point until you reach the swan that lulls so soft under the Trinity spires, you hold your breath.' Nancy's response to this spring-magic landscape is not recorded, but ten years later she visited it again, for halfway between Long Compton and Stratford is the Cotswold village of Ilmington, a place she was to come to know well, and to sketch many times: it was the home of her future in-laws.

But it is Larry's musings on Shakespeare's last years in this same letter that are most interesting, since they highlight his ambivalence about the business of being a writer and what it meant to him. A constant refrain throughout all his letters is a longing *not* to write, a fear of the cost demanded of him and those near him when he pushed his gifts to their limits. It is easy to see this as a meaningless form of self-deprecation, but I think it was more than this, and there is a core of truth in his fear of his abilities – the fear that Anaïs observed. In Stratford during those sunny April days he felt he came close to the 'real' Shakespeare: not the writer of genius, as one might expect, but the solid citizen of a small provincial town who had matured to the point where he no longer needed to write. What others have seen as creative exhaustion or the drying up of inspiration, Larry regarded quite differently. In his opinion Shakespeare had at last outgrown his art and entered his manhood. He writes, 'Across this silence [of the last five years] I seem to hear the quiet lucid notes of musical LIVING fall at last.' It was the state Larry himself yearned to achieve but never did, the place where living – and loving – were all.

Nancy also. As a miserable schoolgirl she had devoured Fielding Hall's account of Burmese Buddhism and its values coloured her life, so she was in complete sympathy with Larry's devotion to the writings of Lao Tzu, that being was more important than doing.

The place where both were able to 'be' most effectively was Corfu. When Larry was fretting in London, Dylan Thomas wrote wanting to know why he was still there. What's the matter, he asked, had they moved Corfu? In spite of the descent towards war, the pull of the island was strong and they returned to the place they both loved more than anywhere else for the last summer of peace.

An illustration for 'The Magnetic Island', a Corfu-inspired legend
that was dedicated to Theodore

'The Magnetic Island' is the title of a strange story Larry wrote that year; it reads as though inspired by the local legends they had heard from Theodore, to whom it was dedicated. Nancy produced three Cocteau-esque line drawings to accompany it. She also provided the black-and-white photographs which accompany the article Larry had published in the *Geographic Magazine* that spring. Her abilities as a photographer had improved since the days of Witch Photos.

From early in their friendship, Larry had been trying to persuade Henry to visit them in Corfu. He sang the praises of the island, painted a picture of lotus-eating and creative ferment, cajoled and tempted, but without success. Henry loathed travel and so long as he had a place to work and enough cash for his basic needs, he saw no need to go scampering off to places unknown. Perhaps it was due to a sense that time was running out, but in July 1939 Henry suddenly turned traveller. He headed south, took the ferry from Athens to Corfu and fell in love with all things Greek. The story of the next few months, in Corfu, Athens and the Peloponnese, inspired *The Colossus of Maroussi*, which many regard as his best book. His intoxication burns on every page.

Kalami was pure pleasure. Larry and Nancy practically lived in the sea, Henry noted, swimming like dolphins. The house was 'ample and gracious', and at night he heard the water lapping under his window. He saw his friends in a new light since 'Larry and Nancy are sort of distinguished here.' They went to the nearby cove of St Arsenius and swam naked. Henry fell into the routine familiar to all their guests, but true to form he was the most enthusiastic of them all, and his enjoyment intensified their own. He revelled in meeting the people he had heard about – the family, Spiro, the schoolteacher, their landlords Totsa and Eleni. They watched shooting stars and Theodore pointed out the constellations. They went by boat along the coast, picnicked, swam, lounged in the sun. Able to unwind, perhaps for the first time in his life, Henry gave himself up to the joy of just being; he wrote nothing, didn't even want to read very much. They went round the island and camped on their favourite beach, sat round a fire in the evening and were woken by goatherds in the morning. Back at Kalami, they spent their evenings on the flat rock in front of the house, lulled by the sound of the sea.

In retrospect, those final weeks in their island paradise were almost the best of all because they were shared with Henry at last. And then it was over.

One of the many aspects of life on the island guaranteed to make the British expat feel at home is the Corfiot obsession with the weather, especially the winds. Each kind of wind had its own name and personality, and Nancy described them lovingly. The Maestro was a strong wind that turned the sea a dark navy blue and beat the waves into white horses; it whipped the olive trees until their undersides showed, 'so they were all shimmering pale grey against this navy blue with white splodges. Maestro was a coolish wind,' she said, 'and always very strong. The master wind.' Then there was the Tramontana ('over the mountains') which was a hottish, sultry sort of wind. The Sirocco was the same as siroccos everywhere in the Middle East: another hot southern wind, also sultry and rather unpleasant. Her favourite was the Kareklas, the only wind to have a Greek rather than an Italian name, and so perhaps the most local to Corfu. *Karekla* means chair, and the Kareklas blew over the chairs on the esplanade. Nancy described it as 'a charming wind – the chair wind'.

The weather was out of joint at the end of August when the King returned suddenly to Athens and the Greek army was mobilised; war between England and Germany had not yet been declared, but it was only a matter of days. Mother Durrell had already headed back to England, warned by her bank that they would no longer be able to guarantee her money once war broke out. Larry and Nancy made the decision to head for the relative safety of Athens. Larry described their last hours in Kalami in a letter to Anne Ridler: they packed up their belongings in the White House while 'vast Japanese craters of cloud' massed over Albania and 'a dazzling thin rain like star-dust' fell. As they stood on their balcony for the last time, 'it seemed like the end of the world. The whole hillside lay with its cheek in a cloud, the cypresses all stiff and priapic with dew.' Totsa and Eleni's children were weeping in the garden, and when they found a boat to take them to Athens the scenes of farewell and separation were heartbreaking. Six weeks later, from the safety of Athens, Larry said simply, 'I am cut to the heart and dumb.'

At about the same time he wrote a letter to Anaïs which aches with homesickness for Corfu and evokes the island in loving detail: 'At tea time the tall shadows from the cypress meet the sea; ultramarine crashes down through fierce blue chords to green and gold. Albania opens into huge dark fissures and becomes strangely Tibet.' He imagines the changing season there: 'autumn with the first thrust of asphodel on the bare tumulus of rock – The lift and kick of the inexpert *Van Norden* the day the squall came up and nearly took us down.' He can't stop thinking about it. 'In my imagination I am always thinking and loving those bare tumps of rock to the north where the sea thrashes and uncoils all the year long. It is a kind of internal catechism of places: the places I have touched there. The scented bay where we landed one morning on our way round; clarid, still, icy, with a thick shock of weed visible in two fathoms. To switch off the engine and glide to anchor is like a spiritual entering of silence.' And for the first time he writes about their sparse encampments on the beach: 'We slept with the sun and connected the dreamless nights to the nescient daytime. At dawn the sheep came down the precipice to water, their bells tonking, the weird cries of the boy in the myrtle like a bird in pain. Daphnis was so real that it was not necessary to mention him ... I never wrote about it, the wildness and desolation of it, because this kind of heartbreak belongs to the morning of the world.' But it is their Kalami home that he misses most acutely: 'I would trade the remotest caravan routes of Asia for a dukedom of Koloura in Corfu, if it were only the rock with the house of white rock built upon it.' *Prospero's Cell*, which he wrote while he was marooned in Alexandria after Nancy and he had parted, is a book powered by yearning.

For both of them, losing Kalami was an ache of bereavement that would not be healed, but they never spoke of it to one another. The pain ran too deep. They might talk about it to others, but seeing their own loss mirrored in the other made them mute, and in this silence the gulf between them grew.

Larry did not return to Corfu until 1966, and by then it was a changed island, a changed, post-war world, and he was a different man. Its memory coloured his writing for decades. Nearly a quarter of a century later his poem 'Summer' celebrates 'Dreamless summer sleeps they once enjoyed / In Adam's Eden long before the Fall.' And that long, almost hallucinatory episode which comes towards the end of *The Alexandria Quartet*, when Darley and Melissa discover the secret island with its mysterious underwater caves, is shot through with images from the little bay of St Arsenius, where they too had dived into underwater caves.

Nancy never went back. For her, Corfu remained always the place where she had been young and free, where she had discovered Mediterranean light and colour, the sensuous joys of swimming naked, a time of hope and promise and belonging. On the deserted beaches and in the clear waters below the shrine of St Arsenius, on the flat rock in front of the White House and aboard the *Van Norden*, she had captured a rare and precious content.

9

THE REFUGEE HABIT

The frontiers at last, I am feeling so tired.
We are getting the refugee habit . . .

Lawrence Durrell, 'In Europe'

On their first morning on the mainland, Larry and Nancy had a massive row. Nothing so unusual in that – they'd argued for years. But this one was different, or so Henry thought.

He described it in *The Colossus of Maroussi*. They were on the terrace of the Hotel Cecil in Patras when a bitter row blazed up between them. Henry was accustomed to what he later called their 'lambasting' of each other, but this was of a different order. Over breakfast, he said, 'a terrible wrangle ensued between Durrell and his wife'. (How Nancy would have appreciated his honesty in registering their quarrel, in contrast to Alan Thomas's fantasy that all was idyllic.) Henry's reaction is typical of him: he makes no judgement, merely laments their wretchedness, saying that he felt quite helpless and that he 'could only pity them both from the depths of my heart'. He tried to explain: 'It was really a private quarrel in which the war was used as a camouflage. The thought of war drives people frantic, makes them quite cuckoo, even when they are intelligent and far-seeing, as both Durrell and Nancy are.' All Henry's compassion is contained in this account, just one of the reasons he always kept a sure place in Nancy's affections. But he could only guess at the causes of the row, which went much deeper than mere war panic.

Henry soon regretted having left Corfu so precipitously and, since the war in Europe was still in that strangely unreal phase now known as the Phoney War, he went back for six solitary weeks of bliss in Kalami. Nancy and Larry moved into a small fourth-floor flat at 40 Anagnostopoulou Street, not far from the city centre; from its balcony they could see across the city to the Acropolis. Soon after they moved in Nancy realised she was pregnant. This pregnancy was planned, but even so, the timing was disastrous. Phoney or not, war had broken out between Britain and Germany. Greece and Italy were still neutral, and so far there was no reason to assume fighting would spread to the Mediterranean, but their carefully constructed world had collapsed: they'd lost their beautiful White House, sitting on its flat rock in Kalami; they had lost Larry's family, whose support meant so much to Nancy; and Nancy's inheritance was almost all gone. From now on Larry was obliged to join the ranks of those who must work to survive, and with the prospect of a baby to support as well.

His first job was with the British Embassy in Athens, working as a temporary staff member in their Information Services. Theodore, also now in Athens, was recruited at the same time. This was Larry's first taste of the world of the diplomatic service and he did not find it congenial, though having his friend working alongside was some compensation. However, after a month the regular embassy staff arrived from London and Larry was unemployed again, until he found a job that was marginally more appealing, working as an English instructor with the British Council. In neutral countries like Greece, Britain and Germany were engaged in what has become known as the 'battle for hearts and minds', so the work of the British Council counted as part of the war effort. But still, after nearly ten years of freedom from financial worries (despite his regular complaints of penury) the daily grind of work came as a shock. He wrote glumly to Alan Thomas, 'Earning a living is a terrible business.'

The Durrells made friends. George Katsimbalis was a towering figure, whose patronage made a huge contribution to modern Greek literature; his friend George Seferis was a remarkable man who was both poet and career diplomat, and they shared a love of mayhem reminiscent of the Villa Seurat days. In a letter Seferis describes an evening spent with Nancy and Larry and a Pole called Max Nimec, who tried to drive his small Morris into the lobby of one of the smartest hotels in Athens. The car got as far as the third step. Seferis wrote that 'the Englishman's young wife was making the faces of a Polynesian savage' and when Katsimbalis's wife appeared in her nightdress, they all bellowed like seals.

Nancy loved being pregnant. When I was expecting my first child, she told me how intensely fulfilled she had felt with both her planned pregnancies. She revelled in the sense of creativity, the new life being formed within her, with no conscious effort on her part. She added ruefully that a new born baby had seemed to her a less appealing proposition, and that once the child was born she would have ideally gifted the infant back to its father for the first few weeks of its life. In the 1940s, the emphasis of all the child-care gurus was on the practical problems; establishing efficient routines of cleaning, feeding and sleeping was all-important, almost an extension of good housework practice, and there was nothing in this to arouse her interest. By the 1970s, when she had devoured the insights into the psychology of infants and small children in the books of Bowlby and Winnicott, she found a whole new way to engage with babies, eagerly imagining their world of perception and need, so she was fascinated by her grandchildren from day one.

While Nancy enjoyed the first weeks of pregnancy, Henry was basking in autumnal solitude in Kalami. But October brought winter storms and the track from the bay up to the road became an impassable torrent. When Nancy came over from the mainland to pick up a few personal belongings he decided to travel back with her that same day. In Athens, his intoxication with all things Greek continued unabated and Henry embraced Larry and Nancy's new friends with his usual gusto. He took to George Seferis at once, and declared that he had caught the spirit of eternity and embedded it in his poems. He was even more impressed by Katsimbalis, and dubbed him the Colossus, a tribute both to his massive physique and his commanding presence. After a short time Henry took off from Athens and travelled around Greece on what he called 'a voyage into the light'. The ancient site at Epidaurus was 'sheer perfection' where he 'heard the great heart of the world beat', while the 'full devastating beauty' of the plain of Thebes moved him to tears. Back in Athens, he visited his friends at Katsimbalis's house and told them he'd had a better holiday than he could ever have dreamed of. He explained that on the Acropolis he'd been so inspired to communicate with God that he had felt an overwhelming urge to masturbate. From the depths of an armchair, Nancy pretended she hadn't heard properly and asked, 'What did you want to make, Henry?' 'Masturbation,' he calmly replied, to the shock of Katsimbalis's more conventional guests.

Miller's Greek odyssey was almost over. He returned to Athens in mid December, and the American consul told him to leave without delay. As Christmas approached, and with a few days before his boat left, there was just time for one last trip. This time, Larry and Nancy went with him.

In some ways Henry's account, in *The Colossus of Maroussi*, of their three-day drive through the midwinter rains of the Peloponnese reads like the holiday nightmare of all time: on the morning of their departure Larry and Nancy are four hours late picking him up from his hotel; the soft-topped car they have been lent by Max Nimec provides no protection from the atrocious weather and they are soon soaked through and freezing; the hotels are full and the food is bad. The climax of awfulness comes while they are having their Christmas lunch in a smoky cellar, enduring abominable food and a jumble of music and propaganda from a German radio station. A drunken diner at the next table 'suddenly turned very white and without a word of warning puked up a heaping dishful of bright vomit and then quietly lowered his heavy head into it with a dull splash'.

On their way to the train, which Henry must catch if he is to make the boat for the US, Max's little car breaks down in a sea of water, whereupon, as Henry writes, 'It was so obvious that the car had given its last spark of life that we sat there laughing and joking about our plight without thinking to make the slightest effort to start her again.'

Yet through it all, in retrospect at least, Henry's enthusiasm never flags. In Corinth they hear 'the queer strains of a flute' through the open door of a house, 'the original music for which no notes have been written and for which none is necessary ... fierce, sad, obsessive, yearning and defiant'. They visit Mycenae and Argos, Sparta and Mystras, and reading Henry's account one senses him cramming in the last precious morsels of his Greek experience before the reality of war and his return to America claim him. When the three friends part in Tripolis, they all know it is the end of their charmed existence. Henry predicts that 'The war will not only change the map of the world but it will affect the destiny of every one I care about.' True, and even more than he imagined.

Nancy never saw Henry again, but his friendship with Larry continued until his death in 1980. But those three days of rain and discomfort revealed an aspect of Larry's personality Henry had not encountered before, what Henry called 'the Englishman' in him, adding that it was 'the least interesting thing about him, to be sure, but an element not to be overlooked'. Driving near Mystras they bump into a friend of Larry's, but he just throws the fellow a casual greeting and does not even stop the car. The gregarious Henry is surprised and wonders if they'd fallen out. Not at all, says Larry, and when pressed he explains, 'What would we do with an Englishman here? They're bad enough at home. Do you want to spoil our holiday?' Later the same day another friend, this time a Greek, attempts to strike up a conversation with them in a café, but Larry rebuffs him in the same way. Henry is perplexed and dismayed. It is Christmas Day and he wants to get into the festive spirit and enjoy himself, but he is continually thwarted by Larry's insistence that they keep themselves separate. Trying to pinpoint what is going on, he says in a telling phrase that it makes him feel as though 'we were building a wall of ice around ourselves'.

He excuses Larry at once. His friend had been in charge of all the driving and the arrangements, he was dropping with fatigue, he was usually the most easygoing and amiable of people. All true. But Henry's experience of the 'wall of ice' that Larry had thrust up between the three of them and everyone else they encountered is an uncanny echo of the phenomenon Nancy had first experienced in Paris: for whatever reason Larry was compelled, sheep-dog-like, to separate his intimates from other people. If Henry, the senior partner in their friendship, tough, outgoing and independent, found himself being confined behind a wall of ice after only three days in Larry's company, what chance did Nancy have of breaking through after more than seven years?

At breakfast on the final morning Larry – 'still feeling somewhat English', according to Henry – demanded two boiled eggs and made a fuss when they weren't prepared to his liking. While Larry was insisting on proper service, Henry and Nancy had tea and toast and smoked several cigarettes. Together but separate behind that ever present wall of ice, there was never any possibility of real communication between them.

After they had said goodbye to Henry, Larry and Nancy did not go straight back to Athens but on to visit Epidaurus, a site of impressive serenity even today, when it is a magnet for tour buses and milling groups of visitors. On one of the last days of 1939, wintry and dark, it was unforgettable. A difficult travelling companion Larry might have been, but this brief trip triggered some of his finest lyric poetry: 'Nemea', with its compelling evocation of stillness, and 'At Epidaurus', which includes the haunting couplet,

Here we are safe from everything but ourselves,
The dying leaves and the reports of love.

Their personal battles seemed more real than the news of conflicts far away, and the pain of this double dislocation was for Larry a potent source of inspiration.

In Athens their social life was expanding and contemporary accounts offer fascinating glimpses of how they appeared to their Greek friends. Seferis recalled his first impressions of the younger couple: 'Durrell is a short sturdy young man, with a clever, satirical mind. His wife Nancy is tall, quiet, something in between a wild

deer, a vine arbour, and a Greta Garbo: her arms and legs fly out
all over the place, clumsy, her husband occasionally gives her an
affectionate smack of the behind.' All her life there was something
awkward in her movements, though its exaggeration in the early
months of her pregnancy probably indicated the increasing strain
she was under: in the privacy of the Anagnostopolou Street flat
their marriage was deteriorating so much that by February Nancy
had decided to return to England to sit out her pregnancy with
Mother Durrell. She took a plane from Phaleron, just south of
Athens, a luxurious and novel experience for her.

The time in Bournemouth was tranquil enough. Nancy enjoyed
being with Margo and Mother Durrell. Theodore's wife Mary had
also taken refuge there with their daughter Alexia, though by the
time Nancy arrived they had already moved elsewhere. Yet after
less than three months Nancy was once more heading back to
Athens. Crossing Europe by train in May 1940 was a dangerous
and uncomfortable undertaking. German troops were advancing
on Paris: the train was constantly being shunted into sidings to
give way to the Axis troop trains so the journey took more than
three days; and she was in the last month of her pregnancy. Why
did she risk it? Larry reported airily to Henry that 'Nancy had got
bored with England and decided to return and have the brat [in
Athens] after all'. Nancy, equally dismissive, always maintained
that Larry had summoned her back because he had some ridiculous notion that it would be romantic for his child to be born on
Greek soil, and he still had hopes that the British Council were
going to send him back to Corfu. There is probably an element of
truth in each account, but there is a third ingredient, one that neither would admit to after they had split up: their separation in
February had been the brinkmanship of a rocky marriage, and
after several weeks apart they were quite simply missing each
other. Nancy destroyed all his letters when she married for the

second time, but a postcard survives, written in February or March of this year. It's written in transliterated Greek script, perhaps a humorous way to evade the censor's eyes. On the back of the photograph of Nancy and Henry on the Acropolis he writes, 'Darling; I have nothing to add to my previous letter except to tell you: that I love you; and miss you horribly; it does me good to write to you.' If he hated being alone, life in wartime Bournemouth had no doubt started to pall for Nancy. They wanted to be together for the birth of their child and to try to be a family in the face of whatever the war might bring. In spite of all the rows and resentment, they were at that stage neither of them ready to face the future without the other.

Henry and Nancy on the Acropolis, not communing with God this time

Once Nancy was back in Athens, Larry's tone in his letters to his male friends was truculent: his wife is being kicked by the baby, and though he doesn't like seeing her being knocked about he is powerless to help. He once tried kicking the baby back but the only effect was on Nancy. As so often, his letters are deliberately upbeat, callous even, and so they only tell half the story. Under the bravado he was anxious and unhappy, as any man in such a precarious position would be. His account obscures as much as it reveals.

The baby was expected at the end of May, but was late in coming. In the last days of Nancy's pregnancy they heard that Spiro had died suddenly in Corfu. The ebullient taxi driver had been an integral part of their life on the island, a life that now seemed part of a different world. Nancy finally went into labour in the first days of June and was admitted to hospital in Athens, where her habitual fortitude was misunderstood: the doctors refused to believe she was in full labour because she wasn't yelling in agony, which was apparently expected. When it became obvious, despite her silence, that the birth was imminent they pressed on her belly to help push the infant out, a process she found distinctly unhelpful. In spite of medical misunderstanding, a healthy girl was born on 4 June. She was called Penelope, a suitably Hellenic name and a good compromise between Larry's determination to have a thoroughly Greek daughter and Nancy's equal determination that her name would not become a liability (as Sappho's would ten years later). However, she was soon given the faux Chinese nickname 'Ping-kû' with which name she is celebrated in the poem 'To Ping-kû Asleep'. Inevitably, Ping-kû became Pinky, a nickname Penelope grew to dislike intensely but which she was unable to shake off for many years.

Both parents had mixed feelings about the arrival of their daughter. Larry, like many first-time fathers, was initially perplexed, telling Henry that 'I'm very pleased but don't quite know what to do with it', adding that in the present climate 'the domestic virtues seem rather an anachronism: household gods at a discount'. Nancy's response was more complicated and reveals deep ambivalence about the maternal role. In a couple of handwritten pages, in which she makes a last stab at unravelling her relationship with her father, she said, 'Would he rather I'd been a boy? I think I felt so later on and that I thought of myself in some inner way as a boy – masquerading as a girl, but I don't think this was very fundamental as it comes to me now as here-say, an echo, rather than a revealed truth.' But then she adds, 'although my reactions to the birth of my children – the feeling that I was making a present for my husband and that it was very hard cheese to have to look after it afterwards' might be inter-preted as 'a very clever thing for a boy to do, and that responsibility should stop there'.

It didn't, of course, but motherhood did nothing to diminish Nancy's ability to raise eyebrows. Soon after Penelope's birth Seferis wrote to his wife that 'Nansopoula' – Little Nancy, as he affectionately referred to her – had been spotted clad in bright red velvet shorts and an orange blouse, with the infant 'some-where, in her hands or on her back, like a package or a rucksack'. He says that the moment he visited their flat he 'left Greece behind. I was in some suburb of London.' He also observed Nancy's involvement in Larry's writing. After dinner at their very English home Larry read the first act of the play he was working on, and Nancy declared it to be 'extremely *Grand Guignol*'; Seferis added that he thought she had the ability to judge.

That summer came to seem almost serene in contrast to what followed. By now the war was anything but phoney. The day of Penelope's birth saw the last Allied troops evacuated from the beach at Dunkirk; all those who remained were captured by the triumphant German army. Continental Europe was now dominated by the Axis powers. Just a week later, the swastika was hoisted over Paris. Greece was still a neutral country, but Larry and Nancy and their new baby were effectively cut off from their homeland for the duration, and the German advance seemed unstoppable. All the same, an air of unreality pervaded those summer months in Greece. While the Battle of Britain was being fought in the cloudless skies over southern England, Larry went on holiday to Mykonos with a couple of friends, and for a long time he clung to the hope that the British Council would send him back to Corfu. At the last moment Corfu was assigned to his friend Paul Gotch and their destination changed. They packed up their few belongings once again, and headed south.

On 21 September *Tharros*, the local Kalamata paper, carried a brief announcement:

> Yesterday the Englishman Lawrence Durrell arrived in Kalamata with his wife in order to oversee the organisation and operation of the Athens Institute of English Studies, which has been established in our city. Both Mr Durrell and his wife will teach the English language. Cheap fees.

Pictures of pre-war Kalamata show it to have been an attractive small port. The town lies between the first and second of the long fingers of land that reach down from the southern end of the Peloponnese towards Crete; surrounded by groves of olives and orange trees, it is encircled by hills. Tall, well-built houses face the sea across a wide esplanade; dozens of caiques are moored along the seafront, their curves lending a timeless grace to the scene.

The British consul in Kalamata had asked for someone to be sent in order to counteract the efficient propaganda machine of the Germans in the town, and Larry's job was to set up a British institute and school. By all accounts he was an energetic and popular teacher during the few months the school was open, and he and his little family had been given a flat overlooking the esplanade and the sea. It could have been an agreeable wartime billet, but at the end of October 1940 Greek neutrality came to a sudden and dramatic end.

At four o'clock on the morning of 28 October, just five weeks after Nancy and Larry had arrived in Kalamata, the Italian Ambassador contacted Prime Minister Ioannis Metaxas and demanded that Italian troops be allowed to occupy strategic positions in his country. Metaxas's reply was instant and unequivocal refusal. Within hours, Italian troops were pouring down into Northern Greece from Albania. What happened next was totally unexpected. Poland, Holland, Belgium and France had all been overrun by the Axis armies, and if Britain was still struggling to hold out she was helped by the fact of being an island, so there was every reason to suppose Greece would fall within weeks. But it didn't. The Greeks – soldiers and civilians, men, women and children – resisted the invaders with supreme courage and determination, and drove the Italian army back. In the snow-covered mountain passes the defenders overpowered the wretchedly equipped Italians, and by Christmas the bells were ringing out their victory peal all over Greece. Despite terrible hardship Greek heroism had given the Allies their first real success of the war. Neutral no longer, the Greek people had become Britain's most triumphant allies, and in Kalamata Nancy and Larry followed events with delight. They were all 'in raptures', as Larry wrote to Henry, adding how gratifiying it was that the two nations were in the fight together: 'with all their faults they both stand for something great'.

The winter euphoria disguised a harsh reality: Mussolini's ill-judged attack on Greece had condemned the Balkans to years of suffering. In 1939 Hitler had no ambitions in that direction, and would probably have let Greece remain neutral while he pursued his territorial ambitions in Russia and the East. But after 28 October 1940 that was no longer a possibility. In early November

British troops occupied Crete, which was vital for the control of the Eastern Mediterranean, and British and Commonwealth troops were shipped from bases in Egypt to the Greek mainland to help defend their ally. The cards that had been dealt would determine the course of Nancy's life for years to come.

Kalamata was already suffering daily air raids. On one occasion an Italian plane flew so close to their home it seemed as if it was going to fly right into their dining room; another time, an explosion in the harbour sent Larry racing out in panic to where Penelope was being pushed in her pram along the seafront. Yet despite these dramas the baby thrived. By early spring her proud father reported that she had 'eight teeth, a vocabulary of two words, and a yell like a hungry starling'.

In February the international situation had grown so threatening that the British Council closed all its schools. Larry passed the time by, among other things, putting together a little handwritten book of limericks, some of them illustrated by Nancy.

> There was a fair maid of Corfu,
> Who blocked up her joy-place with glue.
> With a certain mistrust
> She was widely discussed
> By the two or three people who knew.

It was the only art she managed. The demands of a small baby and anxiety over the war effectively stifled any creativity. By now their friends in Kalamata were urging them to escape while they could, but still they lingered. Partly this was due to their reluctance to tear themselves away from the country they loved, and partly it was down to loyalty, the belief that in some small way their presence in Kalamata and the support they could give to the embattled Greeks counted for something. There were other

Conducted Tour of Greece
(after hear)

There was a fair maid of Corfu
who blocked up her joy-place with glue.
With a certain mistrust
She was wisely discussed
By the two or three people who knew

Nancy and Larry whiled away the time creating a little book of limericks

factors in their indecision: they had no idea where to go, and only a very vague idea of what was going on. The overwhelming impression given by those who were on the Greek mainland in the spring of 1941 was that there was an almost complete absence of reliable information. Larry had a radio, but news broadcasts were erratic and heavily censored. Even in Athens, the writer Olivia Manning – who was later to play a part in Nancy's story – remained unaware of the disaster that was about to overwhelm Greece until it was almost too late.

Palm Sunday 1941 fell on 6 April, cold and bleak. The nation-wide broadcast from Athens Cathedral was interrupted by the news that troops were once again invading from the north. But this time, instead of the badly equipped Italians, it was the German army that was pounding through the mountains. The British Expeditionary Force on the mainland numbered about fifty-eight thousand, many of them from Australia and New Zealand, but they were scattered and ill-prepared and, crucially, they had no proper air support. The German shock troops, by contrast, had one thousand aircraft to back them up. They powered down through Northern Greece and after just two weeks they were advancing on Athens. As the Allied forces pulled out the Greeks threw flowers and shouted, 'Come back soon!' Marooned in Kalamata and with almost no idea what to do for his little family or where to go, Larry cabled his boss in Athens for advice. Instructions came in the form of a two-word telegram that Larry and Nancy never forgot: 'Rule Britannia!' Larry interpreted this as: Stay put! It was only later that he learned the writer of this elliptical telegram had quit the city that very day.

There are differing accounts of what happened next, but perhaps that is only appropriate since muddle and confusion seem to be the most usual condition for civilians in wartime. One version is that the vice-consul in Kalamata arranged for a boat from Pylos to take the refugees across to Crete. Hastily gathering a few items, Larry, Nancy and Penelope drove the fifty-five miles to the ancient port where a sturdy caique, belching sparks, was waiting to carry them via Cape Matapan and Cythera to Crete. At one point in the journey, as Larry describes it in *The Greek Islands*, there was an almost dreamlike interlude while they sheltered in a bay near the southernmost tip of the Mani Peninsula and waited for the safety of darkness to continue their journey. The proud Maniots killed their last two lambs and prepared a feast for the refugees. Their hearts full of pride in the valour shown by the Greeks, and confident that, however long it may take, victory would be the final outcome of this fight, they toasted each other calmly and with love. Perhaps it did happen as Larry describes it, and the villagers were indeed slaughtering their animals rather than letting them fall into German hands (and there's no doubt that it should have happened that way), but each time I read it I hear Nancy's eloquent snort of disbelief.

Her account, which I heard many times, was more prosaic. Starved of any real information, they knew only that the danger was getting closer and they no longer had any means of escape. By great good fortune a friend who was escaping on a caique from further up the coast and who knew they were stranded in Kalamata persuaded the captain to pull in and pick them up. Hastily gathering a few essentials, they left with two suitcases full of nappies and baby clothes and only a small bag containing their own essentials. The journey on the open boat was terrifying and the suitcases, which they arranged on deck to shelter the baby from the night breeze, kept falling over and having to be set upright again. There was very little food and no milk for Penelope. After three nights at sea, exhausted and hungry, they arrived in Crete and found themselves in what was already a war zone, since the Luftwaffe had been bombing the island for days.

I had intended to leave these two accounts just as they were, since there seemed to be no way of reconciling them: either the vice-consul in Kalamata organised their escape, or they were picked up by a friend. It seemed like a good example of how it is impossible to be entirely accurate at such a distance. But then, by great good fortune, I found an article in the *Daily Telegraph* dated 5 May 1941 with the headline 'Escape from Greece in Fishing Boat' and underneath, 'Adventurous 6-Day Voyage through the Islands'. Filed from Cairo, the report tells how an acting British consul, 'a middle aged, sandy-complexioned Scot who served under Lawrence in the last war', had set off from his base in Patras in his little 29-ton diesel-engine fishing boat, determined, in his own words, 'to gather together as many British subjects as I could'. Sailing had been Harold Hoyland's hobby, and he knew the waters well. He set off at dawn on 22 April, spent a night on the island of Oxeia and then headed south to Zante, before going on to Navarino (Pylos). There he learned that there were a number of British citizens in nearby Kalamata and 'I determined to drive there, although it was a poor road. I wasted half an hour bargaining for a car, but when it was obtained, my driver certainly went fast. Before we were halfway there I was more scared of him than of the Germans.' When he returned to Navarino it was with 'a mixed bag of 35'. From Navarino the craft went via Cape Matapan and Anticythera, by which time German parachutists were already landing in Cythera. 'On Sunday morning,' he said, 'my little fishing boat *Hagias Trias* – Holy Trinity – sailed into port at Suda Bay, in Crete, flying the consular flag. I had brought my boat through undamaged and, starting with six passengers, I had finished with 65 without loss of life. They were British, Greek, Australian and Jugoslav, a little League of Nations, in fact.'

It turns out that the apparently conflicting accounts do match up. Nancy was correct in stating that a friend of theirs had arranged for the caique to stop off and collect the British stranded in Kalamata (Henry mentions the impressive British consul whom he met during their brief stay in Patras just as war was being declared), while the consul in Kalamata no doubt organised the fleet of cars that were needed for the dash to the port.

Whatever the precise details, it was terrifying and there is no doubt they were very lucky. The fleeing boats were harried incessantly by the Luftwaffe, and many were bombed by Stukas and sunk with great loss of life. Some didn't even make it to a boat. A

few days after Larry and Nancy scrambled with Penelope onto the
little caique, the Allied troops still stranded in Kalamata surren-
dered, among them a large contingent of Jewish volunteers from
Palestine. They were sent to Stalags in Austria and Germany.

One of Nancy's photographs that was reproduced in the *Geographic Magazine*

There is a postscript. I grew up on the story of the perilous
escape on the little boat, and the very word caique has always had
a kind of magic. When Penelope and I went to Corfu in 1994 she
had with her a few photographs taken by Nancy before the war.
One showed a small, almost deserted bay, a line of caiques drawn

up close to shore. Penelope hoped to find out where it was. She asked at the White House in Kalami, but they were unable to help and suggested she try Agni. That evening we walked along the footpath that leads from the olive groves above Kalami, across a little bay, past the shrine of St Arsenius and round the wooded headland to descend to the pebble beach at Agni. We chose the furthest of the three tavernas, Taverna Nicholas, with its tables set right by the water's edge. An energetic, moustachioed man introduced himself as Perikles. He was delighted to meet Penelope, and told us that when the Durrells were looking for somewhere to live they had first come to Agni, but had been put off sharing a house with his family because there were too many children. After we had chatted for a little while Penelope showed him the photograph of the bay and its line of caiques. His expression changed, and he stared at it for a few moments before asking quietly, 'May I show this to my father?'

'Of course,' said Penelope.

He vanished into the back of the taverna and we relaxed with our drinks. After a few minutes a tall, handsome man in his early seventies came to our table. He was holding the photograph and his face was taut with emotion.

He stood in front of us and pointed at one of the caiques in the picture. Then he struck his chest with his fist. 'My boat,' he said, striking his chest a second time. 'My boat.' There were tears in his eyes.

Perikles explained: 'All the caiques were bombed by the Germans during the war, and the fleet was never rebuilt.' It had been fifty years since Nicholas had set eyes on his precious boat.

'Thank you,' said Perikles. 'You have made my father very happy.'

Later, as the moon rose over the sea, we saw Nicholas standing up in a little rowing boat near the rocks at the edge of the bay.

He was prodding for fish and octopus in the traditional manner and he looked happy and proud; a fragment of his vanished past had been restored.

So, whatever the precise details of the escape, I'm glad it was one of those traditional boats, a caique, in which they got away.

In Crete their troubles were far from over. They had hardly any food for themselves, and none at all for Penelope. Travelling with a ten-month-old baby is stressful enough in peacetime; after three days at sea, it was a nightmare. Half of Athens seemed to be there, and they ran into George Seferis, among others, but there was no food to be had anywhere. This time rescue came from an even more unexpected quarter: two drunken Australian soldiers, alerted to the problem by Penelope's loud crying – that 'yell like a hungry starling' had its uses – cheerfully looted a crate of Carnation milk from a shop in Canea and presented it to Nancy.

Whenever I hear disapproving reports of lawless folk looting from shops after some natural disaster, I think of those two drunken Aussies who may just have saved my sister's life.

After the harrrowing escape from mainland Greece, the crossing from Crete to Alexandria was relatively straightforward. Once again, they got out just in time, a tiny part of the flood of refugees pouring south ahead of the Axis advance on a ship packed with journalists all fretting to file reports of the fall of Greece once they reached Egypt.

Nancy and Larry arrived in the huge port of Alexandria at daybreak. They had baby clothes and nappies – and all that Carnation milk – but none of their own possessions or money and, more importantly, in the rush to leave Kalamata they had brought no papers with them. They were exhausted but Penelope, as is the way with babies, appeared unmarked by the horrors. An enchanting photo has survived, which was taken as they stepped down the gangplank and on to Egyptian soil. Confident and secure, she rides on her young father's shoulders with that rather smug expression of small children who suddenly find themselves higher than the adults around them, and Larry is turning slightly to accommodate her. The photo is all the more poignant for the separation that was to come.

Larry bears Penelope on his shoulders as they finally reach safety

They may have been penniless, and with only the clothes they stood up in, but they soon discovered they were in possession of an asset which would prove useful on more than one occasion: Larry's reputation as a young writer of note had gone before them.

The soldier on port duty who took that photograph of Penelope riding on her father's shoulders was John Braun, who had spotted Larry's name in the ship's manifest and was looking out for him. He described most of the refugees as a pathetic assortment of retired schoolteachers, widows and other expatriates from Athens, but then he spotted a stocky, round-faced man with a wife and child in tow. Years later, Braun remembered their initial exchange:

'Are you Lawrence Durrell?'

'Yes.'

'Once of the Villa Seurat?'

'Yes.'

'Friend of Henry Miller's?'

Here Larry seems to have smelled a rat and one can hear the suspicion in his defensive 'Yes, anything wrong with that?'

But he needn't have worried. Far from fretting about his potential security risk, John Braun had read and admired *The Black Book* and was eager to talk to him. Once all the refugees had been processed, John and Larry spent most of the night talking literature and ideas. How Nancy and Penelope passed the time is not recorded. The next morning they were loaded into an army truck and travelled through the Nile Delta and down to Cairo. A journey of three hours, it was hot, dusty and uncomfortable; those interminable journeys in the back of jolting lorries were to become a grim feature of life, for Nancy and Penelope at any rate, in the years ahead.

That arrival in Egypt was Nancy's first exposure to a non-European city and culture. Even now, in an age of cheap flights and with television bringing images of distant lands into our homes every day, the impact of a North African city experienced for the first time is still overwhelming: the crowds, the noise, the dirt and dust; the huge gulf between rich and poor; the haunting call of the muezzin echoing from the minarets that rise up from the chaos of streets and houses; the colours and smells and the relentless glare and heat of the sun. It was almost exactly six years since she and Larry had escaped from the soggy grey of an English winter to their first Greek spring and summer; then they had been intoxicated by the brilliance of the southern sun, the dazzle of sea and sky, the vibrant colours – a never-to-be-forgotten initiation. This was an initiation of a different kind, unchosen and chaotic, a first taste of what Olivia Manning was to call 'exile from a country not our own'.

They checked in to the Lunar Park Hotel and immediately telegraphed Mother Durrell in Bournemouth for funds. Larry soon found work of sorts, writing a humorous column in the *Egyptian Gazette*, and after a couple of months he was taken on as a press officer at the British Embassy on a salary of six hundred pounds a year. Life had been reduced to a matter of survival, and they were learning how to get by, but after the hedonism of their time in Corfu and Paris, when they had been free to devote themselves to the only activities they considered important, it was a dreary prospect that stretched ahead. So far as they knew the war might drag on indefinitely, with no means of escape and nowhere to escape to; England was an impossible three-month journey by ship round the Cape of Good Hope, and their beloved Greece was overrun by Axis forces. At a time when thousands were facing death and destitution, loss of home and family and country, and when the news from Greece was getting worse by the day – during the 'Great Hunger' of the first winter of occupation, three hundred thousand Greeks died of starvation, including Eleni, whose house they had shared in Kalami – they knew they were comparatively well off, but as Nancy and Larry approached the end of their twenties they had ceased to have any control over their lives. They were learning what it meant to be refugees.

Superficially at least, they had once again landed on their feet.

The impression of wartime Cairo that has survived is of a privileged society, if you were British, full of fascinating people who enjoyed their elevated status to the full. In theory Egypt was a neutral sovereign state with a young king, Farouk, and an independent parliament and prime minister. In actual fact Sir Miles Lampson, the British Ambassador in Cairo, held the real power, backed up by a formidable military force: the vast harbour at Alexandria, the Suez Canal and access to the oil fields in the Middle East meant that Egypt was too strategically important for technical niceties about sovereignty. Lampson was either a racist bully or the last of the great imperialists, depending on your point of view: in the short term he safeguarded British interests in the Eastern Mediterranean, but in the long term the Egyptians' frustration and resentment would erupt in nationalist riots that marked the end of British rule.

Meanwhile there was much to enjoy in the gilded cage: servants were cheap, the war was mostly happening elsewhere and a leisurely expat life revolved around the luxurious Gezira Sporting Club and the British Embassy in the Garden City district. Shepheard's Hotel was legendary both for comfort and the slowness of its service. And Nancy and Larry met up with some old friends including Theodore, now serving with the Royal Army Medical Corps having escaped from Crete after a gruelling march across the island. Even John Gawsworth made an appearance, a reminder of their early days together in London. They met others who were to become firm friends: Olivia Manning and her husband Reggie Smith, Freya Stark, Patrick Leigh Fermor. It could have been a lot worse.

Once Larry had secured his 'proper job' they moved into a comfortable flat with an imposing front door in Zamalek, on Gezira Island where some of the coolest housing was to be found in this hot and dusty city. The flat at 14 Saleh Ayoub became the home of another new friend, Mary Bentley, an enterprising young woman who shared Larry's office in the British Embassy; her boyfriend Dudley Honor, a pilot who was engaged on many daring sorties, joined them whenever he was in Cairo. Mary and Nancy took turns to babysit Penelope (according to Mary) when they went out dancing at the Kit Kat club, where they might be entertained by 'une dance classique' or 'une dance fantastique'. Before long, they discovered a more affordable meeting place than the Gezira Sporting Club or Shepheard's. The large, shady garden of the Anglo-Egyptian Union was close to their flat, and soon became a haven for the impecunious writers and artists who had little in common with society.

Despite the gloss of history, which blurs the edges of the class distinctions and snobberies that were so much a part of expat life, the glittering social scene in wartime Cairo was in many ways antipathetic to Nancy and Larry. 'Other ranks' were barred from Shepheard's Hotel and from many of the better restaurants and nightclubs; the Egyptians were treated at best with tolerant disdain, at worst with rudeness and casual violence; the qualities that were valued were those suited to wartime – valour and patriotism, sacrifice for the greater good. Not just household gods, but the arts and literature were also at a discount. The Durrells shared few interests with the majority of the British in Cairo, which made genuine friendship all the more precious. Robin Fedden was a pacifist poet whom Larry had met in Athens. Together with Bernard Spencer they started a magazine called *Personal Landscape*, its title chosen to emphasise their focus on what was individual and private at a time when the qualities they valued were being discounted by the demands of war. It was, as Fedden wrote, a response to the stagnation and boredom of exile.

If boredom and stagnation were the signature notes of life in Cairo for the poets who collaborated on *Personal Landscapes*, how much more so was it for Nancy, alone for long periods of each day with her small daughter. Since Paris she had been isolated behind that infamous wall of ice. Now motherhood created a further barrier between her and their friends, most of whom were still childless, and by this time Larry had honed his public persona to perfection. One friend described his champagne effect in company, while another said that he seemed to pump oxygen into the air – a valuable accomplishment in the stifling Cairo days. He might have felt that he was stagnating, but outwardly he carried all before him. Mary Bentley, who after all shared a flat with them, knew tensions existed between them, but put it down to stress at having been forced to leave their Corfu idyll. Occasionally Nancy hinted at more serious conflicts, but she had never known how to confide her problems in anyone and maintained her usual reticence through these last months of married life, when the strain of keeping up a convincing façade was becoming ever harder.

As always, she made the best of things, finding respite where she could. One place where she could always be sure of a sympathetic welcome was the home of Amy and Walter Smart. Smartie, as he was usually known, was the oriental councillor at the British Embassy, a man of legendary charm, erudition and expertise, and with a genuine passion for literature. On one of Larry's first afternoons at the embassy this eminent figure dropped by his office. As he had just returned from an extended lunch break Larry feared a ticking off. Nothing of the sort. Almost apologetic for disturbing him, Smartie wanted to discuss a little book of Larry's poems that he and Amy had got the day before. He invited both him and Nancy to supper. His wife – the painter Amy Nimr – came from a long-established Cairene family of Syro-Lebanese Christians, and their large home in Zamalek, with its profusion of books and paintings, manuscripts, rugs, carpets, with a long terrace overlooking a large, shady garden, was Nancy's

first glimpse of that cosmopolitan world that used to exist where
Europe and the Orient merge, a way of life with a breadth and
grace that has all but vanished. Their common interest in painting drew Amy and Nancy together; in the Smarts' welcoming
and cultured home, Nancy discovered a safe haven where she
and Larry were appreciated by people with money and the good
taste to spend it with generosity and wisdom.

But even here, safety was precarious. During the winter of
1941–2 Rommel had taken the port of Benghazi and then the area
known as Cyrenaica, in eastern Libya. The Allied forces, many of
them from Australia and New Zealand, formed a defensive line
south from Gazala which appeared to be impregnable, and in
Tobruk the determination of the Australian garrison had repulsed
all the German attempts to take it. Then, towards the end of June
1942, the unthinkable happened: after holding out for more than
a year, Tobruk fell. An unmitigated disaster, declared Churchill.
Rommel was made a field marshal and the British in Egypt were
appalled. Three days later the Panzerarmee Afrika had reached
the border of Egypt, the 8th Army was in retreat and it seemed as
though nothing could halt the Axis advance. Those Egyptians
who saw the Germans as potential liberators from British oppres-
sion were already preparing to welcome the invaders. At the end
of June Mussolini flew to Derna, in northern Libya, and brought
with him the white charger on which he planned to ride in triumph into Cairo. Rommel had picked out Shepheard's for his
headquarters. Vital shipping was moved from Alexandria to the
safer ports of Beirut, Haifa and Port Said. There had been little
'flaps' before, but this time it was serious. As Cecil Beaton, who
was in Cairo, commented drily, 'Flap is the word of the moment.
Everyone puts a stopper on their panic by calling it a Flap.'

Panic was an understandable response. By 28 June Rommel
had reached Mersa Matrub, and a day later his apparently

unstoppable advance had brought him to an obscure railway halt called Alamein, about sixty miles west of Alexandria. In Cairo women and children crammed into the railway station, anxious to flee before Egypt was overrun by the Germans. Among the crowds were Mary Bentley, Nancy and Penelope. There was just time for hasty, anxious goodbyes, and then the packed train carried them to Jerusalem. They stayed first in the YWCA, which was in a somewhat dreary building in the appropriately named Via Dolorosa. Refugees again – and lucky, again. Even now, the Palestine administration refused to alter the quotas for Jews, who were left with no option but to remain in Egypt. Meanwhile staff at the British Embassy and GHQ were frantically burning files; smoke from the bonfires filled the air, and 1 July became known as Ash Wednesday.

The halt at Alamein

But Rommel had overreached himself. His supply lines stretched for a thousand miles and Axis energies were now being diverted to the invasion of Russia. The fighting continued throughout the summer, but Alamein was as far as he got. Slowly, the refugees began to trickle back to Cairo. Mary Bentley was missing Dudley, who after a week or so had flown up to Jerusalem to visit her, and she came back as soon as she could. But Nancy remained where she was and after a little while went to stay with Olivia Manning, who had also taken up residence in Jerusalem. Her absence could, at least for the time being, be explained away by the continuing danger in Egypt.

At the end of July Churchill flew out to Cairo to assess the situation. A new commander of the 8th Army was soon appointed, Lieutenant-General Bernard Montgomery, and by the end of October Rommel was in full retreat. There was no longer any official reason for Nancy not to return to Cairo. But she never did. Instead she wrote to Larry and told him their marriage was over.

Nancy always maintained that it was a seemingly trivial thing that made her realise she had to get out. Near where she and Larry were staying, presumably in the flat in Saleh Ayoub, a newly married couple had moved in. Observing their tenderness, finding herself close to a couple who were truly in love, who were kind to each other and actually enjoyed being together, brought home to her just how far she and Larry had journeyed from that state. She decided, quite simply, that all love had gone from their relationship. She had to leave.

Writing this now, I wonder if it was Mary and Dudley she was referring to. She lost contact with them after the split, so there was no reason why she would have given them names when she talked to me, but for some months she and Larry had been sharing a flat with Mary, had been witnesses to their ecstatic reunions each time Dudley returned from a flying mission, seen how much Mary missed him when he was gone. The contrast with her own relationship with Larry was stark.

Mary was in the office with Larry when he opened Nancy's letter, and she never forgot his reaction. He was devastated. In spite of all their fights and differences, he had never imagined she would leave him. He was in such a state that a few days later Dudley broke all the rules and flew Larry up to Jerusalem to plead his case, but Nancy's mind was made up. Those weeks apart from Larry had given her a glimpse of what life might be like without him, and she had no faith in his promises to change. Over the years she had become inured to the constant drip-drip of his put-downs: Henry, who after all was one of Larry's closest friends, reports Larry's habitual response to any suggestion of Nancy's was 'Why don't you shut up?' And that was in front of other people. In private, when they quarrelled, he deployed every weapon in his verbal armoury to gain the upper hand, just as he had always done in his battles with Leslie. In the letter Nancy wrote years later to help Penelope understand what Sappho was going through, she tried to convey what it was like to be on the receiving end of Larry's diatribes – 'Scorched with words, muddled with words, bewildered with words and his ever-changing expectations.' She went on, 'When Larry is crossed he lashes out with all the guns he can think of – "Nothing but a dirty Jew" to me – but this only hurt me because he was saying it. Basically not at all because I knew my Myers ancestry was more illustrious than his ... And I have always felt secure in having decent good looks and a fair skin, and except for being too thin, taken pleasure in myself physically. All the same, when Larry was in an angry mood I was "dirty", had "disgusting shadows on my ankles" etc.'

There were rumours among some who knew them in Cairo that he had resorted to physical violence as well. Apart from the one incident in Paris, when he rushed out of the bedroom and charged into her, causing her to fall down the stairs, she never mentioned him hitting her. And in a curious way, even if he did occasionally resort to what she called 'bashes' I don't think that would have caused her to leave. Her picture of a bohemian marriage allowed for behaviour that is now deemed beyond the pale. She was clear about what had brought her to breaking point. It was the 'betrayal, so difficult always to put your finger on, or fight, that is so damaging and hurtful – not the bashes – but the being done down, sold up the river under the pretence of a united front'. Larry was a supreme games player, and while she was with him she was so caught up by his overwhelming personality, his determination to dominate any encounter and his success in keeping her firmly behind that wall of ice, that she was probably unable to contemplate life away from him. After a few weeks away, as she began to discover the relief of being single, she knew she had no choice. In order to recover and grow she had to make a life in which he had no part.

Larry made one final attempt to make her change her mind. She describes a train journey from Beirut to Jerusalem during which he talked all night, trying to persuade her to return. He insisted that he had only been unfaithful to her twice. Once was with Teresa Epstein, whom he had met in Paris, and once was with Dorothy Stevenson, one of the dancers who had spent the summer of 1938 with them in Corfu. When I spoke to her friend Veronica, I mentioned that Larry claimed to have had a bit of a fling with Dorothy. Veronica's response was immediate and unequivocal. 'Balls!' she said, looking me straight in the eye, and then went on to explain that Dorothy was totally committed to her career, and would never have put it all in jeopardy by risking pregnancy. Of course it is quite possible that Dorothy was ashamed of the brief coupling ('behind a rock', as Larry described it to Nancy) and so denied it, but there is also the intriguing possibility that Larry, battling to save his marriage – or maybe out of pique – felt he had not been unfaithful enough during the ten years they spent together, and felt obliged to invent a second infidelity.

It didn't do the trick. Larry returned to Cairo alone, and Nancy did her best to survive with Penelope in Palestine. Gradually heartache was replaced by anger and bitterness. Larry moved to Alexandria and extolled the sensual delights of Alexandrian women, such a contrast to the 'sphincter bound' Anglo-Saxon type. In time he met Eve Cohen, Nancy's opposite in so many ways, and eventually they married. If he mentioned Nancy at all it was in tones of casual contempt, and when *The Black Book* was republished after the war, he dropped her name from the dedication. Sometimes he looked back with a judicious wisdom that had been missing at the time, as in the three lines in his poem 'Conon in Exile':

We never learned that marriage is a kind of architecture,
The nursery virtues were missing, all of them,
So nobody could tell us why we suffered.

Nancy was always dismissive when she talked about him, and maintained his later success was due to his having sold out to commercialism. She claimed never to have read *The Alexandria Quartet* and apparently told her second husband not to bother with anything Larry wrote after *The Black Book*, though their copies of his later books always looked fairly well-thumbed to me.

The façade of indifference masked strong feelings that never quite went away. In one of his notebooks, dated about two years after Nancy had left him, Larry roughed out a poem that seems, unlike so many of his public utterances, to have come straight from the heart. It is a poem saturated with the anguish of loss:

In Athens the hills do not turn
Towards the light their faces nor the sea
Reaching to the moon makes half this tidal wish
Of mine, sitting alone on a stone on a hill,
Waiting, or minding the business of clocks,
But chiefly waiting and wanting by minutes.
Hunting the thought of you, of the letters
I have not written, the house . . .
The quiet room over the sea, the lost
In photographs and diaries hunting envy

The poor self had enough confusion
The mind enough terrors without
Your punishment of going.
My expense was all in you,
Therefore the air is empty now
Too much for poems, or letter

I privately, in another place
Put up this wall of will against the loss of you.

He never worked it up into a state in which he might have chosen to publish it. For me, it is one of the most moving pieces he ever wrote, and offers a glimpse of the kind of poet he might have been if he had allowed his real emotions to shine through, rather than, as was so often the case, masking them in obscurity. Those close to him were not the only ones to be confined by him behind a wall of ice; Larry's own personal wall of ice grew even

more impermeable after Nancy's departure. He wanted passionately to impose his personality on friends and readers, but it was
a carefully edited version of himself that he offered for public
consumption. Nancy was familiar with all his contradictions, and
she was no more immune than he was to the heartbreak of their
parting. He might have been impossible to live with, but she
never ceased to care for him. One afternoon in early January
1967, a quarter of a century after she left him, when she and I
were sitting in the London flat and chatting over tea, the phone
rang. Nancy answered it. It was bad news. Claude, Larry's third
wife, had died suddenly. Nancy had met Claude a few years earlier, when she and my father had travelled down to the south of
France to talk through some anxieties over Penelope with him.
She had been impressed by Claude, and thought that she was just
the kind of tough-skinned, managerial wife that Larry needed.
And now Claude was dead, and Larry was alone again.

She put down the phone and turned to me. 'Who will look
after him now?' she wanted to know, tears spilling from her eyes.

It was the only time I ever saw her cry.

10

AN ATTRACTIVE LEAVE VENUE

Palestine in 1942 was a country of dizzying variety, Jerusalem most of all. The city's ancient walls encircled the aspirations of believers from three of the world's great religions. To the Muslims it was Al-Quds, the Holy City, dominated by the golden Dome of the Rock; almost immediately below that stood the Wailing Wall, symbol for nearly two thousand years of Jewish exile from their promised city; and close by lies the Church of the Holy Sepulchre, said to be built on the very spot where Christ was buried. A small city with a mighty significance, Jerusalem had been a magnet for religious mystics, pilgrims, crazies and all shades in between for centuries. The Christians were represented by Orthodox and Catholic, Syriacs and Ethiopians, Egyptian Copts, Armenians, Melchites, Chaldeans and every kind of Protestant. Some continued the age-old tradition of hospitality to travellers, while others were simply making sure they had a ringside seat when Christ returned to earth in all His glory at the Second Coming.

The massive walls around the Old City had been built by Suleiman the Magnificent when Henry VIII ruled in England, and entry was still through gates with wonderfully evocative names, including Herod's Gate, St Stephen's, Damascus, Jaffa and Zion. Once inside, the traveller plunged into what seemed like hundreds of complicated little streets teeming with figures of picture-book exoticism: the curled ringlets of the orthodox Jew contrasted with the starched headdress of the Catholic nun; Greek Orthodox priests with stovepipe hats and Palestinian women serene under elaborate tall headdresses; Bedouin from the desert, soldiers and sailors from Europe and the Antipodes, Palestinian police and small boys clamouring to sell dirty pictures or images of the '*Toomb Hully Vuggin, two piastres*', as a contemporary of Nancy's noted. The polyglot population had been swelled by refugees from Hitler's Europe: as well as Arabic, Greek, English and Armenian, the cafés now echoed with conversation in Czech, Polish, German and Yiddish.

During the war, the troops in the Middle East had their own weekly magazine, *Parade*. It was large-format, and lavishly illustrated, in the style of *Picture Post*. From their headquarters in Cairo, the editors aimed to convey essential facts about the progress of the war with upbeat reports on civilian life in Britain: pictures of horse-drawn ploughs and cherry orchards frothing with blossom, as well as smiling land girls and women at work in munitions factories. There were also articles on places where soldiers might enjoy their leave. Palestine was shown as the perfect place for a spot of leave, which was just as well since it was really the only place for soldiers who were fighting in North Africa. So *Parade* declared breezily:

Although troops stationed in Palestine complain that the country is dull, men fresh from sandy months in Egypt find Palestine's fresh greenness a welcome change. Its sunny Mediterranean atmosphere, its smart modern towns, its abundance of gay night haunts and restaurants, its low prices and its easy transport facilities make Palestine an attractive leave venue.

This cheery description masked a sombre reality. Palestine was a country moving inexorably towards a massive upheaval, not the Second Coming so fervently awaited by the more extreme sectarians, but the Jewish–Arab conflict that in 1948 led to the creation of the State of Israel, still known to Palestinians as the Nakba – the Catastrophe. This troubled land was the unlikely haven where Nancy was to spend the next five years, longer than she had spent in Corfu and Paris combined. Since Palestine was far from just an attractive leave venue, it is worth touching on the main events which had brought it to this state of precarious tension.

Until the First World War, Palestine had been a part of the Ottoman Empire, loosely ruled and a place where, for the most part, different races and religions co-existed without serious conflict. But in 1917, wishing to gain the support of influential Jews to the Allied cause, the British government issued the Balfour Declaration. This promised British support for the creation of a national home for the Jews in Palestine, with the proviso that the civil and religious rights of the existing population should not be prejudiced: twin aims that were irreconcilable from the start. When the Ottoman Empire collapsed a year later the Allies were left with large swathes of the Middle East to be stabilised; the concept of the mandate was evolved. The theory was that Britain and France would govern Syria, Lebanon, Transjordan and Palestine 'until such time as they were able to stand alone'. Britain took over Palestine with the aim of both developing self-government and promoting the aims of the Balfour Declaration. Since self-governing Palestinians would always oppose the Balfour Declaration, impossible contradiction was piled on impossible contradiction.

The initial suspicions of the Palestinian Arabs were intensified by a rising tide of Jewish immigration. In 1918 there were fifty-five thousand Jews in Palestine, about 7 per cent of the population. By the outbreak of the Second World War the exact number of Jews was impossible to estimate, since there was almost as much illegal as legal immigration, but they made up more than 30 per cent of the population. Axis persecution transformed the tide into a flood: desperate Jews regarded Palestine as 'a land without people for a people without land'. For those who had lived there for generations, it was obvious where this would lead, and they resisted as best they could. British attempts at neutrality only made enemies all round. The Arabs regarded them as Zionist sympathisers while the Jews were convinced they were pro-Arab and therefore to be thrown out. When war between Britain and Germany was declared fighting between Arab and Jew temporarily declined. There was no way that the Jews could support the Axis forces, and while some Palestinians supported Germany on the basis that 'my enemy's enemy is my friend', most simply waited to see who would win. But the problem had been put on hold, not solved. It was not an easy place for a woman to survive on her own with a small child.

Penelope and Nancy relaxing together in Jerusalem

One of Nancy's mantras when I was growing up was the impor-tance of having a marketable skill, 'so that if ever you're alone with a child you can support yourself'. (It did no good; neither my sister nor I ever had a proper trade.) Nancy's attempts to make a living before her unexpected inheritance on her twenty-first birthday had not been particularly successful, and now she also had sole responsibility for Penelope. Just how much Larry contributed over the next few years is impossible to say for sure: less than he made out and more than Nancy credited him with is probably about right. His wages had only just covered their outgoings when they were together, so there was not much to divide. As well as coping with the emotional aftermath of a failed marriage, Nancy had to deal with the practicalities, and she and Penelope often had to fall back on the generosity of friends.

To begin with, they stayed with Reggie Smith and Olivia Manning. Reggie was an ebullient bear of a man, generous to a fault, who was to be immortalised by his wife in her *Fortunes of War* series as Guy Pringle. Olivia seemed to be his opposite in every way: introverted and spiky, and as outspoken in her criticisms as Reggie was generous in his praise. She was never going to be pop-ular, but I get the feeling that it was difficult to be a clever woman in a society that was male dominated in a way that is hard to imag-ine nowadays, especially if you were not prepared – or did not know how – to play the feminine game. For most men in her circle the female sex was divided into beautiful girls and all the rest. It was possible to remain a beautiful girl for quite some time, and while Nancy at thirty definitely fitted that category, Olivia was strange-looking, which contributed to her bad press. But her books are terrific and she was kind to Nancy at a time when she needed it. Reggie, who was controller of programmes at the Palestine Broadcasting Station, gave Nancy small parts in plays whenever he could. Her light voice made her suitable for children's parts.

Nancy and Wallace Southarn in Beirut

For a while she went up to Beirut and stayed with other friends, Wallace and Anna Southarn, where she painted a little picture of the household pottering about their tasks, a painting which has survived. Back in Jerusalem again, she did some work for Nebby Samuels in the Censorship Office, helped out Gershon Agronsky at the *Palestine Post*, got by the best she could. It didn't help that she had never learned to type. In Corfu once, when Larry was confined to bed with 'grippe and a temperature', he was obliged to dictate a letter to Nancy. It was one of the briefest Henry ever received from him, only thirteen lines, because, as Larry explained, 'the faces Nancy is making over the machine are something awful'. In Jerusalem, desperation forced her to gloss over this shortcoming; at an interview for one job she was asked if she could type. 'Yes,' she said without hesitation. On her first day at work the lie was revealed; her boss found her hen-pecking at the keys and put her in a side office for a couple of days while she improved her skills, but she was never very good.

Right at the end of my researches for this book, I discovered that another friend of my mother's was still alive, this time someone she had known during the Jerusalem period. And so, just a week after Penelope died, I went to Jerusalem with my cousin Liz, who knows the city well, and met Lotte Geiger, who had befriended Nancy soon after she arrived in Palestine. It was Lotte who arranged the job in the Censorship Office, Lotte who recommended a suitable kindergarden for Penelope, and Lotte who helped Nancy find somewhere to live.

At ninety-six, Lotte was still a remarkable woman who lived alone in a second-floor flat and stomped up two flights of stairs without help. 'What's the secret to staying so fit when you're nearly a hundred?' we asked her. She grinned. 'Think only of yourself!' she answered firmly. She had left Germany in 1933: on the day of the national boycott of Jewish businesses she noticed a large crowd outside a newsagent's shop and pushed her way through. Inside she found the terrified staff and asked to use the phone. She called up her boyfriend and said, 'We have to get out of this country now.' Her loyalty to Israel had not blinded her to what she saw as its downward trajectory. 'I feel,' she said firmly, 'the same way now about Israel' – that it had reached a point of no return, and if she were younger, she would leave.

She talked about Nancy as she had known her, and we tried to unravel some of the puzzles left by conflicting accounts of that time. Most of them – such as Nancy saying she was always hard up, while Larry claimed to be sending her money – are easy to explain, others less so. The one conundrum I was unable to solve was Lotte's insistence that Nancy claimed Larry had been too mean to pay for a doctor and so she'd been forced to give birth in terrible agony on the floor of a peasant hut. It is possible that Lotte had simply misremembered, and had transposed Nancy's account of the confinements of their Corfu neighbours to Nancy herself. It is also possible that, alone and adrift in an uncertain world, Nancy took a holiday from her usual devotion to truth and created a more dramatic backstory for herself. Remembering my mother's rigorous honesty, I find that hard to believe, but have to accept it as a possibility. Emerging from a marriage that was both difficult and hugely enriching, and which had imposed on her an identity which she now was eager to shake off, Nancy must have been struggling to create a new self, so maybe she did experiment with the kind of manipulation of the past that Larry and Gerry were both to elevate into a fine art. Lies and truth are the threads that run all through her life, from her mother's creation of a false self to her own youthful longing for art that would strip away the 'veils of lies and deceit', so the idea that she might herself have indulged in a bit of creativity with the truth remains a tantalising possibility. And one which, this time, there is no relevant newspaper article to help unravel.

On our second meeting with Lotte, after she'd treated us to an excellent lunch, she was keen to take us by taxi around the places where Nancy had lived. We drove south from the Old City, past the site where the Allenby Barracks had stood, and on towards the hills now covered in suburban housing and blocks of flats where she and Nancy had been living when they first got to know each other. 'Slow down here,' she said to the taxi driver. 'It's just on the left. Turn here.' Then, as we drove down the street, she said, 'No, not this one. It must be the next.' But that wasn't it either. We drove slowly down several streets full of modern houses, the taxi driver infinitely patient, Lotte rueful and apologetic, but the places where Nancy and Penelope had lived were proving elusive. 'All this was desert!' she explained, gesturing towards the dense housing developments that stretched out in every direction. In the end we managed to find a square, bunker-like building where Lotte herself had moved towards the end of the war: it was in a street packed with houses with views across to the bare outline of the Jericho hills far in the distance. 'There were only six houses on this street when we lived here,' she said sadly. 'It was all different. Everything was different.'

We never found a single place where Nancy had lived. It became a kind of journey of lost memories. We returned to her flat to console ourselves with tea and cake, and it was there that Lotte said the most telling thing of all. 'When I met Nancy again in London in the 1950s,' she said, 'she wasn't the same person. She was different.' How? I wanted to know. But Lotte found it hard to pinpoint the precise difference. Had she been warmer, more spontaneous in 1942? 'Well, yes,' said Lotte, 'but it was more than that. She had been different.' More than just the usual progression of someone's character as they age, there had been a fundamental difference between the Nancy she had known in Palestine and the Nancy she had visited when she was married to her second husband (who remained a close friend to Lotte) and living in London.

All of which raises the intriguing possibility that I, who in some ways knew Nancy so well, am in fact trying to write about a pre-1947 Nancy who is essentially a stranger, someone I never knew at all. And there is always the danger that the woman I was so familiar with in the 1960s is being superimposed upon her younger self, however dispassionate I try to be and however much this account is based on her own words.

Some time in 1944, at a party thrown by Reggie and Olivia in their Jerusalem flat, Nancy met the man who was to dominate her life for the next three years. There had been flirtations before; Nancy had a wide circle of friends in Palestine and was attractive – Wallace Southarn said simply that she was the most beautiful young woman he ever met – but this time it was serious. Mike Silver was older than her, dark-haired with a bushy moustache and a hooked nose – in photographs, one can see something piratical in his appearance. He had a strong personality and was the kind of man whose presence was immediately noticed in a room. When Nancy met him he was at a very low ebb, a 'lost person', in his own words, having been badly wounded at Alamein. His vulnerability appealed to Nancy's need to care for someone, while at the same time he was protective and could offer her security of sorts.

Mike was nearly forty. His origins were mysterious, left-wing and Jewish, but the details are obscure. He grew up in England and his father died when he was still at school, but socialist friends of the family stepped in and paid for the rest of his education. When he left school he joined the Communist Party and worked for Claud Cockburn on the *News Chronicle*. All his life he regretted not having fought in the Spanish Civil War, but like hundreds of others he left the Party in 1939 over the Nazi–Soviet pact. In 1941 Mike had been in the Royal Tank Regiment in Crete – at the same time as Theodore Stephanides – and fought in the gruelling rearguard action as the Germans drove Allied troops from the island. From there he fought in the Western Desert as first the Allies forced the Italians westwards and then the Germans under Rommel pushed back. At Alamein his tank received a direct hit; he was the only survivor. Thrown from the turret, he suffered a fractured pelvis and shattered ribs and was in and out of hospital for over a year. The emotional scars took longer to heal. Nancy said when he was picked up in the desert he had been cradling the head of his closest friend in his arms.

Nancy and Mike intended to marry

It was a serious relationship, and one which both thought would lead to marriage, but it was far from tranquil. Both Nancy and Mike were emotionally strung out, suffering from stresses that erupted into physical symptoms: Mike suffered with what he called 'bumps and nervous excitement' while Nancy was during that period afflicted with an involuntary and very noticeable twitch that convulsed one side of her face. She said of him afterwards that 'he always needed something doing, either cheering up or calming down', and in a letter he wrote to her after they had parted, he remembered 'the loveyness of you when I crept to you like a frightened dog full of appeals because I couldn't sleep'.

That same letter provides snapshots of their turbulent times together:

> ... the first time I saw you weep at Halgaberg; the sinister man with the shufflefeet; tea in the YMCA; how affectionate I felt towards you when you displayed jealousy at the kids who crowded round after an ARK broadcast; lovely suppers at Anona; my being boorish with Ellen and Hans because they gave you something I lacked; the sight of you trying to look professional at the Post; the madman with his love letters I frightened off outside the Zion; being a tough with some blacks to show you how brave your man could be; endeavouring to clear away smoke and soot to the accompaniment of Olivia's whining to Reggie in the next room; riding an elephant with Pinkie at the zoo ...

Mike was aware, though, of his own shortcomings: 'Never did I give you any real relaxation and mental happiness: we never spent days on golden sands listening to the lapping sea; even when we went away together it was never to surroundings that might be considered conducive to mingling into one. I continually broke the continuity of our oneness by having to rush off here and there.' At one time, in one of their many emotional scenes, she hurled at him, 'I want a mate!' Both wounded, both needy and frightened, they tried to give each other what they needed but couldn't always manage it.

And Mike was married. His wife was in England with their daughter, who was about the same age as Penelope. No area of his life, or Nancy's, was straightforward. In Palestine his idealism focused on the creation of a socialist Jewish homeland. He had been involved with Haganah, the underground Jewish army, but his links with both the British army and the Jewish underground meant he was regarded with suspicion by both sides. As he recovered from the Alamein catastrophe he started to get radio work, most of it in Cairo.

Life became slightly more secure for Nancy when she was employed by the British Council. She taught English to Polish officers in Jerusalem and, in the second half of 1944, worked with Greek refugees at a camp in the south-west of Palestine. Nuseirat lay between the ancient city of Gaza and the sea. Fourteen thousand Greeks, mostly peasants who had fled starvation and the tyranny of Nazi rule, lived there in a tented city. Most of the men of military age had gone into the services, but women, children and the elderly were cared for with schools and a hospital. Nancy was sent there as her knowledge of Greek gave her an advantage when teaching English. A glowing reference written by the British Council director in Tel Aviv declared that 'Her experience with foreign peoples has brought sympathy and understanding in regard to their difficulties both of language and outlook.' But even here were political divisions to negotiate. Greece was liberated in October 1944, but the Allies quickly crushed the EAM, the left-wing resistance movement, in order to support the royalists. Conflict between the two erupted into bitter civil war, and the animosities spilled over into the Nuseirat camp. In December Olivia Manning wrote to a friend: 'I cannot pretend they are all pro-EAM here – an English girl friend of ours, wife of Lawrence Durrell, who is working at the Refugee camp at Gaza has had stones thrown at her because of her strong pro-EAM feelings.' It was while she was working in Gaza that she and Larry began the tortuous proceedings which would lead, eventually, to divorce.

After the initial shock of Nancy's departure had worn off, Larry strove to give the impression that he was enjoying his new-found freedom. In February 1944 he wrote to Henry that Nancy and the child were well but in another climate. He got no direct news of them and it was nearly two years since he'd seen either of them so he'd almost forgotten what they meant – 'symbolic appendices to walk around with' is how he describes them. He added that he himself was 'devilish gay and empty'. But a few months later he admits that he has met and fallen for a beautiful young Egyptian called Yvette Cohen. (Later she adopted the English variant, Eve.) In many ways Nancy's polar opposite, she was small and dark, beautiful, passionate and troubled, but she was also stateless and Larry's eagerness for a divorce grew more intense as the time came for him to leave Egypt. He needed to marry Eve so she could travel with him.

In November 1944 he wrote Nancy a conciliatory letter. It began with expressions of concern. Floods had been reported in the Nuseirat area of Palestine and he was worried. 'If you or Pinky are in any need please don't hesitate to cable me for anything I can send, or money if you need it.' The reason for his generosity is soon apparent: he wants the divorce to move ahead but 'since the whole subject seems not to arouse a great deal of interest in you' he wants to know if she intends to go ahead immediately. 'If you are doing so, well and good, but if not is it because the whole legal machinery worries and bores you?' In which case, Larry suggests that he could file a desertion plea. If she agrees to let him claim that she left in February, not July, 1942, then he could claim three years' desertion sooner and by March or April 1945 'we would both be free'. He ends by reassuring her that 'you need have no fear that I will try and take Pinky away from you. I promise you that I would not even insist on seeing her. I feel I've grown up quite a lot and would like to settle this business amicably – if you would be prepared to offer your friendly cooperation.'

Most probably Nancy did not reply, and that was the last anyone heard of 'friendly cooperation'. The rest of their correspondence in the divorce file is as bitter and combative as these things usually are, even now when divorce is so much easier. A week after his first letter to Nancy, Larry wrote to her Jerusalem solicitor, presumably in response to Nancy's statement that he had not made any contribution towards Penelope's upkeep. Larry asserts:

Since the date mentioned in your letter
a) My wife has not answered my letters, and has not offered me any news of the child's welfare.
b) Has refused to let me see it.
c) Has refused to visit me in Alexandria (expenses paid) with the child.
d) Has refused information concerning the child to my family.
I was therefore obliged to take the only course open to me – namely to stop her allowance.

However, he now undertakes to pay a regular fifteen pounds per month, but in return he wants to know whether he has any rights: 'I should be entitled to the pleasure of its company for at least 6 months of the year. Also, I have not been consulted as to its schooling. I understand it has been farmed out in Jerusalem and denied any kind of home atmosphere entirely due to my wife's wilful and selfish stubbornness.' He says firmly, 'If my wife's income is inadequate to support it, may I now undertake to support it myself,' and ends with a grandiose flourish: 'It is regretful that this sort of behaviour should be allowed to prejudice the natural growth of the child in propitious surroundings.'

Nancy must have then paid a rare visit to her solicitor's office, because some notes handwritten by him after the meeting form the basis of his next letter to Larry. He writes, 'Your wife is agree-able to your visiting your daughter at any reasonable time at which you desire to do so. She wishes, however, to point out that during several visits by you to Palestine you did not even utter the wish to see your child.' As regards the accusation that Penelope has been deprived of 'home atmosphere', he says that,

> the reason for your child not being with her mother is that Mrs Durrell is at present working at a Refugee Camp, where she considers she cannot properly look after the child. The arrangement is a purely temporary one, and Mrs Durrell intends, as soon as circumstances permit, to resume living with your daughter. We trust that you will agree that a small girl is better looked after in a kindergarden than she would be looked after by you, who is at present living on his own, and presum-ably most of his time out of his house.

The solicitor goes on to state that 'your wife will be glad to con-sult you regarding its upbringing and education, provided you take an interest in this matter, which we understand, you have not done heretofore'. Larry responded with hauteur: 'I regret that when I passed through Palestine I did not attempt to trace the child, but as it would have meant meeting my wife, I forbore to do so. It would have been distasteful.'

The correspondence continues with increasing bitterness, and neither Nancy nor Larry come out of it very well. The accusation that Penelope was being 'farmed out' and deprived of a proper home life was one that stung. In Nancy's defence it can be said that during the Second World War tens of thousands of children were separated from their parents 'for their own good', whether evacuees from bombing in London or children escaping Germany on the Kindertransport, and *Parade* regularly showed photographs of merry tots enjoying life in well-run institutions, safe from city bombing. The crucial importance of the bond between small children and their mothers was hardly going to be emphasised by a ruling class who, for the most part, had been reared by nannies and boarding schools. Still, the decision to leave Larry led to several very difficult years for Penelope, and Nancy always felt bad about this. In the midst of a divorce, however, she was not about to admit that to Larry, and though he tried valiantly to do things differently with his second daughter, in the end he had to admit defeat and Sappho too was brought up by her mother alone.

Albert Spaer was the unfortunate solicitor Nancy had chosen to act for her, and the only light relief in the proceedings comes from his increasing exasperation with both of them. Larry, despite continual reminders that all communication should be made through his own solicitors, insisted on writing to both Nancy and Spaer directly and, as was his custom, never dated his letters. In fact he didn't always use writing paper: one missive was typed on to four separate business cards, which Spaer was obliged to staple onto a sheet of paper in order to keep them together in the file. Nancy was even more infuriating, since what Larry referred to as her 'boredom' with the legal machinery had developed into a pathological inability to put pen to paper and she was maddeningly vague as to facts. 'We do not quite see why,' Mr Spaer scolds her, 'you should be unable to provide us with all the particulars to be inserted in the draft petition. You will have to make an affidavit bearing out these facts, and they must accordingly be within your knowledge.' It turned out that Nancy was unable to remember the date of their marriage, whether it had been in December 1934 or January 1935, and in the end Spaer was obliged to write to the Bournemouth Register Office for the correct information.

On 6 August 1945 the solicitor wrote testily to Nancy that she had not replied to his letters of 9 June, 2 July or 15 July. Two weeks later Spaer had still not heard from her. On 23 August Nancy wrote him a rare letter from the government hospital in Jaffa:

I am very sorry that I have been unable to reply to your letter of 2nd July [she does not mention the others] previously. Last month I went to Egypt and the letter has been following me about – I am now ill but expect to be in Jerusalem in about a week or 10 days' time and will let you know and fix an appointment.

Predictably, she failed to show up, prompting the solicitor to write on 18 September:

We regret very much to note that you have not thought fit to reply to our very numerous letters addressed to you, nor to get in touch as indicated in your last letter. Please understand that all proceedings in your case are now held up because of the lack of diligence shown by you in providing us with the information required by the English solicitors.

His nagging finally did the trick, because at the beginning of October – a mere ten days later – Nancy at last produced the information he needed. She must have been in the habit of drifting into his office, when she did at all, without warning, prompting him to request somewhat pompously that she 'please call on us after fixing an appointment telephonically'.

Divorce in the 1940s, even if all the parties cooperated, was still a long drawn out and farcical business, precisely designed to bring out the worst in both Larry and Nancy. There was the charade of the guilty party, which meant that a friend, in this case Paul Gotch, had to sign an affidavit that he had seen Larry and

Eve sharing a bedroom and the divorce petitions then had to be served on both of them. This meant Nancy had to provide a photograph of Eve, which of course she did not have. The combination of prurience and legalistic manoeuvrings was the epitome of all the Pudding Island bourgeois hypocrisy they both loathed, but the reasons for Nancy's prevarications go deeper than this.

She had as much reason as Larry to want a divorce, since she was now hoping to marry Mike. It wasn't that she didn't want to write to the lawyer, more that she couldn't. Long after the war, when she was far more secure and tranquil than she was in 1945, her second husband was similarly driven to distraction by her inability to put pen to paper when stressed. The most accommodating of men, he said one of the few occasions they rowed was when he discovered she had not been paying bills because of a mental block about writing even her signature on a cheque. His guess was that marriage to two fluent writers had somehow induced a kind of literary paralysis: I think it was more complicated than that, some kind of freeze response in a crisis, but I doubt if even she could have explained it fully.

Palestine in the mid 1940s was an increasingly troubled place, but there were moments of levity. Nancy was popular, with a wide circle of friends, some of whom lasted a lifetime. Chief among these was the third of those larger-than-life, outgoing personalities – like her first love, the flamboyant Roger Pettiward with whom she used to disrupt the art-school dances, like Henry and his baboon-cavorting in the cafés of Paris – she was drawn to, a man who was just beginning what was to become an iconic radio career. Jack de Manio had a gift of spreading happiness, a gift which was more valuable than ever in the midst of bleak wartime restrictions. He exuded warmth and an unquenchable zest for life.

Nancy in 1945

His laugh, his booming, plummy voice and his extraordinary smile provided many of my happiest times when I was a child. But this most English of personalities was not at all what he seemed. For a start, he wasn't English at all.

His father was an Italian aviator who had died before he was born; his Polish mother never remarried but enjoyed a string of admirers while Jack was growing up. She dressed him as Little Lord Fauntleroy for far too long, and he had an undistinguished school career, at the end of which he spent some time in the hotel trade. He applied for a job in the BBC but was turned down, and a caterer he might have remained but for the war. As he himself said, the war was a crucial point in his life, as it was for so many who had no clear idea of the direction their lives should take. He started well and won a Military Cross for his bravery with the British Expeditionary Force in France, when he pulled an airman from a plane 'despite the fact that it was burning fiercely and the ammunition was exploding'. He had, in the words of his citation, 'displayed great courage and coolness'.

Moreover, the airman for whom he had risked his life was one of 'the enemy'. He was then transferred to the Western Desert, where he proved to be an enterprising if eccentric catering officer, capturing vast quantities of Parmesan from the enemy and feeding it to the bemused troops, Italian food being considered by most people in the days of 'meat and two veg' to be inedible.

Some time in 1943 an administrative oversight meant that Jack found himself in receipt of two pay packets. In the atmosphere of living for the moment that prevailed in Egypt during those months when no one knew if they'd survive tomorrow, Jack regarded this as a stroke of unexpected good fortune and omitted to report the error, but on discovering their mistake the authorities took a different view. He was court-martialled and stripped of his lieutenant's rank, which, by the strict code of the day, meant that clubs and bars reserved for officers were now closed to him. In theory. Jack and Nancy enjoyed marching into officers' messes and loudly insisting on being served drinks at the bar. The tutting of the stuffed shirts observing this breach of etiquette only added to their pleasure.

Jack was rare among Nancy's male friends in that, so far as I know, there was never any hint of romance between them. She was with Mike when she could be, and Jack was engaged to Loveday – small, beautiful, with huge blue eyes and an infectious and mischievous giggle. He got work with Forces Radio in Beirut, where Mitzi, the first of the dachshunds that he and Loveday always had, was a familiar figure waddling in and out of the studio.

The end of the war was something of an anti-climax in Palestine, as here the conflict was far from over: the unspoken truce between the Arabs, Jews and British broke down. For

Nancy it meant the end of her work with the British Council, and the need for a new job. This time, her friendship with Henry Miller came to her rescue. In the third year of the war the Special Operations Executive (SOE) had established an Arab broadcasting station in Palestine to counteract the Axis propaganda coming out of Radio Bari and thus retain Arab loyalty to the British. It was called Sharq al-Adna and a certain mystique has grown up around its activities and funding, most of it, as far as I can make out, unjustified. Its second director was Aidan Phillips, who had just read *The Colossus of Maroussi*. A man of passionate enthusiasms, Aidan raved about the book to anyone and everyone, and tried to find out all he could about the author, until one day he happened to be bombarding Olivia and Reggie with questions. 'If you want to know about Henry Miller,' Olivia told him, 'you'd better talk to Nancy Durrell. She knows him well.' Aidan sought Nancy out, took her out for meals, and she talked to him about Henry and his books. When her work with the British Council came to an end he offered her a job. It was almost his last action before handing over the running of the station to his successor, Edward Hodgkin.

Edward – or Teddy, as he was almost universally known in Palestine – had not had a particularly challenging war, despite having enlisted the day after war was declared. He had passed two years in training, night exercises and postings to remote parts of the British Isles, apart from a few months in India in 1940. In desperation he had applied to a friend to get him into SOE. He was sent to Iraq just as the Axis threat in the Middle East had receded; he enjoyed his time in Baghdad and trips north into Kurdistan, but it was hardly demanding. So when, at the end of hostilities, he was offered the prospect of running Sharq he leapt at it; at last he could do something of value. He had loved

Palestine when he visited the country in the 1930s, though now it was obvious the country was anything but peaceful. He was never anti-Semitic, but Teddy's sympathies were definitely pro-Arab.

The newsroom, where Nancy was to work, was in Jerusalem, but in 1945 the headquarters of Sharq al-Adna were still in Jaffa, and that was where she and Teddy first met. He has described their meeting. Nancy had been in Cairo, staying with Mike between jobs, and for some reason, perhaps because she was feeling unwell, she had stopped in Jaffa on her way to Jerusalem. Teddy wrote:

It was one summer evening after dark, about 6.30 or 7, that an army pickup truck stopped outside our gate, and out of it emerged Captain Peter Magaw, the officer in charge of the transmitting station at Beit Gala, who had been driving, and a tall blond girl with a small blond child. The first thing I noticed about Nancy was that she seemed very tired – natural enough for someone who has just completed the 10 or 12 hours road journey from Egypt. She sat in one of the wood-framed, leather-seated armchairs, saying little, with a very noticeable nervous tic on her left cheek. For Nancy it was, for that day at least, the end of the journey, but not so for poor Pinky. After something to eat and drink, Magaw said he ought to be off, and Pinky, who was going back to the Sisters of Zion convent, with him. A brief unemotional goodbye with her mother (the two of them, you could see, used to the frequent partings and impermanent lodgings of war) and the truck had moved off.

The next day Nancy was admitted to Jaffa Hospital (from where she wrote that rare letter to her much-tested solicitor) and for the next few days Teddy and his second-in-command, Jonesey, visited with gifts of fruit and books. She was apologetic at having started her job by falling ill and being a nuisance. They reassured her: not at all, everything is well organised. Teddy will go to Jerusalem to cover a shift. It is what he most enjoys. She tells them her temperature is down and she hopes to be out soon. Teddy was impressed by what another friend later described as

Nancy and Teddy relaxing. Also Jonesey, Teddy's deputy

'her contentment with her solitude' as well as by her particular beauty, 'enigmatic and appealing'. But he was plunged into work which he was enjoying, and for the next two years they were colleagues and friends, nothing more.

As soon as Nancy was well enough she went to Jerusalem to start work as one of three deputies to Louis Lawler, who was in charge of the newsroom. After a while she and Louis shared a flat that was rented in the station's name in the Katamon district. Louis was devoted to both Nancy and Penelope, though he found it a bore when Mike joined them, which he did whenever he could.

Teddy has described the work Nancy was to do for the next two years:

There were five fifteen-minute news bulletins each day and each bulletin was supposed to be supervised by a member of the British staff, normally by an assistant to the head of the news room, of whom Nancy was one. When they were not available Lawler or Chudleigh (Derek Chudleigh, who succeeded Lawler) or myself would stand in for them, and I have an idea that the Arabs were often left unsupervised for the uncomfortably early bulletin which went out at about 7 a.m. and so had to be got ready an hour and a half or so in advance. They would ring up instead to say what was going into the bulletin.

Each bulletin was prepared by a team of three Arabs – an editor (I think we called him though really he was more a sub-editor) who explained the material, if it was in Arabic, to the British supervisor who put agency and other messages into some sort of shape and then passed them on to a junior sub-editor who produced a final draft (in Arabic of course) which he then passed to the third member of the team, who typed it ready for the announcer. I have a picture of Nancy sitting cool-looking and at ease at the head of the table in the vaulted stone room where the news was prepared. Badam Azam is reading from some paper, carrying messages telephoned in from our correspondents in one of the Arab capitals – Damascus, perhaps, 'He says that the municipality of Aleppo have sent a telegram to President Truman protesting against America's vote in the Security Council.'

'No, we don't want that,' says Nancy.

'No, I don't think it is important,' Badam agrees, and moves on to the next item. Although she was extremely diffident about her qualifications as a news editor, maintaining that she knew nothing about politics, Nancy's common sense was pretty infallible. And she was always prepared to ask, 'Well, what do you think, Badam?' Or bringing in Number Two, 'Let's ask Walid. Do you think we should put it in?' So decisions were often reached in a nice democratic way – and of course, the staff loved her because she had not the slightest trace of arrogance or false superiority. They were her colleagues and therefore her friends, and it is not surprising that they valued her judgement on much more than what was to go into Sharq's news bulletins. She was consulted on problems of children's education and health, on difficulties with parents or on love affairs; on what to eat and whether it would be a good idea to emigrate to America. On anything, in fact.

Teddy was writing about Nancy less than a year after she died, and his description of that time is coloured by nearly forty years of loving closeness. He was never the slightest bit critical of those he loved, her most of all; in retrospect, Nancy could do no wrong. He described her part in a visit from the assistant under-secretary at the Foreign Office in charge of Middle East affairs, who was visiting Sharq at Teddy's request: though he enjoyed their independence, he thought London ought to have some input into what they were doing. Ivone Kirkpatrick duly turned up and was shown round the station. "'This," I said, "is the news room, and this is Mrs Durrell who is getting the twelve o'clock bulletin ready to go out." Kirkpatrick's eyes brightened at the sight of this beautiful English girl and he spent longer asking her questions than he had spent with anyone else. "Supposing," said Kirkpatrick, "a piece of news came in which

you were doubtful about – whether it was right to use it – what
would you do?"

"'I would ring up Colonel Hodgkin," said Nancy demurely, to
everyone's satisfaction.'

*

During 1946 Teddy spent more and more time in Jerusalem.
Jewish terrorism had been mounting ever since the danger of
German victory in the Middle East receded in 1943, and the end
of the war was the signal for the Zionists to ratchet up the pressure to get the British out. Sharq al-Adna, being both British
and Arab, was obviously a prime target for their attacks. By the
summer of 1946 Derek Chudleigh had taken over from Louis
Lawler as head of the newsroom and had also taken his room in
the Katamon flat with Nancy. It was Derek's custom, on the way
home from work, to stop for a drink at the King David Hotel,
part of which housed the British civilian administration. On 22
July members of Irgun, the extreme right-wing Zionist underground organisation, blew up part of the hotel, killing more than
ninety people. For some reason Derek Chudleigh had not paid
his usual visit to the bar that day. He returned home to be
greeted by six-year-old Penelope: 'Hello, Derek. You're meant to
be dead.'

The situation deteriorated. Jewish terrorists (or freedom fight-
ers) kidnapped a judge; sergeants were flogged and hanged; Tel
Aviv was put under curfew. Restrictions on the British increased
and, in order to reduce the risk of sabotage, the transmission of
Sharq's broadcasts was moved from Jaffa to Jerusalem, which
meant that instead of seeing Teddy on his two or three visits each
week, Nancy now saw him pretty much every day. By the beginning of 1947 the situation had got so bad that women and
children were evacuated from Jerusalem, though an exemption
was obtained for Nancy. Soon afterwards all British in the main

towns were concentrated in special areas surrounded by Dannert wire and other protections, from which Arabs and Jews were supposed to be excluded. Teddy persuaded the authorities to recognise their radio station buildings as a small secure area with its own special guard, but it meant that they were confined for weeks on end inside their bleak little compound. In the evenings they played cards, drank a good deal and talked. Officers –Teddy was a colonel – were ordered to carry a firearm at all times. The technical chief had a special shoulder holster made for his weapon. Teddy, who was less warlike and always disliked being told what to do, carried his pistol around in a brown HMSO envelope and used to plonk the package on the table whenever he sat down. I doubt it was ever loaded. (His mild contempt for the trappings of militarism, a legacy no doubt from his Quaker forebears, might have been a reason why he was never sent on active service.) Nancy approved of his disdain for regulations, and she admired his directorial style. The door to his office was left open at all times, so that anyone could drop in whenever they wanted. She noted that he wrote with great ease: if a piece had to be prepared he would break off in the middle of a party, or evening of conversation, scribble away for ten minutes in a corner of the room and come back with the job done. Given her tortuous relationship with the written word, Teddy's fluency did indeed seem remarkable.

By the early summer of 1947 there was an awareness that, for the British, life in Palestine was drawing to a close. Mike had already left for South Africa. His movements before this are hard to pin down: there were rumours that he was working as a spy, and that he had to be got away in a hurry and spent some months in Cyprus. Some time in May, Nancy announced that she wanted to leave. She was going to join Mike, who had secured a job with

an advertising agency in Johannesburg. No one was unduly surprised as there was what has been described as a *sauve qui peut*
mood among British nationals. It was obvious that whatever the
outcome of the worsening conflict between Jews and Arabs, the
British could no longer hold the ring. Exhausted by six years of
war, impoverished and over-stretched, the British government
had neither the will nor the means to continue the responsibility of the Palestine mandate. In February 1947 they had referred
the problem to the newly created United Nations. Teddy had
decided to call it a day, and a new director was being sent out to
replace him at the end of the summer.

Then, as he describes it, 'something went wrong' and Nancy
asked if she could rescind her resignation. Teddy telegraphed
Cairo but it was too late: her replacement had been appointed
and there was no work for her at the station. Moreoever, she had
given up her room at the flat. The outlook was dire: she had no
job, no prospects and would soon have no home. The 'something'
that had gone wrong was that communication with Mike had
dried up. He had promised to send her out money and tickets, so
she and Penelope could follow him to South Africa, but these
never arrived. Nor did any word of explanation.

Teddy recalled in detail the events that followed:

It was one hot summer evening, walking back rather tipsy
from a party in Katamon, that we called in at the Public
Information Office for something to eat. I had been wearing an
Old Etonian tie, I suppose because I had earlier to go and see
the Chief Secretary, or some other dignitary I wanted to
impress (would never have worn it otherwise) and as we
walked slowly along I thought it a nice idea to tie it round a
lamp-post; somebody when dawn came might be surprised or
amused by the sight.

(Why, I can't help wondering. How many residents in Jerusalem would have recognised or been remotely interested in an Old Etonian tie? But for some reason they both regarded this detail as central to their story.) In any case, as Teddy said:

Nancy liked the gesture. We sat at a table eating bacon and eggs. 'I like round tables,' I said.

'So do I,' said Nancy.

'We seem to agree about everything,' I said. 'Mightn't it be a good idea to get married?'

'Well, I don't know about *that*,' said Nancy. But there was that mixture of calm and storm, of confidence and excitement, in the air which accompanies rapidly maturing love. I was happy and hopeful.

Teddy always maintained that until that moment in the Public Information Office he had never regarded Nancy as anything but a colleague and a friend. But, as he said, 'It seemed suddenly the most sensible idea I had ever had.'

A few days later, at another party (there were a lot of parties that summer, as everyone got ready to leave and said their farewells), Nancy said she had decided that it would be right to get married. "You ought to be pleased," she said. I was. She thought the first practical step we should take would be to find ourselves a room somewhere so that we could sleep together and get to know each other better – still in so many ways strangers. The next day she arranged this with someone called Sylvia who had a spare bedroom at the back of her house in the German Colony. There we installed ourselves.

Writing about it in 1984, Teddy admitted that it must have looked as if Nancy was desperate and that he felt sorry for her but, a romantic to the end, he said simply that they suddenly, and completely, fell in love. And maybe so. How much was a sudden instinctive recognition that the person sitting opposite them at the table was a person they might be happy with for the rest of their lives, how much expediency, how much that familiar wanting to hang on to someone from a place and time which has been important – like all the couples who marry at the end of their time at university – it's impossible to know at this distance. What I find curious is that for the second time in her life Nancy was about to plunge into marriage with one man while she was still, at least to some extent, pining for another.

They kept their decision pretty much to themselves, but in those final days in Palestine, days of packing up, parties and picnics and sorting out paperwork, they spent as much time together as they could. Penelope was told and for reasons of privacy they did this together in the flat they had borrowed. Nancy said, 'We're all going back to England because Teddy and I are going to get married.' Penelope squirmed with embarrassment. 'Don't be silly, Mummy,' she said.

At nine o'clock on the morning of 27 August 1947 Teddy and Nancy were married by the Assistant District Commissioner of Jerusalem in his office in Katamon. There were two witnesses, one of whom had brought a bottle of champagne. When that had been drunk they picked Penelope up, drove to the airstrip at Lydda and flew to Cairo for a few days of 'sort of honeymoon' before flying to England and their new life together. Which should have been the end of the story, but it wasn't.

Two days after their wedding a distraught Mike wrote, in

pencil, a single-sheet letter to Nancy from South Africa, though in his anguish he scribbled 'Jerusalem' at the top of the page. Given how slow communications were, he must have been responding to a letter that she had sent him, stating her intention to marry Teddy.

Nancy, sweet

Writing the letter must have been difficult; for me to reply is bloody nigh impossible ... you see, dear, I sent off a reply to your lovely, calm and intelligent letter the same day. No, dear, this isn't one of my mental aberrations – it was the longest epistle I'd ever dispatched for I felt so cock-a-hoop at the time. And as the weeks went by and there was no indication as to when you were coming and the inevitable rumours seeped through from Palestine ... ' [Here he started to write, 'I didn't want to' but crossed it out. The rest of the letter is written in a desperate scrawl.] 'All this is bloody silly. Teddy is a hell of a nice person; you are the most wonderful person that's ever come into my life. I'm not going back to England, I love you very much and always will and sincerely hope you get some happiness at last. Nancy, I owe you so much – I do want you to be happy – Bless you, dear. Mike.

The following day he wrote another, more considered letter, but the gist of it remained the same. He understood her decision, respected it, but would always love her. And indeed, twenty years later, when his own marriage had been patched up and his wife and daughter had long since joined him in South Africa, he still maintained that Nancy had been the love of his life.

I was reared on this story of my parents' unlikely courtship, that their marriage and thus my existence all hinged on a letter, containing money and tickets for Nancy and Penelope, that had been lost in the post. By the time I got to hear about it, it made a good story, and their solidly contented marriage made it safe to talk about, part of the collective family myth. But what Nancy's feelings were when she read Mike's heartbroken words, one can only guess. What I find impressive about the few letters he sent her after she returned to England is his total acceptance, right from the start, of the decision she made. He never tries to persuade her to change her mind. He is even generous enough, when he writes more calmly the following day, to acknowledge that she has perhaps made a good decision. 'For the first time in years,' he writes, 'you have achieved a path which shows a clear road ahead: I envy you your clear vision; but I envy Teddy more. Come to think of it, I used to envy Teddy in Jerusalem ... comparing myself to his calm, cool detachment and balanced kindliness. But I never thought that I would be jealous of him because of you. Louis, yes, possibly because I saw in his neurotic frustrations and make-believe a reflection of me.'

By the time Mike's letters reached Nancy she was in England and determined to make this second impetuous marriage a success, which, in the end, it most triumphantly was. But in the early months it nearly foundered entirely.

11

AND AFTER

At the end of August 1947 Nancy flew back to England with her
new husband and Penelope. By then Larry had completed a two-
year stint as public information officer in Rhodes with Eve and
was also back in England, looking for new employment. They
had been happy in Rhodes. After the long war years in Egypt,
much of it in Alexandria, returning to the colours and culture of
Greece had been for Larry a kind of rebirth. It gave rise to
Reflections on a Marine Venus, which brilliantly describes Rhodes
at a critical moment in its history.

Over the next ten years the obligation to make a living took
Larry to Argentina, Yugoslavia and Cyprus. He was building a
reputation as a fine poet and his island books were highly
regarded, but the all-important financial independence continued to elude him.

Sappho, his second daughter, was born in 1951; a difficult time
followed for both him and Eve. They were living in Tito's
Belgrade, a closed and bleak society where neither felt at home.
When Sappho was eighteen months old Eve had a serious breakdown and was hospitalised in Germany. For a while it was by
no means certain that she would recover. When he first went to

Cyprus the following year, Larry was struggling to hold down a job, care for his daughter and write at the same time. In the end, even though his mother came out to help, he was forced to admit defeat. Eve made a complete recovery but the marriage was beyond fixing and Eve returned to England, taking Sappho with her. For the second time he had lost both wife and daughter, though Sappho was usually able to join him during the holidays.

Larry's hopes of making a permanent home in Cyprus were blighted when the battle for union with Greece became serious and he was forced to leave, but by then he had met the woman who was to become his third wife. His marriage to the Alexandrian-French Claude was generally considered a success. Claude was tough, beautiful, hard-drinking, talkative and capable, and as Larry reported cheerily to Henry, if he hit her, she hit him right back. They set up home in Provence, where Larry was to live for the rest of his life.

In 1957 his career finally took off. *Bitter Lemons*, his third and some think the best of his island books, won the Duff Cooper Prize, which was presented by the Queen Mother. Penelope accompanied him to the ceremony – I remember the frantic hunt for a suitably grown-up dress and Penelope anxiously practising her curtsy before the event. Even more significant was the publication earlier that year of *Justine*, the first of the extraordinary sequence of books which make up *The Alexandria Quartet*. Early reviews were mixed: some were puzzled by the strangeness of it, while others recognised a mature and explosive talent. By the time *Clea* came out in 1960 Larry's place in the literary canon was assured. What he described as 'an exploration of modern love' charted the lives and relationships of an exotic group of people living in Alexandria before the war. Now that so much of what was revolutionary in his work – the unreliable narrator, shifting perspectives, a refusal to offer up a single truth – has been absorbed into the mainstream, it is easy to forget just how groundbreaking his novels were at the time. For a whole generation of readers his early novels were a revelation, just as *Tropic of Cancer* had been for him twenty years before.

Claude's death on the first day of 1967 was a desperate blow. And early in 1985 Sappho committed suicide, an appalling loss for all those who loved her. His fourth marriage was brief and unhappy; during his last years, despite the loving companionship and care of Françoise Kestsman, he was drinking heavily and often depressed. Yet his passion for literature, his devotion to Buddhist practice and his extraordinary charm and humour were undiminished, as I discovered when I spent a week with him and Penelope in Sommières two years before he died. He continued to write poetry to the end.

During the first autumn of their marriage, when Penelope had been deposited in a boarding school and they were staying with Teddy's mother in the Cotswolds, Teddy glimpsed on the writing desk in their bedroom a fragment of a letter Nancy had begun to Mike. 'If I had known this,' he read, 'I would never have taken this step . . . '

This step. Teddy was haunted by the phrase. Was this what their marriage meant to her? But, he writes, 'I did not know what to do or say, and predictably did and said nothing, partly from a feeling that I should not take advantage of evidence which I was clearly not meant to see. But I should have confronted her, admitted that I had seen the letter, and then we could have said some of the things which we both so dangerously withheld from each other.'

It is possible that when she spoke of 'this' Nancy was simply referring to the fact that Mike's letter had gone missing in the post, but Teddy always thought she was referring to her lack of preparation for what life with him in England entailed. The astonishing thing is that throughout their two-year friendship in Palestine, and in spite of all those long evenings cooped up behind barbed wire and guards, when there was nothing to do but play cards and talk, she had learned almost no facts about him. In a way, this harked back to her youthful belief that family and background had to be left out of the equation: a dangerous assumption, as it turned out. Arriving in England she quickly discovered that Teddy had a huge and close-knit family – over forty first cousins, many of whom were close friends – into which she was supposed to be absorbed, but with whom she had, to begin with, no point of connection. Unlike the chaotic and bohemian Durrells, Teddy's extended – very extended – family were ferociously academic, self-confident and with a dedication to public service that sometimes shaded into smugness. Heads of Oxbridge colleges, bishops, future ambassadors, headmasters and top civil servants, they had no idea what to make of a tall, beautiful, enigmatic divorcee who had a young child in tow and had never been to university. The incomprehension was mutual. Nancy found them 'overpowering and constricting', and years later wrote a brief note which attempted to describe her feelings during those early years. 'I remember a time long ago – but after we came back to England – saying to myself "Even the id respects a survival crisis (Palestine) but when it's over, wants freedom and expression" or something on those lines. Importunate id – breaking away and shouting "Now, why not now?"'

Teddy always reproached himself for his inability to raise the topic of her unhappiness, and rightly so. She never posted that letter to Mike. On the contrary, when she did write to him it was to emphasise her happiness. In September 1947 Mike wrote, 'Your letter oozed contentment and serenity', and three months later he says, 'Thank you for your letters . . . I must confess envy: they mirror such happiness and contentment.' My guess is she *wanted* Teddy to find that never-posted letter; it was her attempt to try and open a dialogue with this man who had been in so many ways a stranger when they married, of letting him know how she was struggling to find a foothold in his family.

As eventually she did. In later years she said they could have got off to a better start if they had lived abroad at the beginning of their marriage; she had lived in the Mediterranean through most of the previous twelve years, and post-war Britain, with its grey skies and bomb sites, rationing and austerity and recent memories of a war that had been very different from hers, seemed a chilly and unwelcoming place. She had no ties there. Her mother had died in an asylum just before the end of the war. Her father was still living in Gainsborough. When she and Teddy bought a pleasant house near Watford shortly after I was born in 1949, they invited him to live with them. It was not a success. In fact, it triggered in Nancy a lingering flu-like illness that was probably severe depression. In my earliest memories of my mother she is a remote and unresponsive figure, and during those first years it was Teddy who provided the abundant love, while his mother offered structure and simple fun (she relished children's games). Through this period Nancy was struggling to adjust to her new life, and perhaps also coming to terms with no longer being a 'beautiful girl'. In 1952, when Nancy was forty, that signalled the start of middle age – 'mutton dressed up as lamb' was her damning verdict on women who resisted the limitations of their years.

At the suggestion of Teddy's godmother, Margery Fry (the former principal of Somerville College, Oxford, prison reformer and sister of Roger Fry), she went to see a psychiatrist called Dr Torre, a kindly Quaker who became a father figure whom she visited fairly regularly until his death some time in the 1960s. With him she was able to start unravelling the tangle of her toxic childhood family, the scars left by her first marriage and the years struggling in Palestine, and probably of the world in which she now found herself as well. 'Mum's gone to see Dr Torre' was a frequent refrain when I was small. Once I asked her in what way he was helpful. She was vague, telling me that on the whole he didn't say much. 'But he has said one or two things that helped,' she said. 'Such as?' I wanted to know. She thought for a moment before explaining, 'He once said I wasn't the worst mother in the world.' (I could have told her that.) But of course, his remark echoed the family mantra that had dogged her for so long: 'Your mother's the best woman in the world.' Best-worst – the old dichotomy remained. Many of her friends were undergoing full-scale psychoanalysis during the 1950s. One of them insisted on only being treated by someone who had been breastfed, and reduced one analyst to such infantile anguish that he crawled round the consulting room on all fours whimpering for his mother. At least that was the story.

In 1953 the family moved back to London (without Nancy's father) and she went back to art school, this time to focus on sculpture. She loved it. The slow accretion of clay, the chance to work and rework a piece for months on end, appealed to her craving for perfection. I find it impossible to view her work objectively since I grew up with it and earned my first pocket money modelling for her, and to my mind all other sculpture succeeds or fails according to her principles. Financially secure at last, she never tried to sell or exhibit her work except for two pieces that were shown in the Royal Academy's summer exhibition. As she emerged from the gloom of the early 1950s she became more demonstrative and involved as a mother; she was always a conscientious and good housekeeper, and a tender nurse when anyone was ill. Her love was often expressed through creativity: when I was very young she made robust and wonderful soft toys, and later built a fine wendy house.

My parents bought a television so I would sit still and be modelled.
Seemed fair to me

While writing this I found a letter she wrote to Teddy in September 1965, when she had remained in London with Penelope while my father and I went to my grandmother's. It shows how close they had become, as well as her anxiety caused by Larry's sudden appearance in London. After describing her hunt for a cheap teapot and shoe racks of the right size (she was always a dedicated shopper) she says she was only just back in time to help Penelope get ready for going out:

She got a p.c. this morning with the time of meeting and a telegram in the middle of the morning to tell her not to be later as he [Larry] has tickets for Covent Garden. It is rather upset-ting – but I don't really think he will do her any harm. It is more the stirring up of old ghosts and not being sure of my own reactions – He seems to be taking a very gay and gallant line, both towards past and present, and P came back from the picnic full of all the stories he had told her about our adventures and life in the past, making everything sound daring and romantic and constant nymphish – which is, I suppose, all very well if you can do it – and makes everything very charming. She criticized his chain smoking and volunteered that he probably drinks too much, and was intrigued that he made her take her shoes off to see whose feet she had – He said they were his. He painted a vivid picture of the house in Bournemouth, which he calls the mad house and said everybody in it was drunk, mad, illegitimate etc (Sapphy is apparently there now because Eve is 'too nervous' to look after her and he has custody). I think he will invite P for a weekend. Gerry has written a funny book about the family life in Corfu, caricaturing and exaggerating it into a wild farce. I feel it might be a tremendous bestseller (coming out this month). Mother Durrell he says has sunk into befuddlement unable to cope any longer – I don't blame her. Oh dear … Jill [Penelope's great friend who was a favourite model of Nancy's] is coming again tomorrow after class and will stay one night with us so I ought to have a good long session. I feel that in the end I'll get something worthwhile out of it, but it's a most complicated and elusive thing.

I hope you had a lovely ride today, both you and Jo. I do miss you a lot. I feel very upside down and rather horrid. It will be nice to hear your voice tonight. Thank goodness for the telephone. With all my love, Nancy.

After four years in London we moved to a house in the Chilterns and got a dog. It was there, on walks and in the evenings when my father was working late, that she began talking to me about her life before I was born. Of course I was flattered. As a young adult my own ease with the listening role of the counsellor or therapist surely dated back to those walks through the beech woods with our determined Welsh collie. From that time, our relationship evolved into a relaxed and open sharing of experience in which most topics were open for discussion. She was always good at knowing what books to recommend: during my animal-obsessed childhood we shared a love of Konrad Lorenz and Desmond Morris, before moving on to more people-focused books.

Penelope remained behind in London, only joining us at weekends, when to my dismay she seemed to be asleep for most of the time. She was at last devoting herself to classical dance training, which had been a cause of ructions between her and Nancy, a deep sadness for them both. In the 1950s the rules about the height of dance students were rigid. Nancy feared that Penelope would be tall like her and had discouraged her passion for dance, with the result that she started training too late ever to reach the front rank. She did have some success until a foot injury, sustained when she was taking part in the opening of Liverpool's Catholic Cathedral, ended her dance career. With her second husband Penelope worked for some years as a potter, and they combined that with farming in the West Country. Those years in Cornwall when we were both newly married and struggling, without notable success, to make our way in the world, were when Penelope and I became close.

Nancy's health continued to be fragile. 'What can you expect at your age?' was her GP's unhelpful response to her ailments (she was in her forties). But in 1963 a more rigorous doctor diagnosed a problem with her pancreas, so she underwent surgery which was risky and experimental, but which ultimately gave her a new lease of energy and strength. This was the beginning of the best period in our family life; for her, I think, it must have seemed as though the world, the questioning, challenging, inquisitive world of the 1960s, had finally caught up with the freedoms of the Villa Seurat. Henry Miller and Anaïs Nin, so long regarded as little more than pornographers, had become iconic figures at last. Nancy loved the tumble of ideas and devoured the books of people like Robert Ardrey, R. D. Laing, Bruno Bettelheim and Alan Watts. They all fed into her experience and we discussed them endlessly. Always there was a questioning and exploration, a sense that her inner journey was at least as significant as what was taking place on the surface of her life. Someone who got to know her at about this time said she often gave the impression of listening to inner music, which just about sums it up.

Feeling physically robust for the first time, she decided after much thought to emerge from what she called her ivory tower and engage more directly with the world. She worked for a while as a ward aide in Paddington General Hospital and then, through work with the wives of men who were serving prison sentences, she gradually became involved with prisoners and ex-cons, most notably with two US schemes – the Manhattan Court Project and New Careers – which she worked to publicise in the UK. Her own sense of being always at odds with mainstream society gave her a useful way to connect with renegades, even when she had assumed the outward trappings of a respectable middle-aged woman. On one of her visits to California, to work with ex-convicts in Los Angeles, she saw Anaïs for the first time in more than a quarter of a century. Anaïs was struck by the change in her: she was absorbed in 'good works'. Their rackety days in Paris seemed a lifetime away.

Penelope nursed Nancy when she was battling the cancer that killed her. At about the same time she met her third husband, John, with whom she spent twenty-seven contented years. They were married at the Tibetan Buddhist centre in Samye Ling and divided their time between their homes in Rhodes and Hereford. After both Nancy and Larry had died, she devoted considerable

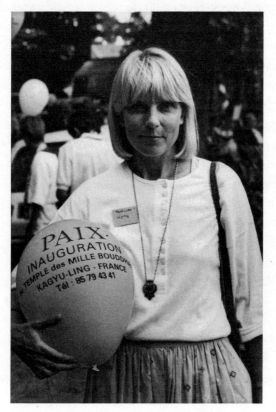

Penelope at the Buddhist centre in France

energy to piecing together the story of her early years – meeting the people who had known her as a child in Greece and Egypt and Palestine. Her researches, and the support of John, who survives her, have been a huge help while I was writing this.

*

When he was first posted to Belgrade in 1949 Larry wrote to Nancy explaining why his payments for Penelope were now irregular: 'owing to a very confused system here, by which one is paid quarterly in dinars; and I have only just done my life certificates for this quarter. Of course, there is no reason to bother you with my problems.' Then he says, 'I relish your threats. Why don't you go ahead and sue me? I'm sure you'd win your case and enjoy doing so. Your letter reminds me so vividly of the good old days.' His challenge can be read in so many different ways, but it would have evoked in Nancy memories and references which only she and Larry would ever really know, that private alchemy of love and hurt and broken dreams that remain always unknowable to anyone else.

There are so many ways to tell the story of a marriage, especially one between two individuals as complex and mercurial as Larry and Nancy. You could say they were a couple who married too young, simply because that was what people did in those days when 'living in sin' was an embarrassment, even to a woman as unconventional as Mother Durrell; maybe they simply weren't compatible; or maybe, as Larry said, it was 'just the war I guess' and their relationship might have survived if the circumstances had remained favourable – it was the stress of being refugees which caused their marriage to buckle. Or maybe, as Nancy sometimes implied, their marriage was poisoned because Larry had a terrible destructive ambivalence to anyone who got close to him, and Nancy was his first victim. Then again, as some of his admirers suggest, she was not a worthy mate for the great man and should have understood his tortured needs better. None of these ways of looking at their life together gives more than a fraction of the real picture, whatever that might be. I would be hard pressed to give a real explanation for the story of my own marriage, and its failure after thirty years, so hesitate to make a final judgement about anyone else's.

It is better to end with an image. In the summer of 2000 the Durrell Society, a US-based collection of admirers and academics, held their biennial conference in Corfu and I went with Penelope, who was to give a talk. One of the highlights of the week was a trip by boat up the coast from Corfu town to Kalami. It was hot July day. En route, the boat pulled in to the deserted cove where the shrine of St Arsenius still presides over rippling rock formations and deep blue water. Margo, who also attended that year, threw cherries over the side of the boat and the more aquatic delegates tried to replicate Nancy's fabled accomplishment of diving through the clear water to bring the cherries up in their teeth. I have a feeling that the only successes were due to the ones that helpfully floated up to the surface, but memory, as my researches for this book have shown, can be fickle.

From there we rounded the headland to Kalami and the taverna that now sits on the slab of rock where Nancy and Larry lounged and sunned and worked on their boats during those few summers before the war. A lavish meal of local fish, replicating the one so lovingly described in *Prospero's Cell*, was served by Larry's godson Giorgos and his family. The highlight of the afternoon was the unveiling of a plaque at the front of the White House in celebration of its famous lodger. A small band trooped up and played cheerful Greek music while a group of dancers in bright costumes tripped up and down in the road. The mayor and other local dignitaries made speeches. Margo and Penelope were guests of honour, Margo every short inch a blue-eyed Durrell charmer, Penelope blonde and shy with a classic Princess Grace kind of beauty. The plaque was unveiled and everyone burst into loud applause and it was all very jolly.

And suddenly, amid all the music and laughter and gaiety, I found tears were streaming down my face as I thought of that couple of unknowns, so determined and courageous, life-loving and flawed and unique, who had made this their home when barely out of their teens, who had loved this place as they never loved anywhere else again, who had tried to live life differently, in a way that was dedicated to art and literature and freedom, but who had tried and failed, the way ultimately we all try and fail, but who had created a myth and a mystery that lived long after their laughter and their fights and their loving had faded to silence, who wanted to create something valuable and lasting, something of real worth. Who had brought all these people to this place at this particular moment. It seemed like quite an achievement.

SOURCES AND ONWARD READING

These are not intended as technical footnotes: this is a personal memoir, based largely on family material and conversations, and makes no claim to be an academic text. Still, a task that I expected to be quick and impressionistic turned out to demand vast amounts of reading and research, most of it fascinating, so for those who want to explore further, the following bibliographical notes are offered on a chapter-by-chapter basis.

1: Of Introspection Got
Most of the material in this chapter is based on the memoir that Nancy started to write, and on her spoken memories which were taped and transcribed by my father after her death. For topographical detail the Local Studies section of Eastbourne public library was very helpful.

2: A Harum-Scarum Schoolgirl
Similarly, Nancy's schooldays and her worsening relationship with her parents were explored in detail in her unfinished memoir. Margaret Kennedy's novel *The Constant Nymph*, which had such a profound impact on Nancy, is very readable and still in some ways shocking, especially now when the much older Lewis Dodd might well be stigmatised as a paedophile for his affair with the fourteen-year-old Tessa.

3: *Seeing Life*

Part of this is based on Nancy's written memoir, and part on the transcribed tapes. Supplementary information on Roger Pettiward is mostly derived from his entry in the *Dictionary of National Biography* and the introduction by Ruari McLean to *The Last Cream Bun*, a wonderful collection of his cartoons that was published in 1984. As Roger wanted to keep his real name for his paintings, his cartoons appeared either under the name Paul Crum, or with a simple spiral as signature.

4: *'This Odd, Sideways Way'*

From now on Nancy's memories are supplemented by those of Larry and other contemporaries, and there is a mass of secondary information, not least Ian MacNiven's magisterial biography which came out in 1998. Larry writes about John Gawsworth in one of the pieces collected by Alan Thomas in *Spirit of Place*, which is a good introduction to Durrell's writings about people and places – but always with the caveat that he was interested in poetic rather than actual truth: his disregard for dates and details was at least consistent.

Peter Fleming's *Brazilian Adventure*, which was published in 1933, is a light-hearted and engaging account of the extraordinary trip he made with Roger Pettiward the previous year. Well worth tracking down and enjoying. Likewise the film of *Mädchen in Uniform*, though of course dated – it was made eighty years ago, after all – is still powerful and moving.

My skills as a genealogist being just about nil, I was much helped in my discoveries of Louise's secret family by Patricia Earle. It is a great sadness that she died in September 2011 and so cannot seen my gratitude in print.

5: Provincial Life

The story of censorship in the mid twentieth century is a sad tale of prejudice and misplaced zeal, nowhere more than in the fate of Geoffrey Potocki de Montalk. His story has been told by his cousin Stephanie de Montalk in her 2002 biography *Unquiet World*.

Durrell's first novel, *Pied Piper of Lovers*, is mainly of interest now for its autobiographical details – just as he was never strictly accurate when writing about himself, so also he was never entirely fictional in his fiction – and for the glimpse of a writer learning his craft. The same is true of his second novel, *Panic Spring*, a curiosity rather than a riveting read.

6: Prospero's Island

I can't imagine that the two Durrell books on Corfu will ever be bettered; essential reading for anyone visiting Greece who wants to delve a bit deeper than just the pool and the taverna. *Prospero's Cell* evokes a landscape and a people still permeated with ancient myth and magic, while Gerald's *My Family and Other Animals* is a glorious description of the island's abundant wildlife and the young naturalist's eccentric family.

A charming description of that period has just been published by the Durrell School of Corfu and the International Lawrence Durrell Society. *Autumn Gleanings* by Theodore Stephanides combines his reminiscences with a selection of his poetry and gives a vivid impression of the humour and warmth of this remarkable man who was so important to the two fatherless brothers.

Lawrence Durrell's letters are a rich source of material and many of them are in print, those to Alan Thomas in *Spirit of Place*, and those to Henry Miller in two editions, the first edited by George Wickes in 1962 and the second, a more comprehensive selection, by Ian MacNiven in 1988. He was a brilliant letter writer, incapable of ever being dull. The originals are scattered between the British Library, the University of California Los Angeles and the Morris Library at Southern Illinois University Carbondale. My mother destroyed all his letters to her when she married for the second time: all that remains are brief notes he wrote on the back of photographs, mostly while she was back in England in early 1940.

Tropic of Cancer has lost none of its raw energy or its power to shock. My feeling is it's a book to be dipped into, rather than attempting to read it through like a novel. The language still explodes on the page, but too much at a time can be somewhat indigestible. The same is true of *The Black Book*, extraordinary, extravagant writing best savoured in small amounts. Even Henry Miller said pretty much the same thing in one of his early letters of praise. Both books are brilliant and fearless firework displays, containing much to admire and enjoy.

7: Safe from Everything but Ourselves

The title of this chapter is taken from Lawrence's poem 'At Epidaurus', which he wrote some time late in 1939, early 1940. His lyric poetry is second to none, and I think it deserves to be better known: Peter Levi wrote that his was without doubt the best English poetry about Greece, adding that his only rival was the combination of Yeats and Sophocles, praise indeed. Perhaps the extraordinary success of *The Alexandria Quartet* somehow led to his poetry being undervalued: whatever the reason, poems like 'At Epidaurus' or 'Nemea' are more than enough to guarantee his immortality.

The Villa Seurat era has been widely documented. I never met Henry Miller, but one of his short pieces, 'Via Dieppe-Newhaven', an account of his disastrous attempt to travel from

France to England, conjures up his hobo-seer personality better than anything else I've read. It's published in a collection of short pieces called *The Cosmological Eye*.

Where to begin with Anaïs Nin? She's too often known for her least good work, the erotica she wrote for money and which was published as *Delta of Venus* and *Little Birds*. Selections from her diaries were first published in Britain by Peter Owen, edited by Gunther Stuhlmann. Later selections have been published posthumously by Rupert Pole, whom she had married while still technically married to Hugo Guiler. Her books provide a sometimes painful insight into the difficulties of being a woman artist in a world dominated by men.

8: *Time Tasted*

Some of Durrell's letters to Anne Ridler are printed in *Spirit of Place*, others are in archives as mentioned above. There is a plan to publish *The Magnetic Island*, with Nancy's illustrations, but so far it has not seen the light of day.

9: *The Refugee Habit*

Henry Miller's account of his few months in Greece in the second half of 1939, *The Colossus of Maroussi*, brims over with his enthusiasm and love for all things Greek. George Seferis managed to combine a distinguished diplomatic career with Nobel Prize winning literary achievements. Roderick Beaton's biography *George Seferis, Waiting for the Angel*, covers both strands of his life, and Edmund Keeley has published translations of his poetry. There is a vivid account, quite different from Nancy's memory, of their escape from Kalamata in *The Greek Islands*; he even gets the year of their escape wrong, but like everything else he wrote about Greece, this is evocative and entertaining. Theodore Stephanides's account of the chaos surrounding the fall of Greece and his horrific march across Crete was published in 1946 as *Climax in Crete* but is now out of print; more's the pity. It is one of the most intense accounts of the experience of war I have ever read, a small classic. A different and better known perspective is given by Olivia Manning in the six books that make up *The Balkan Trilogy* and *The Levant Trilogy*, both excellent. The most recent biography, *Olivia Manning: A Woman at War* by Deidre A. David is published by Oxford University Press.

10: An Attractive Leave Venue
Parade magazine, which was produced in Cairo for the troops fighting in the Middle East, provides a fresh perspective on wartime experience. The origins of Sharq al-Adna are described by its first director in *The House at Herod's Gate*, which was published in 1947: John Connell was the pseudonym of John Henry Robertson. Much of the information in this chapter comes from my father's unpublished memoirs, and remembered conversations with both him and Nancy. The divorce file, which had been stored for half a century by the long-suffering Albert Spaer, was passed to Penelope by Lotte Geiger.

11: And After
The 1950s were the decade when Lawrence Durrell's career took off. *The Alexandria Quartet* was a massive success worldwide: perhaps it was overrated then; it is certainly under-read now. My feeling is that it is his poetry, especially his wonderful evocative lyric poems, that should be more widely known, as well as the three island books. After *Prospero's Cell*, he wrote *Reflections on a Marine Venus* about Rhodes immediately after the war, and then *Bitter Lemons*, which some consider the best of the three, about Cyprus. The best of his work is infused with the love of Greece and the Greek people, which he and Nancy shared.

Since then, Lawrence has been much written about. As well as the official biography by Ian MacNiven, there is Gordon Bowker's *Through the Dark Labyrinth* and a discussion of his work in Richard Pine's *Lawrence Durrell: The Mindscape*. A new biography by Michael Haag, *Lawrence Durrell: A Life*, is published by Yale. A series of interviews with Marc Alyn were published as *The Big Supposer* and give a flavour of his beguiling talk. The man and his work were sufficiently contradictory and intriguing to inspire debate and study for years to come, but my feeling is that it is in his poetry that he is at his triumphant best.

The main weblinks at present are:

www.lawrencedurrell.org
www.durrell-school-corfu.org
www.amateursineden.com

PICTURE CREDITS